SPECTRUM®

Test Prep

Grade 8

Published by Spectrum®
An imprint of Carson-Dellosa Publishing LLC
Greensboro, North Carolina

Spectrum®
An imprint of Carson-Dellosa Publishing LLC
P.O. Box 35665
Greensboro, NC 27425 USA

ISBN 978-1-4838-1375-2

01-349147811

Table of Contents

What's Inside?

Spectrum Test Prep is designed to help you and your eighth grader prepare and plan for success on standardized tests.

Strategies

This workbook is structured around strategies. A strategy is a careful plan or method for achieving a particular goal, such as succeeding on a test. Strategies can be broad, providing general ways to approach a test as a whole or a category of skills. Strategies can also be specific, providing step-by-step instructions on how to tackle a problem or offering guidelines on how to answer a question about a story. Learning how to apply a strategy gives test-takers a plan for how to approach a test as a whole and how to answer questions.

This workbook offers a set of broader strategies and very specific strategies. General test-taking strategies apply to all tests, and should be used to help prepare for the test. Specific strategies for English Language Arts and Mathematics tests are divided into larger categories of skills students will encounter, such as reading literature or performing calculations. On each practice page, you will find even more specific strategies that apply to the skills.

Test Tips

Test Tips are included throughout the practice page. While strategies offer a plan for answering test items, Test Tips offer ideas for how to apply each strategy or how to approach a type of question. There are Test Tips that apply to all tests and Test Tips for English Language Arts and Mathematics tests.

Practice Pages

The workbook is divided into two sections, English Language Arts and Mathematics. Each section has practice activities that have questions similar to those that will appear on standardized tests. Also included are strategies and Test Tips to guide students. Students should use a pencil to complete these activities.

Strategy Review Pages

Strategy review pages give your student an opportunity to review and practice important strategies in each content area. These strategies cover the important skills students will encounter on tests in English Language Arts and Mathematics.

Answer Key

Answers for all of the practice pages and strategy review pages are found in an answer key at the end of the book.

Test-Taking Strategies

Being prepared is key to doing your best on test day. Read the tips below to help you prepare for tests.

In the days before the test...

- Keep up on your reading, worksheets, and assignments. Completing all your assigned work will help you be better prepared for the test.
- Don't wait until right before the test to review materials. Create a study schedule for the best result. That way, you can study a bit at a time and not all at once.
- Take advantage of sample items and practice tests. Complete these to practice for your test. If you run into concepts or skills that are new, ask a teacher or other adult.

The night before the test...

- Don't try to study everything all over again. If you've been studying in the days before the test, all you need the night before is a light review of your notes. Remind yourself of the key ideas and practice a few skills, but don't study late into the night.
- Make sure you have all the materials you will need for the test, such as pencils, paper, or a calculator. Check with your teacher to make sure you know what tools to bring. Having everything ready the night before will make the morning less stressful.
- Get a good night's sleep the night before the test. If you are well rested, you will be more alert and able to do your best.

On the day of the test...

- Don't skip breakfast. If you are hungry, you won't be thinking about the test. You'll be thinking about lunch.
- Make sure you have at least two sharpened pencils with you and any other tools needed.
- Read all directions carefully. Make sure you understand how you are supposed to answer each question.
- For multiple choice questions, read all the possible answers before choosing one. If you know that some answers are wrong, cross them off. Even if you have to guess, this will eliminate some wrong answers.
- Once you choose or write an answer, double check it by reading the question again. Confirm that your answer is correct.
- Answer every part of a question. If a question asks you to show your work or to explain how you arrived at an answer, make sure you include that information.
- If you are stuck on a question, or are unsure, mark it lightly with a pencil and move on. If you have time, you can come back. This is especially true on a timed test.
- Breathe! Remind yourself that you've prepared for the test and that you will do your best!

Strategies for English Language Arts Tests

Read the strategies below to learn more about how they work.

Use details from the text to make inferences, understand theme, and draw out meaning.
Writers carefully choose details to include in their writing. Every detail matters. Each one is included for a purpose. As you read stories, look for details that help you understand what the writer is saying about characters, events, and the overall meaning, or theme. As you read passages, look for details that give reasons that support any opinions or facts the writer shares, as well as the central or main idea.

Identify literary or structural elements and use them to understand the meaning of a text.
Writers use literary elements such as figurative language to bring more meaning to their writing. They choose a structure that reflects their purpose for writing. Read carefully for ways that these elements can help you understand the meaning of a story, poem, or passage.

Look carefully at visuals such as illustrations, diagrams, or graphs to see how they connect to the text.
Visuals are always related to the text. It is up to readers to figure out the connection. Does the visual explain something that is difficult to say in words? Does it add detail? As you read stories and passages, look carefully at visuals to see what information they provide.

Reread texts to make comparisons, draw conclusions, or support inferences.
Every reader has his or her own ideas about a text. If you are asked to draw a conclusion about what the writer means or thinks, however, you need to rely on details in the text, not your own opinions. When you have drawn a conclusion or made an inference, reread the text to make sure you can support it with facts, examples, and other information from the text.

Use word clues in a text to identify its structure, to see how ideas in a text are related, and to clarify word meanings.
Some words are signals that a text has a particular structure. For example, the words cause and because often signal a cause-and-effect structure. You may also be able to use words as clues to the meaning of unfamiliar words.

When writing, use details to support, explain, or clarify your main ideas.
In persuasive and informational writing, it is important to make sure you support and explain each main idea with details. Facts, examples, and logical reasoning can all be used to make your main ideas strong and clear.

Use an outline to plan your writing.
Prewriting activities such as outlining can make writing clear and make your ideas easy to understand. A simple outline that lists main ideas or claims followed by their supporting details is enough to make your writing flow more easily.

Use transitions to show how ideas are related.
As you write, use transitions to help your reader follow your train of thought. You may know how your ideas are related, but readers need a little extra help! For example, the transition *As a result* shows that you are explaining a cause and an effect. The transitions *Next* and *Finally* help readers see that you are explaining a process or events that happen in a certain order.

Revise to make sure your writing is clear and makes sense. Then, edit to fix errors.
After you finish your draft, you may have time to revise and edit. First, revise to make sure your words say what you wanted them to say. Then, check spelling, capitalization, punctuation, and grammar to catch and fix errors.

Name ______________________________ Date ______________

English Language Arts

Cite Text Evidence to Support Analysis

Reading: Literature

DIRECTIONS: Read the story. Then, answer the questions that follow.

From "The Red-Headed League" by Arthur Conan Doyle

The portly client puffed out his chest with an appearance of some little pride and pulled a dirty and wrinkled newspaper from the inside pocket of his greatcoat. As he glanced down the advertisement column, . . . I took a good look at the man and endeavoured, after the fashion of my companion, to read the indications which might be presented by his dress or appearance.

I did not gain very much, however, by my inspection. Our visitor bore every mark of being an average commonplace British tradesman, obese, pompous, and slow. He wore rather baggy grey shepherd's check trousers, a not over-clean black frock-coat, unbuttoned in the front, and a drab waistcoat with a heavy brassy Albert chain, and a square pierced bit of metal dangling down as an ornament. A frayed top-hat and a faded brown overcoat with a wrinkled velvet collar lay upon a chair beside him. Altogether, look as I would, there was nothing remarkable about the man save his blazing red head, and the expression of extreme chagrin and discontent upon his features.

Sherlock Holmes' quick eye took in my occupation, and he shook his head with a smile as he noticed my questioning glances. "Beyond the obvious facts that he has at some time done manual labour, that he takes snuff, that he is a Freemason, that he has been in China, and that he has done a considerable amount of writing lately, I can deduce nothing else."

Mr. Jabez Wilson started up in his chair, with his forefinger upon the paper, but his eyes upon my companion.

"How, in the name of good-fortune, did you know all that, Mr. Holmes?" he asked. "How did you know, for example, that I did manual labour. It's as true as gospel, for I began as a ship's carpenter."

"Your hands, my dear sir. Your right hand is quite a size larger than your left. You have worked with it, and the muscles are more developed."

"Well, the snuff, then, and the Freemasonry?"

"I won't insult your intelligence by telling you how I read that, especially as, rather against the strict rules of your order, you use an arc-and-compass breastpin."

"Ah, of course, I forgot that. But the writing?"

"What else can be indicated by that right cuff so very shiny for five inches, and the left one with the smooth patch near the elbow where you rest it upon the desk?"

"Well, but China?"

"The fish that you have tattooed immediately above your right wrist could only have been done in China. . . . That trick of staining the fishes' scales a delicate pink is quite peculiar to China. When, in addition, I see a Chinese coin hanging from your watch-chain, the matter becomes even more simple."

Mr. Jabez Wilson laughed heavily. "Well, I never!" said he. "I thought at first that you had done something clever, but I see that there was nothing in it after all."

Name ______________________________ Date ______________

English Language Arts

Cite Text Evidence to Support Analysis

Reading: Literature

DIRECTIONS: Use the story to answer the questions.

Strategy As you read, use details from the story to make inferences and cite specific details that are strong enough to support your ideas.

Test Tip Be sure that the details you choose strongly support your ideas. Choose the details that best show why your ideas are valid.

1. **Part A: Why does the narrator, Dr. Watson, try to make his own deductions about Mr. Wilson?**
   - (A) Jabez Wilson is an exceptionally interesting person.
   - (B) Watson wants to see if he can make as many deductions about Wilson as Holmes does.
   - (C) Holmes relies on Watson's first impressions to decide whether to take on a new client.
   - (D) Holmes and Watson are suspicious of their new client and are testing him to see if Wilson is lying to them.

   Part B: Write the sentence from the story that supports your answer to Part A.

   ____

   ____

   ____

   ____

Test Tip

Substitute the word you chose from question 2 into the original sentence to see if it has the right meaning.

2. **Read the following excerpt from the passage:**

> "The fish that you have tattooed immediately above your right wrist could only have been done in China. . . . That trick of staining the fishes' scales a delicate pink is quite peculiar to China."

The word *peculiar* usually means "odd" or "unusual." However, it can have other meanings. Which meaning best fits the way the word *peculiar* is used in this excerpt?

- (A) common
- (B) familiar
- (C) traditional
- (D) unique

Write how you know.

____

____

3. **After Holmes explains his method, Jabez Wilson says "there was nothing in it after all." Do you agree that there is nothing remarkable about Sherlock Holmes' deductive ability? Cite at least two pieces of evidence from the story to support your opinion.**

____

____

____

____

4. **Write the sentence from the story that would best support the inference that the narrator does not think the man visiting Sherlock Holmes is special or interesting.**

____

____

Name ______________________________ Date ______________

English Language Arts

Determine Theme and Summarize

Reading: Literature

DIRECTIONS: Read the story. Then, answer the questions that follow.

The Zen Farmer

Once upon a time, there was an old Chinese farmer who had only one horse. One day, the mare broke through the fence and ran away. Upon hearing the news, his neighbors came to console the old man. "Now you have no horse to help you plant your crops. Such bad luck," they said sympathetically.

"Maybe good, maybe bad," the farmer replied.

The next morning the horse returned, bringing with her two wild stallions.

"Now you are rich—you have three horses. What good luck!" the neighbors exclaimed.

"Maybe good, maybe bad," replied the old man.

The following day, his son tried to ride one of the untamed horses. The stallion threw him and the youth broke his leg. The neighbors again came to console the farmer. "Now you have no one to help you plant your crops," they commiserated.

"We are sorry for your bad luck."

"Maybe good, maybe bad," answered the farmer.

The next day, officers of the emperor's army came to the village and drafted every able-bodied young man. Seeing that the old man's son had a broken leg, they passed him by. The neighbors, weeping for the sons who had been taken from them, congratulated the farmer. "At least your son had the good luck to avoid the draft," they said.

"Maybe good, maybe bad," said the old farmer.

Strategy Evaluate each detail to make sure it is strong enough to support your theme. If the detail is weak, look for another detail.

Test Tip This passage is a Zen teaching story. The theme is a lesson. The lesson is taught by the way the old farmer reacts to what happens.

1. Which sentence best summarizes the story?

Ⓐ A mare escapes from his fence and runs away, returning the next day.

Ⓑ A man's neighbors wish bad luck on an old Chinese man who is negative and mean.

Ⓒ An old Chinese farmer accepts the good and bad events that happen to him and his family.

Ⓓ A son is not asked to serve in the army because he has a badly broken leg.

Write how you know.

____

____

____

2. What is the main difference between the old farmer and his neighbors?

____

____

Name ________________________________ Date ________________

English Language Arts

Determine Theme and Summarize

Reading: Literature

DIRECTIONS: Read the story. Then, answer the questions using details from the story.

Strategy When you determine a theme, find at least two details in the story that supports it. If you can't find any details, look for a new theme.

Test Tip Remember that the theme is the overall message or lesson in a story. It is not the topic, or what the story is about. It is also not the plot, or what happens in the story.

3. If the story continued, what would you expect to happen next?

Ⓐ an event that seems to be bad luck

Ⓑ an event that seems to be good luck

Ⓒ another visit from the army officers

Ⓓ a shift from the farmer's point of view to his son's

Write how you know.

____

____

____

____

____

____

____

____

4. What detail tells you the story is set in China?

Ⓐ Wild horses live near the village.

Ⓑ Farmers do not use tractors to plant crops.

Ⓒ Young men are drafted into the emperor's army.

Ⓓ Someone with three horses is considered wealthy.

5. State the main lesson, or theme, of the story in your own words.

____

____

____

____

____

Write two details from the story that supports the theme you wrote above.

____

____

____

____

____

____

Name ______________________________ Date ______________

English Language Arts

Interpret Figurative and Connotative Language

Reading: Literature

DIRECTIONS: Read the poem. Then, answer the questions that follow.

O Captain! My Captain! ***by Walt Whitman***

O Captain! my Captain! our fearful trip is done,
The ship has weather'd every rack, the prize we sought is won,
The port is near, the bells I hear, the people all exulting,
While follow eyes the steady keel, the vessel grim and daring;
But O heart! heart! heart!
O the bleeding drops of red,
Where on the deck my Captain lies,
Fallen cold and dead.

O Captain! my Captain! rise up and hear the bells;
Rise up—for you the flag is flung—for you the bugle trills,
For you bouquets and ribbon'd wreaths—for you the shores a-crowding,
For you they call, the swaying mass, their eager faces turning;
Here Captain! dear father!
The arm beneath your head!
It is some dream that on the deck,
You've fallen cold and dead.

My Captain does not answer, his lips are pale and still,
My father does not feel my arm, he has no pulse nor will,
The ship is anchor'd safe and sound, its voyage closed and done,
From fearful trip the victor ship comes in with object won;
Exult O shores, and ring O bells!
But I with mournful tread,
Walk the deck my Captain lies,
Fallen cold and dead.

Strategy To gain a deeper understanding of poetry, reread a poem and identify the nonliteral meanings of figurative language. Then, determine the connotative meaning of words and phrases.

Test Tip Historical events may be part of a poem or story's theme. This poem was written to mark the death of Abraham Lincoln, shortly after the Civil War ended. As you read, connect words in the poem to what you know about Lincoln.

1. **The author uses the word *exulting* to describe the people waiting for the ship to arrive. Use the context to choose the phrase that best explains the connotative meaning of *exulting*.**

   Ⓐ negative: amazed surprise
   Ⓑ positive: nervous excitement
   Ⓒ negative: deep sorrow and grief
   Ⓓ positive: great happiness and joy

   Would the word *cheering* have the same meaning? Write how you know.

   ____

   ____

   ____

   ____

Name ______________________________ Date ______________

English Language Arts

Interpret Figurative and Connotative Language

Reading: Literature

DIRECTIONS: Use the poem to answer the questions.

Strategy Use context clues to determine the meaning of figurative language as well as the poem's theme or main message.

Test Tip Keep examples of figurative language in mind as you read. Similes use a comparison word, such as *like* or *as*. Use these words as clues to identify and interpret similes. Metaphors just compare two unlike things without any word clues.

2. If Lincoln is the Captain, what is the ship?

Ⓐ the North
Ⓑ the South
Ⓒ the United States
Ⓓ the White House

What type of figurative language is used? Write how you know.

____

____

____

____

3. Which phrase from the poem means almost the same thing as the word *object* in the following line from the poem?

"From fearful trip the victor ship comes in with object won"

Ⓐ "our fearful trip is done"
Ⓑ "the prize we sought is won"
Ⓒ "Rise up—for you the flag is flung"
Ⓓ "its voyage closed and done"

Write how you know.

____

____

4. How would replacing the word *mournful* with the word *saddened* in the lines below affect the meaning of the poem?

Exult O shores, and ring O bells!
But I with mournful tread,
Walk the deck my Captain lies,
Fallen cold and dead.

____

____

____

5. The metaphor comparing a country to the Ship of State goes back to the Greek philosopher Plato. Identify an example of how Whitman alludes to the Ship of State in this poem.

____

____

____

6. Whitman uses the phrase "dear father" in the poem. Whitman is comparing Lincoln's presidency to being a parent. The citizens of the United States are children, and Lincoln is the father. How are Lincoln and the captain of a ship fathers?

____

____

____

Name ______________________________ Date ______________

English Language Arts

Analyze Characters

Reading: Literature

DIRECTIONS: Read the story. Then, answer the questions that follow.

Thinking resentfully about the history report that was due tomorrow, Jana heard her teacher's voice replay inside her head: "Don't just copy something from Wikipedia; write about something that made a difference."

She wanted to stomp up the steps and slam her front door, but instead she stopped to wave to her neighbor, who was moving a covered box to her car. The wind blew the lid off the container, and photos and newspaper clippings, caught in the gust, were soon swirling everywhere. Jana ran after them, collected them, and brought them back to Ms. Colvin.

"Thank you, dear," said her neighbor. "I had these all sorted to donate to the historical society, and I would hate for some of this history to go missing."

As Jana handed her a newspaper from 1955, she noticed a teenager who looked a lot like her neighbor pictured on the front page under the headline "Girl Held Guilty of Refusing to Move to Back of Bus."

"Is that you, Ms. Colvin?" asked Jana, pointing to the picture.

"Why, yes, dear, it is," her neighbor replied. "I was 15 at the time. I was sitting in the segregated section of the bus when the driver asked me to move so a white woman wouldn't have to sit close to me. We had been studying about black history, and I knew I wasn't breaking a law. So I stayed put."

"How did you have the courage to stay in your seat?" asked Jana.

"Actually, I couldn't have moved," said her neighbor. "It felt like Sojourner Truth's hands were pushing me down on one shoulder and Harriet Tubman's hands were pushing me down on another shoulder."

"So you knew even then that you were doing something that would make a difference," said Jana.

"Oh, yes," replied her neighbor. "And if I didn't then, I certainly knew when Rosa Parks did the same thing nine months later. And Rosa and I, and all of us, knew for certain when the Supreme Court ordered Alabama to desegregate its buses in 1956."

Jana was silent for a moment, trying to imagine what it would have been like to live in the segregated South. Thinking of her history assignment, Jana said, "Mrs. Colvin, would you mind if I asked you some more questions?"

Claudette Colvin, also known as "the other Rosa Parks," smiled at her neighbor and prepared to recall her memories of the Alabama bus boycott of 1955.

Name ______________________________ Date ______________

English Language Arts

Analyze Characters

Reading: Literature

DIRECTIONS: Use the story to answer the questions.

Strategy Use details about what characters say, do, and think to draw conclusions about them.

Test Tip Notice how Mrs. Colvin's conversation with Jana explains her reasons for staying in her seat on a segregated bus.

1. At the beginning of the story, Jana wants to do one thing, but instead does another. What does this show about her character?

____

____

2. When explaining why she stayed in her seat, Ms. Colvin refers to Sojourner Truth and Harriet Tubman. What is the significance of these references? Choose the two best answers.

Ⓐ Colvin was inspired by the example of Truth and Tubman.

Ⓑ Colvin wanted to become as famous as Truth and Tubman.

Ⓒ Colvin saw herself as carrying on the fight for freedom begun by Truth and Tubman.

Ⓓ Colvin admired Truth and Tubman, but she felt activists needed to find new ways to work for justice.

3. Write the line from the story that shows what event inspired Claudette Colvin to take her stand for justice. Write how you know. Think about Claudette Colvin's feelings and thoughts in that moment.

____

____

____

____

____

____

____

4. What role did her study of black history play in Claudette Colvin's decision to stay in her seat?

____

____

____

____

5. Why did Colvin's refusal to give up her seat make a difference?

____

____

____

____

6. What makes Jana stay and continue her discussion with her neighbor?

____

____

____

Name ______________________________ Date ______________

English Language Arts

Compare Text Structures

Reading: Literature

DIRECTIONS: The letter below is part of a historical story written as a series of letters. Read it and answer the questions that follow.

A Great Blow for Liberty

December 20, 1773

Dearest Cousin,

You have often read my complaints about the British efforts to force us to buy tea from the British East India Company, which has been given a monopoly on the beverage. Since the Tea Act was passed, every purchase of British tea admits Parliament's right to tax us without granting us representation. I, like many true Patriots, now drink coffee instead of tea.

Our protests have now gone a step further. On November 27, three ships brought their loads of tea into our harbor. When we did not allow them to land, Governor Hutchinson said that if the ships were not unloaded by December 17, he would break out the cannons and force us to accept the tea.

The night before the deadline expired, your uncle and I went to a meeting of the Sons of Liberty. We then formed three boarding parties. On the ship our party boarded, the captain gave us the keys as soon as we demanded them. He asked only that we do no damage to his ship, and we honored his request. We pulled the chests of tea on deck, and using tomahawks, broke them open and threw the tea into the harbor. Then, we silently disappeared into the night, having struck a great blow for Liberty.

With affection,

Daniel

Strategy

As you read stories, poems, and passages, look for one of the typical text structures: chronological, cause and effect, compare and contrast, question/answer, and problem/solution. Knowing how a text is organized will help you find main ideas, details, and theme.

Test Tip

When reading a story, notice how the author moves from one idea to another. One transition in this story is "The night before…" This is a clue about chronological sequence. Find other words related to time.

1. **Part A: What pattern does the author use to organize events in the letter?**
   - (A) compare-contrast
   - (B) problem-solution
   - (C) cause and effect
   - (D) chronological

   Part B: Write a sentence from the letter that supports your answer to part A.

   ____

   ____

   ____

Name ______________________ Date ______________

English Language Arts

Compare Text Structures

Reading: Literature

DIRECTIONS: Use the letter to answer the questions.

Strategy To identify text structure, ask yourself how you would organize the information in a chart. Would you organize information chronologically or sequentially? Or would you create a chart that compares and contrasts?

2. The organizational pattern is important in this letter because it helps readers understand:

Ⓐ which idea in the letter is the most important.

Ⓑ how a series of events led up to the Boston Tea Party.

Ⓒ where the tea ships were positioned in Boston Harbor.

Ⓓ why the governor refused to listen to the colonists' objections to landing the tea.

3. What would be the best organizer to use to summarize this letter?

Ⓐ a cause-effect chart

Ⓑ a map

Ⓒ a timeline

Ⓓ a Venn diagram

Write how you know.

____

____

____

____

____

4. Why do you think the author chose to describe the Boston Tea Party in a first-person letter instead of in a third-person report?

____

____

____

____

____

____

5. Which two text structures, or methods of organizing text, would also work with the details of this letter?

Ⓐ cause and effect

Ⓑ question/answer

Ⓒ compare and contrast

Ⓓ problem/solution

Write how you know.

____

____

____

____

____

____

____

Name ______________________________ Date ______________

Compare Text Structures

Reading: Literature

DIRECTIONS: Read the scene. Then, answer the questions that follow.

Setting: *A kitchen in Boston, Massachusetts, 1774. Young Nathan Cooper, about 12, talks with his father, Ephraim, and his uncle Jeremiah about the British reaction to the Boston Tea Party.*

NATHAN: Why are the British closing our port, Father?

EPHRAIM: They wish to punish us for the tea that was dumped into Boston Harbor, son.

JEREMIAH: But the Governor wouldn't listen to us. What else could we do to show the King that we will pay no more taxes until we have a voice in Parliament?

EPHRAIM: I agree our cause was just, brother. However, I do believe we should pay the cost of the 354 chests of tea that were destroyed.

JEREMIAH: That will not be enough to blunt the wrath of the British. They call us "lawless thugs" and attempt to destroy our shipping and break our spirits by shutting up the harbor. We may no longer hold town meetings or elect our own provincial officials or judges.

NATHAN: Don't they realize that this is making more and more people think we need to be independent of Great Britain?

JEREMIAH: They believe that if they can get the people of Boston to back down, the other colonies will stop resisting.

NATHAN: But what more can we do to keep resisting? Do we have to choose between going to war and letting the British take away our rights?

EPHRAIM: The Committee of Correspondence has sent a letter to all the other colonies, warning that they too may suffer the loss of their charter rights. We propose a boycott of all British goods, and we ask our sister colonies to stand with us.

JEREMIAH: One good thing has come out of these Intolerable Acts. This September, representatives of all the colonies will meet in Philadelphia. The British will learn that they have pushed us too far!

Name ______________________________ Date ______________

English Language Arts

Compare Text Structures

Reading: Literature

DIRECTIONS: Use the scene to answer the questions.

Strategy When comparing two passages, read each one and analyze them individually. Then, reread both passages and compare structure, setting, characters or individuals, events, theme, and main ideas.

Test Tip Each text structure includes specific words. For example, notice the date on which this conversation takes place. Dates are clues to chronological text structures.

1. What is the main conflict in this scene?

Ⓐ Nathan's desire for independence and his fear of war with the British

Ⓑ Bostonians who want to keep protesting and the other colonies that want to avoid war

Ⓒ Jeremiah and Ephraim argue about whether the colonists should pay for the cargo destroyed during the Boston Tea Party

Ⓓ the colonists who are angry at Britain's attempt to take away their rights and the British who are angry about the Boston Tea Party

2. What pattern does the author use to organize the dialogue in this scene?

Ⓐ argument-counterargument

Ⓑ comparison-contrast

Ⓒ question-answer

Ⓓ time order

Write how you know.

____

____

3. Why do you think the author chose to describe the British reaction to the Boston Tea Party in a dramatic scene rather than in an objective report?

____

____

4. The dramatic scene could be seen as using a problem/solution text structure. What is the problem? What is the solution?

____

____

____

5. Which two things do the the characters in the letter and in the drama have in common?

Ⓐ They believe that war with Britain cannot be avoided.

Ⓑ They are living through events leading up to the American Revolution.

Ⓒ They are angry with the British government and want to protect their rights.

Ⓓ They know that the conflict will end with the colonists forming a new independent

6. The letter focuses on one person's experience of the Boston Tea Party. In the drama, characters speak from many points of view. How does the difference affect the content of the two passages?

____

____

____

____

____

Name ______________________ Date ______________

English Language Arts

Analyze Point of View

Reading: Literature

DIRECTIONS: Read the poem. Then, answer the questions that follow.

Ah, Are You Digging on My Grave?
by Thomas Hardy

"Ah, are you digging on my grave,
My loved one?—planting rue?"
—"No: yesterday he went to wed
One of the brightest wealth has bred.
'It cannot hurt her now,' he said,
'That I should not be true.'"

"Then who is digging on my grave,
My nearest dearest kin?"
—"Ah, no: they sit and think, 'What use!
What good will planting flowers
produce?
No tendance of her mound can loose
Her spirit from Death's gin.'"

"But someone digs upon my grave?
My enemy?—prodding sly?"
—"Nay: when she heard you had
passed the Gate
That shuts on all flesh soon or late,
She thought you no more worth her
hate,
And cares not where you lie."

Then, who is digging on my grave?
Say—since I have not guessed!"
—"O it is I, my mistress dear,
Your little dog, who still lives near,
And much I hope my movements here
Have not disturbed your rest?"

"Ah yes! You dig upon my grave . . .
Why flashed it not to me
That one true heart was left behind!
What feeling do we ever find
To equal among human kind
A dog's fidelity!"

"Mistress, I dug upon your grave
To bury a bone, in case
I should be hungry near this spot
When passing on my daily trot. I am
sorry, but I quite forgot
It was your resting place."

Strategy Identify who is speaking in a poem and what the speaker (or speakers) and the reader know to understand dramatic irony.

Test Tip Dramatic irony is created when someone who witnesses a character's words or actions knows more than the character. Often, it is the reader who knows more than the characters. In this poem, the situation is slightly different. One speaker knows more than the other.

1. Part A: Who is answering the questions asked by the first speaker in the poem?

Ⓐ the man who loved her
Ⓑ the relatives who survive her
Ⓒ her worst enemy
Ⓓ her pet

Part B: Write the lines from the poem that support your answer to Part A.

____

____

____

____

Name ______________________ Date ______________

English Language Arts

Analyze Point of View

Reading: Literature

DIRECTIONS: Use the poem to answer the questions.

Strategy Make a list of what each character in a story or poem knows, including the narrator of a story and the speaker of a poem. Use the list to determine the point of view used.

Test Tip Authors of stories and poems often ask readers to make inferences about events. Use what you already know and details to infer what characters or speakers know, reasons for their actions, and the theme of the story and poem.

2. What is the main difference in the point of view of the two speakers?

(A) The woman's point of view is limited; the other speaker's is not.

(C) The woman now sees the events of her life from a new perspective.

(C) The woman's point of view is trustworthy; the other speaker's is not.

(D) The woman cares about the other speaker; the other speaker does not care about the woman

Write how you know.

____

____

3. How does the woman's lack of understanding set up the ironic ending?

(A) The woman misinterprets her pet's motives for digging on her grave.

(C) The woman realizes that petty disputes no longer matter after death.

(B) The woman realizes she should have known her faithful pet would not forget her.

(D) The woman learns that the woman she thought was her enemy really admired her.

4. What happens each time the woman gets an answer to her first 3 questions?

(A) She finds out that someone she trusted has lied to her.

(B) She learns that the people who loved her still care about her.

(C) She finds out how her life affects the lives of the people to whom she was close.

(D) She discovers that her expectation of how she would be remembered after death is wrong.

5. What does the second speaker know that the first speaker does not?

____

____

____

____

Test Tip

Authors use dramatic irony to create a sense of suspense or to use humor.

Name ______________________________ Date ______________

English Language Arts

Connect Modern and Traditional Stories

Reading: Literature

DIRECTIONS: Read the traditional fairy tale. Then, answer the questions that follow.

Little Red Riding Hood

There was once a sweet little maid who lived with her father and mother in a pretty little cottage at the edge of the village. At the further end of the wood was another pretty cottage where her beloved grandmother lived.

Her grandmother gave the child a red cloak with a hood that she wore so much people started calling her Little Red Riding Hood.

One morning Little Red Riding Hood's mother said, "Put on your things and go to see your grandmother. She has been ill; take along this basket of goodies for her."

Little Red Riding Hood was walking through the woods, stopping occasionally to pick wildflowers, when a gruff voice said, "Good morning, Little Red Riding Hood." When she turned around, she saw a great big wolf, but Little Red Riding Hood did not know what a wicked beast the wolf was, so she was not afraid.

"What have you in that basket, Little Red Riding Hood?"

"Eggs and butter and cake, Mr. Wolf."

"Where are you going with them, Little Red Riding Hood?"

"I am going to my grandmother, who is ill, Mr. Wolf."

"Where does your grandmother live, Little Red Riding Hood?"

"Along that path, past the wild rose bushes, then through the gate at the end of the wood, Mr. Wolf."

The wolf raced to the cottage and knocked on the door. When the grandmother asked who was there, he said, "Little Red Riding Hood." So the grandmother invited him in. He made one leap at her, but she jumped out of bed into a closet. Then, the wolf put on the nightcap that she had dropped and crept under the bedclothes.

In a short while Little Red Riding Hood knocked at the door, and walked in, saying, "Good morning, Grandmother, I have brought you eggs, butter, and cake.

As she came nearer the bed, she said, "What big eyes you have, Grandmother."

"All the better to see you with, my dear."

"But, Grandmother, what a big nose you have."

"All the better to smell with, my dear."

"But, Grandmother, what a big mouth you have."

"All the better to eat you up with, my dear," said the wicked wolf as he sprang at Little Red Riding Hood to devour her.

Just at that moment Little Red Riding Hood's father was passing the cottage and heard her scream. He rushed in, swung his ax, and chopped off Mr. Wolf's head. Then, he carried Little Red Riding Hood home and they lived happily ever after.

Strategy

Use the features of a traditional story, such as a fairy tale, fable, legend, or myth, to analyze how they compare to modern stories.

Test Tip

Fairy tales often contain magical elements or elements of fantasy—events that could not happen in real life. Fairy tales also have a hero and a villain. Ask yourself, *Who is the hero of this fairy tale? Who is the villain?*

1. Which two reasons tell you this passage is a fairy tale?

Ⓐ The wolf can talk to the girl.

Ⓑ The father is brave and strong.

Ⓒ Little Red Riding Hood is very polite.

Ⓓ The good characters live happily ever after.

Write how you know.

____

____

____

Name ______________________________ Date ______________

English Language Arts

Analyze Influence of Traditional Stories

Reading: Literature

DIRECTIONS: Use the fairy tale to answer the questions.

Strategy Reread a modern story and look for repeating or familiar themes often found in traditional stories, such as good versus evil, overcoming challenges, or reinventing yourself. Use these themes to determine how features of traditional stories are present in modern stories.

Test Tip Traditional stories often have themes about good and evil or right and wrong. How to behave and how to treat people are also common themes.

2. Write the line from the story that tells why Little Red Riding Hood answers the wolf's question about where her grandmother lives.

____

____

____

____

3. Describe the villain in this story. Use at least two details from the passage in your answer.

____

____

____

____

4. Part A: Who is the hero of this story?

(A) the father

(B) the mother

(C) the grandmother

(D) Little Red Riding Hood

Part B: Explain your answer to Part A.

____

____

____

5. What is a theme of this story?

(A) Be kind to your grandmother.

(B) Villains in real life are easy to identify.

(C) Always be polite when you're talking to people.

(D) Learn to recognize danger so you can protect yourself.

Write how you know.

____

____

____

____

6. Why does the author include the line "they lived happily ever after" at the end of the story? Use what you know about the elements of traditional tales to answer.

____

____

____

____

____

____

Name ______________________________ Date ______________

English Language Arts

Connect Modern and Traditional Stories

Reading: Literature

DIRECTIONS: Read the modern version of "Little Red Riding Hood." Then, answer the questions that follow.

Little Red Riding Hood Meets the Wolf

Hi. My name is Little Red Riding Hood, but you can call me Red. I live in the woods, which are very pretty to look at, but which harbor some pretty nasty creatures.

One of them is Big, Bad, and Ugly. He's a scrawny looking wolf with a deep, gruff voice and a nasty habit of trying to catch little girls and eat them.

Normally my mother doesn't let me go into the woods by myself, but my grandmother has been ill and my mother is worried about her getting enough nourishment. So here I am, walking through the woods with a basket of goodies instead of being stuck at home doing chores. Wonder when Mr. Big, Bad, and Ugly will show up?

Sure enough, I hear him creeping up behind me on the path. He tries to act friendly and make conversation, but I know he's just trying to find out where I'm going. As soon as he sees the big "For Grandma" tag tied to the basket, he takes off down the path with a fake toothy grin.

I figure if he's heading to Grandma's, I'd better get there as fast as I can. As I reach the end of the path and run through the gate, I see the wolf knocking on the door and squeaking, "It's Little Red Riding Hood" in a pathetic attempt to sound like a little girl.

"Come in, dear," coos Grandma, as she opens the door and positions herself behind it. The wolf starts slinking up the steps. Just as he gets inside, Grandma hefts her cast iron skillet and clouts him a good one. "Here, Red," she says, handing me a broom. "Poke that varmint in the stomach and get him off my porch."

"You got it, Grandma," I say, brandishing the broom. With each swat, I scream as high and loud as I can.

"Stop, please stop," begs the wolf, holding his ears in agony.

"What big, sensitive ears you have," I say. "Why don't you use your big, long legs and run away? Bothering a peaceful old woman and her granddaughter, and trying to turn us into dinner! You scat, or I'll scream louder!"

Trying to cover his ears and hold his sore head at the same time, the wolf slithers down the steps and scuttles off into the forest.

"Nice work with the broom, dear," says Grandma. "You're ready to have your father show you some of his staff–fighting moves."

"Mother says that's not ladylike," I say.

"Ladylike, schmadylike," retorts Grandma. "You can have wonderful manners and still stand up for yourself. Now let's have some of that cake."

Name ______________________________ Date ______________

English Language Arts

Connect Modern and Traditional Stories

Reading: Literature

DIRECTIONS: Use the fairy tale to answer the questions.

Strategy To determine if a story is a traditional story or a modern story that retells a tale, identify the setting. Ask yourself if this story could happen today.

Test Tip A traditional story is one that has been shared for many years, such as a fairy tale, a fable, or a folktale. Consider how the characters, setting, tone, point of view, and plot events in the two stories compare.

1. **Contrast the way Little Red Riding Hood and Red react the first time they meet the wolf. What does this show about their characters?**

____

____

____

____

2. **Modern fairy tales often have a twist, or an unexpected turn, to the ending. What is the twist in this tale?**

____

____

3. **Write a line from the modern version that reminds you of the original version.**

____

____

4. **Part A: According to "Little Red Riding Hood," what two qualities were young women expected to have at the time the tale was written?**

   Ⓐ courage
   Ⓑ innocence
   Ⓒ intelligence
   Ⓓ politeness

Part B: How does Red differ from a typical female character in a traditional fairy tale? Use your response to Part A to explain.

____

____

____

____

____

____

____

____

5. **Which statement best expresses the message, or theme, of the modern version of the story?**

   Ⓐ People only live happily ever after in fairy tales.
   Ⓑ Young girls cannot learn to recognize signs of danger.
   Ⓒ You can be kind and polite without letting others take advantage of you.
   Ⓓ If you are good and sweet, someone will always come along to rescue you from danger.

Name ______________________ Date ______________

English Language Arts

Use Text Details to Support Inferences

Reading: Informational Text

DIRECTIONS: Read the article. Then, answer the questions that follow.

Maternal Fish Fathers

In the warm and temperate waters of the world live two unusual fish: the sea horse and its relative, the pipefish.

The sea horse, so-called because its head resembles a horse, is a small fish about two to eight inches long. It swims by moving the dorsal fin on its back. It is the only fish with a prehensile tail, which it uses like a monkey, to coil around and cling to seaweed.

The pipefish is named for its long snout, which looks like a thin pipe. When its body is straight, the pipefish resembles a slender snake. Its body forms an S shape and is propelled by its rear fins.

But it is not appearance that makes the sea horse and pipefish unusual. It is their paternal roles. With both fish, the female's responsibility ends when she lays and deposits her eggs. From that point on, the male takes over and, in a manner of speaking, gives birth to the babies.

Both the male sea horse and pipefish have pouch-like organs on their undersides in which the female deposits her eggs. Here the young fish stay and are nourished for either a few days or for several weeks, depending on the species. When the baby sea horses are ready to be born, the father sea horse attaches itself to a plant and actually goes through the pangs of childbirth. As the sea horse bends back and forth, the wall of its brood pouch contracts. With each spasm, a baby fish is introduced into the world of the sea. The birth of the baby pipefish is less dramatic. The father's pouch simply opens, and the offspring swim off on their own.

Strategy When making inferences, look for evidence in the passage to support each conclusion you draw. Reread to make sure inferences have enough support.

Test Tip Use what you know about word parts to determine the meaning of words.

1. The Latin word for "father" is *pater*. Write a definition of the English word *paternal*.

____

2. The Latin word for "mother" is *mater*. Write a definition of the English word *maternal*.

____

Name ______________________________ Date ______________

English Language Arts

Use Text Details to Support Inferences

Reading: Informational Text

DIRECTIONS: Use the article to answer the questions.

Strategy Reread the passage and ask yourself if you know any information about the topic from previous readings. Then, use what you already know to help you make inferences.

Test Tip To answer questions about which inferences are supported by the passage, first eliminate answers that are contradicted by the passage.

3. Write the sentence from the fourth paragraph that best explains how a male fish can be maternal.

____

____

4. Which sentences from the passage support the main idea that sea horses and pipefish are unusual because of their appearance and how they reproduce?

____

____

5. Write the words from the sentence below that tell you what the word *prehensile* means.

"It is the only fish with a prehensile tail, which it uses like a monkey, to coil around and cling to seaweed."

____

6. In the last paragraph, this sentence provides a clue to the meaning of a word in the next sentence: "As the sea horse bends back and forth, the wall of its brood pouch contracts. With each spasm, a baby horse is introduced into the world of the sea."

Write the word that is defined in context.

____

Which words helped you determine the meaning?

____

____

7. Part A: Which of these inferences can be supported by the passage?

Ⓐ Male fish form strong bonds with the eggs in their pouch.

Ⓑ Male fish that give birth protect their newly hatched offspring.

Ⓒ The male sea horse can be described as more maternal than the male pipefish.

Ⓓ Male fish that give birth survive because female sea horses and pipefish find food for them.

Part B: Use two details from the passage to support your answer to Part A.

____

____

____

____

Name ______________________________ Date ______________

English Language Arts

Use Main Ideas and Details to Summarize

Reading: Informational Text

DIRECTIONS: Read the passages. Then, answer the questions using details from the passages.

Mathew Brady: The Father of Photojournalism

Mathew B. Brady opened his first photography studio in 1844. The images he produced were daguerreotypes, recorded images on sheets of copper, coated with silver. They required long exposures to produce the image, so a person being photographed would have to stay perfectly still for three to fifteen minutes. That made daguerreotypes impractical for portraits. By 1855, though, Brady was advertising a new type of image that had just been invented: a photograph made on paper.

From the beginning of his career, Brady thought that photography could serve an important purpose. His images could create a record of national life. When the Civil War broke out, he wanted to create a photographic record of the war. Although his costs were prohibitive and his friends discouraged him, he assembled a corps of photographers to take photos of the battlefield and surgeons' tents. He also bought photographs from others returning from the field. Near the end of his life, he reflected, "No one will ever know what [those photographs] cost me; some of them almost cost me my life."

At the time, photographs could not be reproduced in newspapers, so Brady displayed them in his gallery in New York City. His efforts culminated in an 1862 display of photographs made after the Battle of Antietam. The bloodshed shocked the exhibit's visitors, most of whom had never known what warfare was like. A reviewer for *The New York Times* wrote, "These pictures have a terrible distinctness. By the aid of the magnifying glass, the very features of the slain may be distinguished. We would scarce choose to be in the gallery, when one of the women bending over them should recognize a husband, a son, or a brother in the still, lifeless lines of bodies, that lie ready for the gaping trenches."

Brady's goal was to use powerful photos to end all war. Brady did not stop warfare, of course. He did not even earn enough money to pay for his venture. Still, Brady recorded one of the most important episodes in American history, the Civil War. In doing so, he created the first photodocumentation of a war and achieved his lifelong goal: to make photography "a great and truthful medium of history."

Strategy Identify the central idea and key supporting details, and use these to summarize a passage.

Test Tip Read the title and use it to help you identify the central idea. Remember that the central idea is the most important idea of the passage.

1. Part A: What is the central idea of this passage?

Ⓐ Brady used photography to create a truthful record of history.

Ⓑ Brady did not let his friends discourage him from taking battlefield photographs.

Ⓒ Brady exhibited photographs of Antietam that were more realistic than any New Yorkers had ever seen.

Ⓓ Brady took photos on Civil War battlefields because he believed there was little danger to people who weren't actually fighting.

Part B: Write a sentence from the story that supports your answer to Part A.

____

____

____

____

Name ______________________________ Date ______________

English Language Arts

Use Main Ideas and Details to Summarize

Reading: Informational Text

DIRECTIONS: Use the passage to answer the questions.

Strategy When you summarize, make sure to only include the most important ideas. Any details that you use should relate only to the central idea. Avoid adding your personal opinions.

2. What is the most likely reason the author included the quotation from *The New York Times* reviewer?

- (A) to show the amazing technical quality of Brady's photographs
- (B) to explain why so many New Yorkers came to Brady's exhibits
- (C) to emphasize the emotional impact of Brady's battlefield photographs
- (D) to show that people recognized the importance of Brady's innovative photojournalism

3. Write the sentence in the second paragraph that supports the idea that using photography to capture history was Brady's "lifelong goal."

____

____

____

4. Part A: Which definition of the word *medium* best fits the way the word is used in the last sentence of the passage?

- (A) a way of communication
- (B) the midpoint between extremes
- (C) material used in a work of art, such as acrylic
- (D) substance in which scientists grow bacteria

Write how you know.

____

____

____

5. Use the central idea and key supporting details to summarize how Brady's photography achieved historical importance.

____

____

____

____

____

____

____

____

____

____

____

____

Name ______________________ Date ______________

English Language Arts

Analyze Text Structure

Reading: Informational Text

DIRECTIONS: Read the passage. Then, answer the questions that follow.

"Yankee Doodle": From Insult to Anthem

Singing a song in Revolutionary America could get you in trouble. At the time, almost everyone sang in public on occasion. People might sing hymns in church or entertain themselves by singing popular songs. However, songs were also important instruments of satire. People used them to make fun of public figures, to pass ugly rumors, or to playfully insult their enemies.

As opposition to British rule in the American colonies heated up, satirical songs took on a new edge. Rebellious colonists sang songs insulting Britain's king, George III, as a drunken tyrant. British soldiers answered with songs ridiculing the Americans as ignorant backwoods yokels.

One of these songs told the story of a poorly dressed Yankee simpleton, or doodle. An early version used the insulting term *Yankee* to refer to the colonists:

Yankee Doodle came to town
Riding on a pony,
Stuck a feather in his hat
And called him Macaroni.

The song was so popular with British troops that they played it as they marched to battle on the first day of the Revolutionary War. However, the rebels quickly claimed the song as their own. They created dozens of new verses that mocked the British, praised the new Continental Army, and hailed its commander, George Washington. One anti-British version declared

Yankee Doodle is the tune,
That we all delight in;
It suits for feasts, it suits for fun,
And just as well for fighting!

By 1781, when the British surrendered at Yorktown, the colonists no longer considered being called a Yankee Doodle an insult. The song had become the unofficial national anthem of their new country.

Strategy Analyze the structure of the passage and use it to understand the central idea of a passage.

Test Tip Look for ways that the meaning of "Yankee Doodle" changes.

1. How is the passage structured?

Ⓐ cause-effect
Ⓑ comparison-contrast
Ⓒ least important to most important
Ⓓ time order

Write how you know.

____

____

Name ______________________________ Date ______________

English Language Arts

Analyze Text Structure

Reading: Informational Text

DIRECTIONS: Use the passage to answer the questions.

Strategy Determine how information is organized to identify which text structure is used.

Test Tip Use text structure to find information. Problem–solution passages introduce a problem and then describe a solution; compare-and-contrast passages organize information into how things are alike and how they are different.

2. The structure helps you understand the passage because it

Ⓐ establishes the order in which events took place.

Ⓑ signals that the most important information will be at the end of the passage

Ⓒ alerts readers to pay attention to the difference between the two versions of the song.

Ⓓ explains the reason that the rebels began singing anti-British verses to "Yankee Doodle."

3. What other text structures would work for the passage? Write two other structures and explain how they would work to organize the information.

____

____

____

____

____

4. Where in the passage does the author shift from writing about the British version of "Yankee Doodle" to the colonial version of the song?

Ⓐ the last sentence of the first paragraph

Ⓑ the entire third paragraph

Ⓒ the first two lines of the fourth paragraph

Ⓓ the first sentence of the last paragraph

5. What claim does the author support by including a verse from "Yankee Doodle" in the fourth paragraph?

____

____

____

____

6. Below is an incomplete outline of the passage. Fill in the blank.

I. Introduction

A. Singing in Colonial America

B. Satirical Songs

II. Example of a Satirical Song: "Yankee Doodle"

A. _____

B. Colonial version

III. Conclusion

A. New meaning

B. "Unofficial national anthem

____

Name ______________________________ Date ______________

English Language Arts

Determine Author's Purpose

Reading: Informational Text

DIRECTIONS: Read the passage. Then, answer the questions that follow.

The Myth of Multitasking

Do you pride yourself on your ability to multitask? You may not be as efficient as you think.

Dr. Clifford Nass did a study of 262 college students in 2009. He found that students who constantly switched their attention from texting to Facebook to television to music thought they were excellent multitaskers. They also believed multitasking made them more efficient.

The truth is just the opposite. Dr. Nass and his colleague Eyal Phir found that multitaskers were constantly distracted. Even as they worked on one thing, they were thinking about what they weren't doing. As they gathered information from many sources, the information got jumbled together in their minds. And, while students who multitasked while doing homework felt they covered more material than those who focused on one thing at a time, multitaskers don't remember what they study as well as students who are less distracted.

Dr. Russell Poldrack, professor of psychology at UCLA, told NPR's Lynn Neery that "when you learn while you're focused on a task, you engage...the hippocampus" (a part of the brain that stores conscious memories). Those who try to learn while doing many things at once engage the basal ganglia (a part of the brain that builds habits). As a result, multitaskers are less able to remember what they learned. They also have trouble applying what they learned in new situations.

Another reason multitaskers are less efficient is that it takes at least a few tenths of a second to stop doing one task and start doing another. That doesn't sound like much, but it can add up to 40% of your study time, according to cognitive scientist Dr. David Meyer.

When you're driving, those seconds count even more. In the five seconds it takes you to answer a text, your car can travel 120 yards—the length of a football field. The reaction time of a young driver distracted by a cell phone can be as slow as that of a seventy-year-old.

You might think that these statistics would encourage people to focus when they're in the driver's seat. But people tend to assume that they're good at multitasking, according to Dr. David Sabonmatsu; it's only other drivers who become dangerously distracted. The reality? The better you think you are at multitasking, the more dangerous you are behind the wheel.

When you look at all the evidence, the idea that multitasking makes you more productive is a myth. Focusing on one thing at a time helps you learn better, save time, and stay safer on the road.

Name ______________________ Date ______________

Determine Author's Purpose

Reading Informational Text

DIRECTIONS: Use the passage to answer the questions.

Strategy Identify words and phrases that tell what a writer thinks or how a writer feels about the topic. Use these words as clues to determine the writer's purpose, or why he or she wanted to write the passage.

Test Tip Words like *On the other hand* and *Nevertheless* signal when an author moves from one side of the argument to another side.

1. **The author makes three arguments against multitasking. Complete the chart by adding evidence from the passage.**

Argument Against Multitasking	Supporting Evidence
interferes with learning	Nass:
	Poldrack:
is less efficient	Meyer:
is dangerous	Sabonmatsu

2. **Which statement best summarizes the author's position on multitasking?**
   - Ⓐ Multitasking saves time.
   - Ⓑ If you think you are good at multitasking, you're probably right.
   - Ⓒ People who focus on one thing at a time are more productive than multitaskers.
   - Ⓓ Good multitaskers can change focus so quickly they lose very little time when they switch tasks.

3. **Why might the author have mentioned common beliefs about multitasking in the second paragraph?**

____

____

____

4. **Which statistic would make the sixth paragraph stronger?**
   - Ⓐ About 80% of cell phone users send text messages.
   - Ⓑ Ninety percent of American adults have a cell phone.
   - Ⓒ Forty-four percent of cell phone users sleep with their phone next to their bed.
   - Ⓓ Drivers who text are 23 times more likely to crash than undistracted drivers.

5. **What advice might the author have for students who want to improve their study habits?**

____

____

____

____

Name ______________________________ Date ______________

English Language Arts

Evaluate Arguments

Reading: Informational Text

DIRECTIONS: Read the passage. Then, answer the questions that follow.

Do Animals Have Emotions?

For people who have pets, the answer to the question of whether animals have emotions may seem obvious. "Of course they do," a dog-lover may assert. "Fido can sense when I'm sad, and he'll come sit beside me and lay his head on my knee to comfort me." For scientists, however, the question gets a little more complicated.

When humans try to interpret animal behavior, we tend to assume that animals think and feel the same way we do. For example, when her owner, Heather, went back to work, a Rottweiler named Blue began getting into trash cans and destroying electrical cords. Heather assumed Blue was trying to punish her for being left alone so much. Actually, explains Jon Katz, the dog was frightened and didn't know what rules to follow. When Heather used a crate to teach Blue how to behave when left alone, the dog's anxiety eased and the bad behavior stopped.

Blue's story illustrates the danger of interpreting animal emotions by human standards. The assumption that animals think and feel as humans do is called *anthropomorphism*. In an attempt to avoid anthropomorphism, one group of psychologists, the behaviorists, insists that only measurable results can be used to interpret animal emotions. They consider animal emotions to be simple instinctive responses to various stimuli.

Recently, a new discipline called *affective neuroscience* has begun exploring the processes that cause and control emotions in both people and animals. Researchers into these processes have found evidence of emotion in several species, including dogs, rats, ducks, baboons, elephants, and dolphins. For example, a 2014 study by Christine Harris and Caroline Prouvost showed that when dogs were ignored while their owners played with a stuffed dog, they started snapping or tried to get between their owners and the toy. The researchers interpreted these behaviors as signs the dogs were feeling jealous.

Although a growing number of researchers believe animals experience genuine emotion, they still are cautious about interpreting animal emotions by human standards. As affective neuroscientist Dr. Jaak Panksepp explains, feelings like love and joy help both animals and humans survive. However, he cautions, "this doesn't imply that animals think about their feelings like people do." Nevertheless, Panksepp believes people and animals "do experience [emotions] in similar ways."

So the question of how animals experience emotions hasn't been fully answered. Some scientists still say that dogs show affection only because affectionate behavior encourages humans to keep feeding them. But if you choose to interpret your dog's playful smile as a sign of genuine happiness, a growing number of scientists would agree.

Name ______________________________ Date ______________

English Language Arts

Evaluate Arguments

Reading: Informational Text

DIRECTIONS: Use the passage to answer the questions.

Strategy Decide whether a claim is valid by evaluating the strength of the evidence that supports it.

Test Tip Look for evidence to support each claim an author makes. Also, consider the source of the evidence. Is it reliable? Is it valid?

1. **Part A: Which statement accurately summarizes the author's claim about animal emotions?**
   - (A) Those who say animals don't experience real emotions are wrong.
   - (B) No reputable scientists still reject the idea that animals have real emotions.
   - (C) We cannot say whether animals have real emotions without judging them by human standards.
   - (D) Scientists disagree about whether animals have real emotions, but a growing body of evidence suggests they do.

   Part B: Which two types of evidence are used to support this claim?
   - (A) expert opinion
   - (B) personal experience
   - (C) scientific research studies
   - (D) statistics

   Write how you know.

   ____

   ____

   ____

   Part C: Would a pet owner's story about how well her dog understands her feelings add support to this claim? Why or why not?

   ____

   ____

2. **Which two reasons tell why the author disputes the behaviorists' claim that animals do not experience genuine emotions?**
   - (A) Their point of view is outdated.
   - (B) Their criteria for studying animal behavior are too strict.
   - (C) Their point of view is no longer accepted by any reputable scientists.
   - (D) Their belief that we cannot study animals without judging them by human standards is too cautious.

3. **Suppose the author decided to revise the article "Do Animals Have Emotions?" to include a claim that elephants experience grief. If this claim were added to the article, which would be the best evidence to support it?**
   - (A) A newspaper article reports that a baby elephant cried for five hours after his mother rejected him.
   - (B) A zookeeper reports that an elephant weeps whenever her companion is taken out of their enclosure.
   - (C) Jeffrey Masson's 1996 book *When Elephants Weep* includes several anecdotes about elephants that were said to cry.
   - (D) Elephant expert Joyce Poole has observed elephant mothers in the wild that refuse to leave the bodies of their dead infants.

Name ______________________________ Date ______________

Evaluate Arguments

Reading: Informational Text

DIRECTIONS: Read the passage. Then, answer the questions.

Can Pets Help Keep You Healthy?

Exploring the Human-Animal Bond

You take good care of your pet. But what's your pet done for you lately? Scared intruders from your door? Fetched your slippers? Given you a loving nuzzle? People have lots of reasons for owning pets. Now, a small but growing body of research suggests that owning or interacting with animals may have the added benefit of improving your health.

It's true that scientific study of the human-animal bond is still in its infancy. Several small or anecdotal studies have uncovered intriguing connections between human health and animal interactions. However, more rigorous follow-up studies have often shown mixed results. "The general belief is that there are [psychological] health benefits to owning pets, as well as physical health benefits," says Dr. James Griffin, a scientist at the National Institutes of Health (NIH). "But there have been relatively few well-controlled studies. That's the state of the science, in a nutshell."

Some of the largest and most well-designed studies in this field suggest that four-legged friends can help to improve our cardiovascular health. One NIH-funded study looked at 421 adults who'd suffered heart attacks. A year later, the scientists found, dog owners were significantly more likely to still be alive than were those who did not own dogs, regardless of how severe their heart attack had been.

Several studies have shown that dog owners may get more exercise and other health benefits than the rest of us. One NIH-funded investigation looked at more than 2,000 adults and found that dog owners who regularly walked their dogs were more physically active and less likely to be obese than those who didn't own or walk a dog. When my neighbor broke his foot and couldn't walk his dog Jasper, a Labradoodle, he gained five pounds. Another study supported by NIH followed more than 2,500 older adults, ages 71-82, for 3 years. Those who regularly walked their dogs walked faster and for longer time periods each week than others who didn't walk regularly. Older dog walkers also were better able to move around their homes.

Several research teams are examining the potential benefits of bringing specially trained animals into clinical settings. These animal-assisted therapies are increasingly offered in hospitals and nursing homes nationwide. Although little solid scientific evidence confirms the value of this type of therapy, clinicians who watch patients interacting with animals say they can clearly see benefits, including improved mood and reduced anxiety.

Berger and Barker recently wrapped up a preliminary clinical study looking at how well animals help hospitalized cancer patients cope with pain. The data have not yet been analyzed, but the researchers hope it will serve as a launching point for future investigations.

"I think we're just at the tip of the iceberg in terms of what we know about the human-animal bond and its potential health benefits," Barker says.

Name ______________________________ Date ______________

English Language Arts

Evaluate Arguments

Reading Informational Text

DIRECTIONS: Use the passage to answer the questions.

Strategy Decide whether a claim is valid by evaluating if the evidence that supports the claim is relevant and sufficient. Does the evidence make sense? Is there enough evidence?

Test Tip Relevant evidence is directly related to the claim. Ask yourself, *Does this evidence really prove what the author says it does? Am I convinced? Did the author include enough evidence or examples?*

1. Part A: Which statement below best expresses the claim made in the passage on the benefits of owning pets?

Ⓐ It has been definitely proven that owning pets improves people's physical and mental health.

Ⓑ New types of animal-assisted therapies are being used to help patients deal with difficult situations.

Ⓒ People believe their pets make them feel better, but there is little evidence to support this idea.

Ⓓ Some good evidence suggests that animals can improve people's physical and mental health, but more studies are needed.

Part B: Cite two sentences that helped you answer Part A.

____

____

____

2. Part A: Which detail should be omitted from the fourth paragraph because it is not relevant?

Ⓐ More than one study has found that dog owners get more exercise.

Ⓑ Walking a dog helps people control their weight.

Ⓒ A man who couldn't walk his Labradoodle because of a broken foot gained weight.

Ⓓ Elderly dog walkers kept their ability to move around better than less active older people.

Part B: Explain your answer to Part A.

____

____

____

DIRECTIONS: Read the paragraph below. Then, answer the question.

Scientists are studying how animals help humans stay healthy, and they're finding a lot of ways. Just petting a dog can be good for you. Several studies have shown that stroking a dog lowers people's blood pressure. Thirty-five percent of Americans households own at least one dog, according to the American Veterinary Medical Association. Just over 30% of homes have at least one cat. These households are expected to spend at least $58.51 billion on their pets in 2014. Walking a dog also has health benefits. Owners who walk their dogs get more exercise and have fewer weight problems than people who didn't walk as often. Dogs also make people feel less anxious. So the money people spend on pets isn't wasted.

3. Which two details are relevant to the claim that animals help humans stay physically healthy?

Ⓐ how petting a dog affects blood pressure

Ⓑ how many households own dogs

Ⓒ how many households own cats

Ⓓ how owning a dog affects the amount of exercise people get

Name ______________________________ Date ______________

English Language Arts

Determine the Meanings of Words and Phrases

Language

DIRECTIONS: Choose or write the correct answer.

Strategy Use details, context, and word clues to determine the meaning of unknown words.

Read the paragraph. Then, answer the questions.

Propaganda is the distribution of ideas and information to persuade people or to intensify specific attitudes and actions. Although massive wartime propaganda techniques began with World War I, propaganda activities escalated greatly during World War II. The Axis powers tried to weaken the morale of the Allied armed forces and civilian populations by radio propaganda and by dropping leaflets onto civilians and Allied troops. The Allies, in turn, attempted to separate the citizens of the Axis nations from their governments, whom they blamed solely for the war. Radio broadcasts and leaflets dropped from the air carried Allied propaganda to the enemy.

1. **The literal meaning of the word *propaganda* comes from the Latin word *propagare,* which means "to spread." However, because propaganda is typically one-sided, people often think of propaganda messages as biased or deceitful. Which sentence best uses this connotative meaning of *propaganda*?**

   Ⓐ Advertising agencies once referred to their campaigns as propaganda.

   Ⓑ Examples of propaganda have been found in the writings of the ancient Romans and Persians.

   Ⓒ One of the earliest uses of the word was in the name of a Christian missionary group, the Society for the Propagation of the Faith.

   Ⓓ During World War II, Nazi Propaganda Minister Joseph Goebbels falsely claimed that Czechoslovakia had asked to be annexed by Germany.

   Write how you know.

   ____

   ____

2. ***Bene* comes from a Latin word meaning "well" or "in the right way." What effect are beneficial bacteria in our digestive system likely to have on human health?**

   Ⓐ They cause stomach upsets.

   Ⓑ Their role in digestion is unknown.

   Ⓒ They help us digest carbohydrates.

   Ⓓ They make us vulnerable to viruses.

3. **Part A: Read the definitions below. Then, write your own definition of the prefix *counter–*.**

   counterargument: an attempt to prove an argument against your claim is wrong

   counterclockwise: moving against the direction of the clock

   counterpoint: two melodies that are played against each other at the same time

   ____

   Part B: What does the word *counterfactual* mean? Write a definition based on your response to Part A.

   ____

   Write how you know.

   ____

   ____

Name ______________________ Date ______________

English Language Arts

Determine the Meanings of Words and Phrases

Language

DIRECTIONS: Read the passage and answer the questions that follow.

Satellites Used to Save Species

No satellite can detect a lizard from space. But biologist Chris Raxworthy is using satellite data to predict where previously undiscovered species of chameleon might live in Madagascar.

Raxworthy's colleague Ned Horning always believed that satellite data could be useful for ecological niche modeling—predicting the unique locations, or niches, where species or ecological communities exist. He got the idea when he was working at NASA's Goddard Space Flight Center.

Horning and Raxworthy worked together to build a computer model that combined data from old maps with satellite observations. They developed a formula to predict where new species of chameleons might be found. Exploring sites indicated by the model, they have so far found seven new species of chameleon.

"Madagascar is vast," said Raxworthy, "and much is being lost. Any tool that makes describing the island's biodiversity more efficient will be welcomed." In their fight to save species from extinction, conservation biologists need all the tools they can get.

Strategy Use word parts—prefixes, suffixes, and roots—to determine the meanings of words.

1. Why is the work Horning and Raxworthy did in Madagascar an example of ecological niche modeling?

____

____

2. The prefix *bio-* means "life." The word *diversity* means "variety." What does the word *biodiversity* mean?

____

____

Write how you know.

____

____

3. Based on the information in this article, what do conservation biologists do?

- (A) They study chameleons and other reptiles.
- (B) They work to save species from extinction.
- (C) They visit unexplored areas to hunt for new species.
- (D) They use computer models instead of traditional scientific tools.

Write how you know.

____

____

____

____

Name ______________________________ Date ______________

English Language Arts

Understand Word Relationships

Language

DIRECTIONS: Choose or write the correct answer.

Strategy Use a variety of strategies to understand how words are related in a passage. Use details, context, and word clues to make connections between words.

1. Read the passage below.

Oily rags packed tightly into a box or a silo filled with damp grain suddenly bursting into flames appear to be mysterious, for the flames have no apparent cause. But there is one cause of fire that many people don't understand or even think about—spontaneous combustion.

All fires are caused by the heat that is given off when oxygen combines with some material. Fast oxidation gives off much heat and light very quickly and causes things to burn. Slow oxidation gives off no light and very little heat, not nearly enough to cause a fire. But when this little bit of heat is trapped, it cannot escape into the air. Instead, it builds up. As more and more oxidation occurs, more heat is trapped. As the material gets hotter, it oxidizes faster, and the faster oxidation produces even more heat. Finally, things get so hot that a fire starts. Damp or oily materials and powdery substances are the most likely things to produce spontaneous combustion because a little moisture makes them oxidize more quickly.

1. Write the words in the first sentence that help you understand what the term *spontaneous combustion* means.

____

2. Identify the type of comparison in this figure of speech: Jordan's temper is like spontaneous combustion: his anger heats up slowly and then bursts into flame.

Ⓐ analogy

Ⓑ hyperbole

Ⓒ irony

Ⓓ metaphor

Write how you know.

____

____

3. If someone is described as a "young Einstein," what does that suggest about what the person is like?

____

____

4. Which detail in the passage can you use to understand the meaning of the word *oxidation*?

____

____

5. Explain the different between fast and slow oxidation.

____

____

____

6. Why did the author include information about both fast and slow oxidation?

Ⓐ to share examples of fires that could be prevented

Ⓑ to give the reader background information on oxidation

Ⓒ to explain both causes for how fires start spontaneously

Ⓓ to highlight the fact that fires all start for a reason

Name ____________________ Date ____________

English Language Arts

Understand Word Relationships

Language

DIRECTIONS: Choose or write the correct answer.

Strategy Identify figurative language and ask yourself why the author included it in the sentence. Does it add a new meaning? Does it help explain an idea through comparisons

1. **Part A: A pun is a joke based on the different possible meanings of a word. They often rely on homophones—words that sound the same but have different meanings. Which of the following is an example of a pun?**

   Ⓐ I think of you a million times a day.

   Ⓑ Seven days without laughter makes one weak.

   Ⓒ My sister has a mind like a computer.

   Ⓓ My dad is so tall, Sir Edmund Hillary tried to climb him!

   Part B: In this excerpt from Shakespeare's *Romeo and Juliet*, Mercutio and Romeo are at a ball. Romeo is feeling sad about a woman, but Mercutio encourages him to dance anyway. Identify the homophones used in the passage. Then, explain how Romeo uses the pun to explain to Mercutio why he doesn't want to dance.

> Mercutio: Nay, gentle Romeo, we must have you dance.
> Romeo: Not I, believe me. You have dancing shoes
> With nimble soles; I have a soul of lead
> So stakes me to the ground I cannot move.
> Mercutio: You are a lover. Borrow Cupid's wings
> And soar with them above a common bound.
> —*Romeo and Juliet*, Act I, Scene IV

____

____

____

____

2. **Which of these synonyms for the word *untruth* has the most negative connotation?**

   Ⓐ bluff

   Ⓑ fib

   Ⓒ lie

   Ⓓ whopper

3. **Part A: Read the excerpt from "The Cloud" below. Identify the figure of speech that creates the most vivid picture of the cloud in your mind.**

> I bring fresh showers for the thirsting flowers,
> From the seas and the streams;
> I bear light shade for the leaves when laid
> In their noonday dreams.
> From my wings are shaken the dews that waken
> The sweet buds every one,
> When rocked to rest on their mother's breast,
> As she dances about the sun.
> I wield the flail of the lashing hail,
> And whiten the green plains under,
> And then again I dissolve it in rain,
> And laugh as I pass in thunder.
> —from "The Cloud,"
> by Percy Bysshe Shelley

____

   Part B: Based on your answer to Part A, describe what you would draw if you were to illustrate this poem.

____

____

____

Name ______________________________ Date ______________

English Language Arts

Write an Argument

Writing

Strategy When you are asked to write an argument, state your position and back it up with evidence.

Test Tip An argument is more convincing if you support your opinion with facts and reasons.

DIRECTIONS: Choose a topic that reasonable people might disagree on. You might propose a change to a school policy or take a stand on what we should do to reduce the number of distracted drivers. Then, complete the organizer by writing your answers for each step in the space provided.

STEP 1: Make a claim.	
My claim:	
STEP 2: Consider the evidence.	
My list of evidence for my claim:	**My list of evidence against my claim:**
STEP 3: Organize your evidence logically. For example, you might use time order or problem-solution. Begin each item on your list with transition words, such as *first* or *most important*. 1. 2. 3.	
STEP 4: Write a conclusion that sums up what you want your reader to do or to remember.	
My Conclusion:	

Name ______________________________ Date ______________

English Language Arts

Write an Argument

Writing

DIRECTIONS: Read the passage. Then, answer the questions that follow.

[1] All but six states have laws banning texting while driving, but laws and fines aren't the best way to end distracted driving. [2] There is no doubt that texting while behind the wheel is dangerous, especially for teenagers. [3] Teens who text while driving are four times more likely to be involved in an accident than undistracted drivers. [4] So the laws against distracted driving should stay on the books, but states should do one more thing. [5] States should send a message that other drivers disapprove of texting while driving. [6] Psychologist Robert Cialdini found that people are more likely to break rules when they think other people are breaking them. [7] People are more likely to litter in areas where others have left trash and stuff lying around.

1. The first sentence is an example of how to

Ⓐ use scientific data as evidence.
Ⓑ state your claim in one sentence.
Ⓒ preview each main point of your argument.
Ⓓ acknowledge arguments that can be made against your claim.

2. Which of the words or phrases below could be added to sentence 7 to connect it more smoothly to sentence 6?

Ⓐ Although
Ⓑ For example,
Ⓒ On the other hand,
Ⓓ Then,

3. Rewrite sentence 7 so it matches the formal tone of the rest of the passage.

____
____
____
____
____
____
____

4. Write a conclusion to the passage on distracted driving. If you support bans on cell phone use and texting while driving, you may write a conclusion for the passage. If you do not support the bans, write a conclusion that expresses your point of view on what to do about distracted driving.

____
____
____
____
____
____
____
____
____
____
____
____
____
____
____
____

Name ______________________________ Date ______________

English Language Arts

Write an Informative Text

Writing

DIRECTIONS: Read the passage from a student's informative essay. Then, answer the questions that follow.

> One of the most fascinating figures on ancient artifacts is that of Kokopelli. Kokopelli is compelling, not only because he is cute and vibrant, but because he is everywhere. Several Native American tribes, including the Hopi, Zuni, Winnebago, and Anasazi, tell stories and depict images of the flute playing, hunch-backed little man. Each tribe's ideas about Kokopelli are a little different. Some say his back is humped because he is carrying a sack. In some versions, the sack is filled with trade goods like parrot feathers. In others, the sack holds rain clouds that water the crops. Whatever his origin, images of the little dude are now popular throughout the Southwestern United States. His image appears on t-shirts and in artworks, and he has even been turned into a doll. Kokopelli has replaced the howling coyote, the lizard, and the saguaro cactus as the main symbol of the Southwest.

Strategy Plan the structure of your informative writing before you begin to write. Common structures are main idea and details, cause and effect, and problem-solution.

1. **What structure did the student use to organize this introductory paragraph?**
   - (A) compare-contrast
   - (B) main idea and details
   - (C) space order
   - (D) time order

2. **The student summarizes two different explanations of why Kokopelli carries a sack. What idea is supported by these examples?**

   ____

   ____

3. **The student describes several versions of the Kokopelli based on different tribes. Why is that important to include?**
   - (A) Including details that disagree is a feature of main idea and detail structure.
   - (B) The details are not important to the main idea, but they are very interesting.
   - (C) Each tribe has dramatically different descriptions and ideas of Kokopelli.
   - (D) Including all the tribes' descriptions gives a complete picture of Kokopelli.

4. **Most of the language the student uses is formal. How would you rewrite this sentence to replace the informal expression with more formal language?**

   "Whatever his origin, images of the little dude are now popular throughout the Southwestern United States."

   ____

   ____

5. **Why is the last sentence important to the passage?**

   ____

   ____

Name ______________________________ Date ______________

English Language Arts

Write an Informative Text

Writing

6. What word could be added to the draft to connect the fourth and fifth sentences more smoothly?

Ⓐ Because,
Ⓑ However,
Ⓒ In addition,
Ⓓ Next,

7. If the student wanted more information on Native American myths, which two search terms would return the most relevant information?

Ⓐ Ancestral Pueblo
Ⓑ Native American myths
Ⓒ Native American myths Southwest
Ⓓ symbols

Strategy

Take notes to support your main ideas with relevant details. When taking notes, you must put words taken directly from the source in quotation marks. Use your own words—paraphrase—as much as you can.

8. Part A: A search for "Native American Legends" returned collections of myths from several sources. Which source would be the most credible?

Ⓐ "Cuckoo for Kokopelli" (a newspaper article)
Ⓑ "Myths and Legends to Read for Fun" (a librarian's personal site)
Ⓒ "Our Favorite Trickster Tales" (Mrs. Smith's fifth-grade class site)
Ⓓ Native American Indian Legends and Folklore (Native Languages of the Americas)

Part B: Explain your answer to Part A.

____

____

Test Tip

When paraphrasing this quotation, you do not need to put technical terms like *petroglyph* or *Pueblo* inside quotation marks.

9. A student took notes on this passage from an article:

"Kokopelli, the humpbacked flute player of ancient Pueblo mythology, is represented by figures on the petroglyph panel at Sand Island. Test your skill at identifying him. The easily accessible rock art panel at Sand Island is extensive and represents images from 800 to 2500 years old."

The student wrote, "How old is Kokopelli? Based on rock carvings of him found at Sand Island, he may be anywhere 'from 800 to 2500 years old.'" Explain why this is a good way to take notes on the information in the passage.

____

____

____

____

____

____

Name ______________________________ Date ______________

English Language Arts

Write an Informative Text

Writing

Test Tip

If you have a hard time paraphrasing a source, start with an idea from the middle or at the end.

"Petroglyphs are images and designs made by engraving, carving or scratching away the dark layer of rock varnish on a rock's surface to reveal the lighter rock underneath. Images can be of varying depths and thicknesses. Images can be pecked, carved, incised, scratched, or abraded."

10. How might this quotation be paraphrased? Remember that any words you take directly from the source must be put in quotation marks, except for technical terms.

____

____

____

____

____

____

Test Tip

When listing sources, follow the correct format. MLA style is often used to cite sources. You can get help with MLA style at the Purdue OWL or from Citation Machine.

This is an example of how to cite a source from the Internet using MLA style

Author. "Article Name." *Title of the Website*. Posting Date. Publisher (if available). Web. Date you accessed the material. <URL> (optional)

Bureau of Land Management. "Sand Island Petroglyphs." *Places to Visit*. 29 June 2011. BLM. Web. 29 July 2014. < http://www.blm.gov/ut/st/en/prog/more/cultural/archaeology/places_to_visit/sand_island.html>.

11. Create an MLA-style citation for this source:

Author: National Earth Science Teachers Association (NESTA)

Article name: "Coyote."

Title of the website: *Windows to the Universe.*

Posting date: 2012

Publisher: NESTA.

Date of access: 29 July 2014

Medium: Web.

URL: < http://www.windows2universe.org/mythology/coyote_milkyway.html>.

____

____

____

Name ______________________________ Date ______________

English Language Arts

Write an Informative Text

Writing

DIRECTIONS: Write three paragraphs about a character in a Native American myth or another informational topic. Include the following:

- Information from at least two sources
- Facts about your topic
- Definitions and examples to help readers understand your topic
- A correctly formatted list of all the sources you used at the end

Plan your informative article by looking up at least two sources on your topic. Then, choose an organizational plan (cause-effect, compare-contrast, time order, etc.) Use your organizational plan to put your notes in order.

Name ______________________ Date ______________

English Language Arts

Write a Narrative

Writing

DIRECTIONS: Read the fable and then, answer the questions.

[1] A lion used to prowl about a field in which four oxen grazed. [2] Every time he tried to attack one, they turned their tails to one another. [3] Whichever way he approached, he was met by horns. [4] The oxen began quarrelling among themselves, and each went off in a huff to his own corner of the field. [5] The lion then attacked them one by one and soon made an end of all four.

Strategy Plan your narrative writing by deciding on characters, setting, and plot events. Who will be in your story, and what conflict will they face? How will they resolve the conflict?

Test Tip You can use narrative techniques such as dialogue and descriptive details to make stories more interesting.

1. What does the first sentence do?

Ⓐ describe the time and the place
Ⓑ establish a second-person point of view
Ⓒ introduce the characters and the conflict
Ⓓ preview the order in which events happen

2. Which phrase could be added to sentence 4 to create a better connection with sentence 3?

Ⓐ Next,
Ⓑ Even if,
Ⓒ Instead,
Ⓓ After a time,

3. Rewrite sentence 3 so that it includes descriptive details.

____
____
____
____
____
____

4. Add one or more sentences before sentence 5 to show what the lion thinks to himself after the oxen stop working together.

____
____
____
____
____

5. Fables usually end with a moral that states the lesson readers are intended to learn. Write a moral for this fable.

____
____
____
____

Name ______________________________ Date ______________

Write a Narrative

Writing

DIRECTIONS: A narrative is a story that tells about real or imagined events. Write a narrative about a challenge you overcame. The challenge can be real or imagined. Write your paragraph on the lines. Your paragraph should have the following:

- A narrator and/or characters
- A natural sequence of events
- Dialogue
- Descriptions of actions, thoughts, and feelings
- Time words and phrases to show the order of events
- Concrete words and sensory details
- A sentence to end your paragraph

Strategy Plan a narrative by choosing people, places, and events that will be in the story. Use an outline to keep your ideas organized and to make sure you have details.

Test Tip Choosing the right words makes a narrative more interesting to read. Use exact words and phrases and figurative language.

Name ______________________________ Date ________________

Understand Editing and Revising

Writing

DIRECTIONS: Read the passage. Then, answer the questions that follow.

Concrete Arrows and Guiding Lights

On July 7, 1924, Frank R. Yager, a pilot with the U.S. Air Mail Service, took off from Cheyenne, Wyoming, and headed east to Lincoln, Nebraska. Yager was an experienced pilot, but this was no ordinary flight. Six days earlier, the U.S. Air Mail Service had begun transcontinental day and night mail service between San Francisco and New York. Frank Yager had volunteered to fly a nighttime segment of the flight.

When Yager is leaving Cheyenne, he was hoping to outrun an approaching thunderstorm. But he was still 300 miles from Lincoln when the weather began closing in fast. He decided to land at the emergency field at Chappell, Nebraska. Just seconds before landing, a gust of wind struck his plane, snapping his seatbelt and throwing him from the open cockpit of the plane. Yager suffered no major injuries, but the airplane was totally destroyed. Flying in the early days was difficult enough, but for Frank Yager and the other air mail pilots, flying at night would turn out to be a real adventure.

In preparation for night flying, a lighted airway had been constructed between Chicago and Cheyenne. It was later extended from New York City to Salt Lake City. The airway was illuminated by lighted beacons and floodlights. The beacons were installed on towers built on 50-foot-long concrete arrows pointing the way to the next beacon. On a clear night, the beacons could be seen from 60 to 150 miles away, depending on there size and weather conditions.

The beacons guided air mail pilots safely across the country and signaled a major advancement in flight. The U.S. Air Mail Service was short-lived. However, its network of routes and its experienced pilots played a major role in the development of commercial air service in the United States.

Strategy

Revise to clarify your ideas and ensure your reader can understand your meaning. When you are satisfied with your revision, then edit your final draft for errors.

Test Tip

Don't worry about spelling and punctuation when you revise. You can fix those errors when you edit.

Name ______________________________ Date ______________

English Language Arts

Understand Editing and Revising

Writing

1. **Part A: Which sentence contains a gerund?**
   - (A) "When Yager was leaving Cheyenne, he was hoping to outrun an approaching thunderstorm."
   - (B) "Flying in the early days was difficult enough, but for Frank Yager and the other air mail pilots, flying at night would turn out to be a real adventure."
   - (C) "The beacons were installed on towers built on 50–foot-long concrete arrows pointing the way to the next beacon."
   - (D) "On a clear night, the beacons could be seen from 60 to 150 miles away, depending on their size and weather conditions."

   Part B: Write a sentence that uses the word you identified in Part A as a gerund as a different part of speech.

   ____

   ____

   ____

2. **What punctuation mark should you use to show that words have been left out of a quotation?**
   - (A) colon
   - (B) dash
   - (C) ellipses
   - (D) hyphen

3. **What verb form should be used in the first sentence of the second paragraph?**
   - (A) left
   - (B) had left
   - (C) were leaving
   - (D) would have been leaving

4. **Part A: Suppose the third sentence in the second paragraph was rewritten to read "Chappell, Nebraska, was where he landed." How would the change from active to passive voice change the emphasis of the sentence?**

   ____

   ____

   ____

   ____

   PART B: Change this sentence from passive to active voice: "The airway was illuminated by lighted beacons and floodlights."

   ____

   ____

   ____

   ____

5. **How would you correct the spelling error in the last sentence of the third paragraph?**

   ____

   ____

Name ______________________ Date ______________

English Language Arts

Strategy Review

DIRECTIONS: Each strategy below is followed by a review, a passage, and one or more questions. Use these to review important strategies.

Strategy Use details from the text to make inferences, understand theme, and draw out meaning.

"But someone digs upon my grave?
My enemy? – prodding sly?"
– "Nay: when she heard you had passed the Gate
That shuts on all flesh soon or late,
She thought you no more worth her hate,
And cares not where you lie."

A theme can be a lesson learned. For example, a fable ends with a moral that is directly stated. However, a theme can also be a general view of life, as in the story of "The Golden Goose."

Three brothers are sent into the forest to see what they can find. The oldest has a lunch of a fresh cake, which he refuses to share with a little gray man he meets in the woods. The second oldest also refuses to share his treat. The youngest brother, Dummling, has only a stale biscuit, but he shares it willingly. As a reward for his kindness, the little gray man gives him a goose that lays golden eggs.

1. **Reread the stanza, taken from "Ah, Are You Digging on My Grave?" Then, state the theme of the poem in your own words.**

____

____

____

____

Strategy

Identify literary or structural elements and use them to understand the meaning of a text.

Poets choose from a variety of elements to create meaning. Some, such as figurative language, use levels of meaning to create imagery and humor. Some, such as rhyme and alliteration, create the music of the poem.

Read the stanza from "A Red, Red Rose" by Robert Burns.

O my Luve's like a red, red rose,
That's newly spring in June:
O my Luve's like the melodie,
That's sweetly play'd in tune.

2. **Part A: Which poetic elements does Burns use in "A Red, Red Rose"? Choose all that apply.**
   - (A) rhyme scheme
   - (B) simile
   - (C) regular meter, or rhythm
   - (D) alliteration

   Part B: What effect do these poetic elements have on the poem?

____

____

____

____

____

Name ______________________ Date ______________

English Language Arts

Strategy Review

Strategy Reread texts to find details that support inferences.

"You see, Watson," Sherlock Holmes explained, in the early hours of the morning, as we sat over a glass of whisky and soda in Baker Street, "it was perfectly obvious from the first that the only possible object of this rather fantastic business of the advertisement of the League, and the copying of the 'Encyclopaedia,' must be to get this not over-bright pawnbroker out of the way for a number of hours every day....."

"You reasoned it out beautifully," I exclaimed, in unfeigned admiration. "It is so long a chain, and yet every link rings true."

—"The Red-Headed League," Sir Arthur Conan Doyle

This excerpt is one of many tributes to the deductive abilities of Sherlock Holmes. How do we know Holmes is a brilliant detective? Watson praises his reasoning directly, but the author also provides clues that let readers draw their own conclusions.

1. **Reread the passage to find details that explain how Holmes and Watson differ in their understanding of the crime. Write the clues you find on the lines below.**

____

____

Make an inference based on the details you identified.

____

____

Strategy

Use word clues in a text to identify its structure, to see how ideas in a text are related, and to clarify word meanings.

Extremophiles are microorganisms that live in extreme conditions. Consider the thermophiles—"thermo" for heat, "phile" for lover—that live in Yellowstone National Park. When Yellowstone's geysers erupt, they shoot water heated to over 200 degrees F over 100 feet into the air. This hot water provides the energy and chemical building blocks thermophiles need to build communities. Thermophiles do not survive despite the heat of Yellowstone's geysers. Instead, they thrive because of the resources provided by their extreme environment.

Transitions are words or phrases that show how ideas are connected. Words like *before*, *following*, or *next* can signal how events are related in time. Transitions like *because* or *as a result* can show a cause-effect relationship. An Internet search for "transition words" will turn up lists of many more kinds of transitions.

2. **Write the sentence that expresses the relationship between the thermophiles and their habitat.**

____

Context clues are words or phrases within a passage that help you understand unfamiliar words. Sometimes, the writer will make the definition obvious by using phrases like: The word *phantasmagorical* means "dreamlike" or "imaginary." In other cases, you must find hints to the word's meaning in the sentences close to it.

3. **Part A: Write the phrase from the excerpt that helps you learn the meaning of the word *thermophile*.**

____

Part B: Write a definition of the word *thermophile*.

____

____

Name ______________________________ Date ______________

English Language Arts

Strategy Review

Strategy When writing, use details to support, explain, or clarify your main ideas.

Despite their name, jellyfish are not true fish. They are really zooplankton—simple animals that spend their lives floating in water. The hundreds of jellyfish species vary greatly in size. Some are about the size of a fingernail, while others are over 7 feet long. The blue whale, which is the largest mammal on earth, is over 110 feet long. Despite this variation in size, most jellyfish have a similar structure: transparent bodies shaped like a bell, with tentacles dangling below. Jellyfish are simple creatures, lacking bones, brains, blood, or hearts. They do have an elementary nervous system, or nerve net, that allows them to smell, detect light, and respond to other stimuli.

Details can be either helpful or distracting. If your readers have never seen a jellyfish, adding relevant details can help them understand these unusual creatures. However, adding details that don't relate to the main idea may confuse readers.

1. Which in the list below would be least helpful to readers who want to know more about jellyfish?

Ⓐ Jellyfish are about 95% water.

Ⓑ Like jelly shoes, jellyfish are sometimes called "jellies."

Ⓒ Jellyfish can sting, although their sting is not usually fatal to humans.

Ⓓ Jellyfish are members of the same animal kingdom as sea anemones and corals.

2. Identify the irrelevant detail that could be left out of the paragraph.

____

Strategy

Use an outline to plan your writing.

Scratch Outline for Argument

My claim: Solar energy is a green energy source that could reduce the need to use fossil fuels to produce electricity.

Evidence for my claim

1. Solar power is a green energy source.
2. Homeowners who install solar panels can create their own free electricity
3. Solar power is a renewable energy source.

Evidence against my claim

1. Solar power pollutes less than coal or natural gas, but making solar panels produces hazardous waste.
2.
3.

Conclusion: The U.S. government should promote efforts to increase the percentage of electricity generated by solar power.

While you can do a formal outline, complete with Roman numerals *I*, *II*, and *III*, often a scratch outline is enough. These outlines get their name from the way they're written—very quickly and informally. A quick look at Robbie's outline shows that his arguments are not balanced.

3. Based on the outline, what does Robbie need to do before drafting his argument on wind energy?

____

____

____

Name ____ Date ____________________

English Language Arts

Strategy Review

Strategy Use transitions to show how ideas are related in an argument.

People usually assume that cats purr because they're happy. In reality, the sound is far more complex. Cats purr when recovering from injury, and scientists suspect the sound helps strengthen their bones. Cats also purr when they want food. In fact, some have perfected a "manipulative meow," which embeds a sound like a baby's cry inside their normal low-frequency purr. They use the sound to influence humans to give them food.

When your assignment is to write an argument, you may be asked to include a *counterargument*. A counterargument is an argument against your position. One reason to include a counterargument is to give you a chance to show why the other side is wrong. To do this, you need to use transitions that signal disagreement. Transitions that show contrast include *but, on the other hand, actually*, or *the truth is*....

1. **Write the phrase from the passage above that is used to contrast the counterargument and what the author believes to be the truth.**

____

Strategy

Revise to make sure your writing is clear and makes sense. Then, edit to fix errors.

In *Bird by Bird*, writer Anne Lamott describes how she begins writing. She advises, "Start by getting something—anything—down on paper." This first step is the "down draft": at this stage, you're just trying to capture your ideas, or get them down, in some format. The next draft is the "up draft." At this stage of the process, you go back and "fix up" your first draft to make it clear and complete once your ideas are clear, it's time for the "dental draft." In this draft, you check your writing for punctuation, spelling, and missing words as thoroughly as your dentist checks your teeth.

2. **Why does Lamott write more than one draft?**

____

____

____

____

3. **Part A: Which sentence in the paragraph contains an error?**

   Ⓐ "*In Bird by Bird*, writer Anne Lamott describes how she begins writing."

   Ⓑ "She advises, 'Start by getting something—anything—down on paper.'"

   Ⓒ "At this stage of the process, you go back and 'fix up' your first draft to make it clear and complete once your ideas are clear, it's time for the 'dental draft.'

   Ⓓ "In this draft, you check your writing for punctuation, spelling, and missing words as thoroughly as your dentist checks your teeth."

   Part B: Rewrite the sentence to correct the error.

____

____

____

____

____

____

Strategies for Mathematics Tests

Read the strategies below to learn more about how they work.

Use rules, properties, or formulas to solve problems.

You can use rules, properties, and formulas to solve a variety of problems. For example, if you know the formula for the area of a rectangle, you can use a given length and width of the rectangle to quickly find its area. If you understand the commutative and distributive properties, you can rearrange an equation to solve it. If you understand the rules of the order of operations, you can correctly evaluate a mathematical expression.

Use drawings, graphs, or number lines to understand and solve a problem.

Many problems on a test can be modeled with a quick sketch, graph, or number line. These drawings can help you visualize the problem, figure out what you are being asked to find, or solve word problems.

Read word problems carefully to identify the given information and what you are being asked to find.

Whenever you encounter a word problem, you should first ask "What is the given information?" Then, you should ask "What question am I being asked to answer?" or "What am I being asked to find?" Don't start your calculations until you know the answers to these questions!

Look for key words in word problems that help you know which operation to use.

Key words in problems are signals that you should use certain operations. For example, the words *how much less* indicate subtraction. The words *total* and *altogether* often indicate addition. If you are asked to split something into equal portions, use division.

Organize and display data in order to interpret it.

Interpreting data means finding meaning in it. One way to find meaning in data is to organize it in a visual way. For example, dot plots are great for understanding data from a survey or poll. Line graphs show how two sets of data are related.

Apply prior knowledge and basic operations to solve problems.

Using what you already know about numbers and about the basic operations addition, subtraction, multiplication, and division, you can solve problems involving decimals, fractions, geometry, and converting units of measurement. For example, you can use your understanding of division, multiplication, and place value to find area and to convert meters to centimeters.

Write and solve equations to solve real-world problems.

Translating everyday language into equations that use numbers, variables, and operations signs is an essential strategy. You will need to combine your understanding of several strategies to write and solve these equations, including understanding basic operations; applying rules, properties, and formulas; and looking for clues in the words to find needed information.

Name ______________________________ Date ______________

Math

Understand Rational and Irrational Numbers

The Number System

DIRECTIONS: Choose or write the correct answer.

Strategy Differentiate between rational and irrational numbers using prior knowledge of division, roots, and fractions.

Test Tip Keep in mind that any number that can be expressed as $\frac{a}{b}$ is rational.

1. In the table, list three rational and three irrational numbers.

Rational	Irrational
1	$\frac{1}{3}$
2	$\sqrt{2}$
3	$\sqrt{48}$
	π

Explain the difference between an irrational and a rational number.

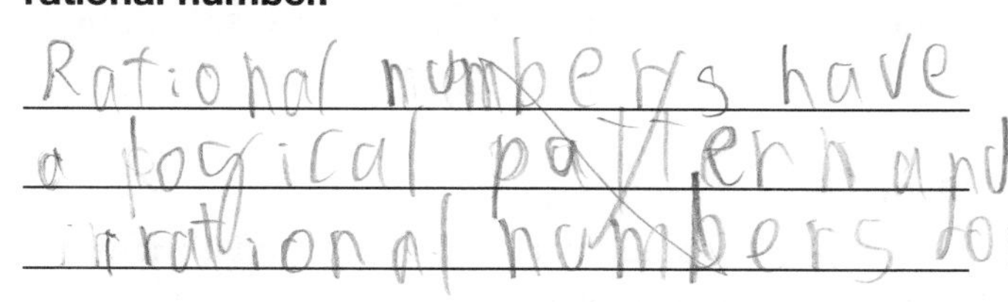

____

2. Which are rational? Choose all that apply.

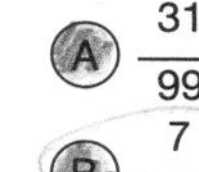

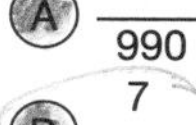

Ⓐ $\frac{314}{990}$

Ⓑ $\frac{7}{28}$

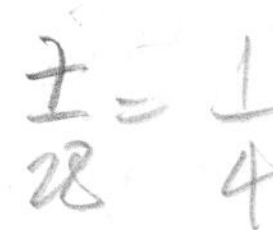

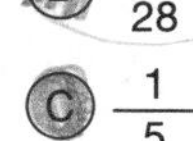

Ⓒ $\frac{1}{5}$

Ⓓ $\sqrt{2}$

3. Which are irrational? Choose all that apply.

Ⓐ $\sqrt{25}$

Ⓑ $\sqrt{4}$

Ⓒ $\sqrt{3}$

Ⓓ $\sqrt{100}$

4. Which of the following operations will result in a rational number?

Ⓐ $\sqrt{3} \times \sqrt{3}$

Ⓑ $\sqrt{3} + (\sqrt{2})^2$

Ⓒ $(\sqrt{3})^3$

Ⓓ $\sqrt{3} - \sqrt{2}$

5. Which of the following operations will result in a rational number?

Ⓐ $\sqrt{2} + \sqrt{2}$

Ⓑ $(\sqrt{2})^3$

Ⓒ $(\sqrt{2})^2$

Ⓓ $\sqrt{2} - \sqrt{2}$

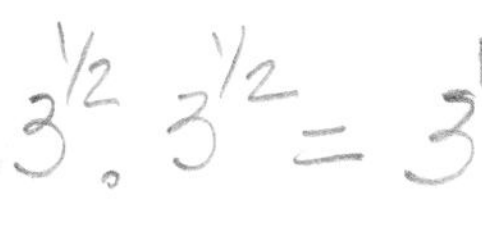

Name ______________________ Date ______________

Math

Understand Rational and Irrational Numbers

The Number System

DIRECTIONS: Choose or write the correct answer.

Strategy Use characteristics of rational and irrational numbers to classify fractions and decimals.

6. Which are rational? Choose all that apply.

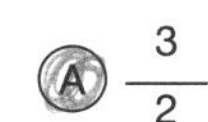

(A) $\frac{3}{2}$

(B) 0.25

(C) $\frac{1}{56}$

(D) 0.99

7. Which are irrational? Choose all that apply.

(A) $\sqrt{99}$

(B) π

(C) $\sqrt{9}$

(D) $\sqrt{36}$

8. Which are irrational? Choose all that apply.

(A) $\frac{1}{3}$

(B) $\frac{5}{0}$

(C) 2.75

(D) $\frac{\sqrt{2}}{3}$

9. Is $\frac{13}{5}$ rational or irrational? Explain how you know.

rational because it is a fraction

10. Explain why $\frac{\sqrt{3}}{2}$ is an irrational number.

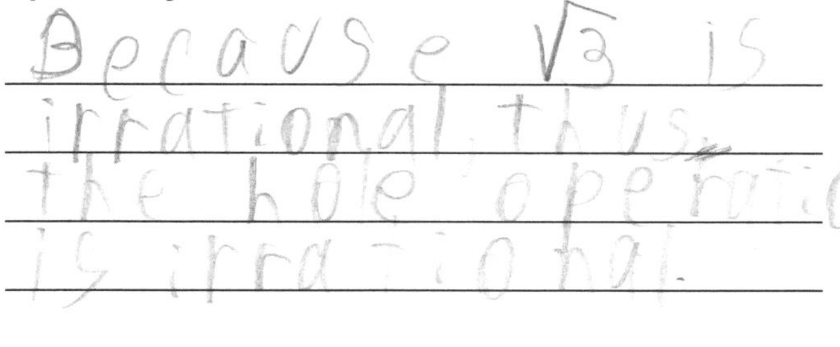

11. Is there an operation you can perform with the irrational number $\sqrt{2}$ that would result in a rational answer? Explain.

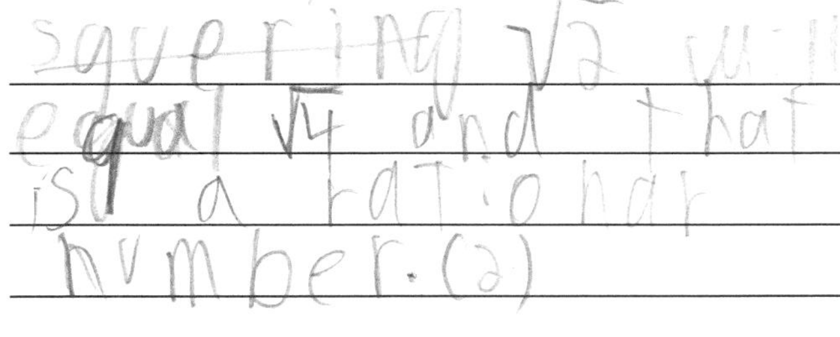

Name ________________________ Date ______________

Math

Expand Rational Numbers

The Number System

DIRECTIONS: Choose or write the correct answer.

Strategy Convert rational numbers from decimals to fractions and from fractions to decimals using basic operations.

Test Tip Remember that you can convert a fraction to a decimal using division.

1. Write each number in decimal form.

$\frac{1}{2}$ 0.5

$\sqrt{25}$ 5

$\frac{147}{3}$ 49

$\frac{1}{3}$ $0.\overline{3}$

What do all of these numbers have in common?

they are rational

2. Convert each decimal expansion into a fraction.

$0.\overline{666}$ $\frac{6}{9}$

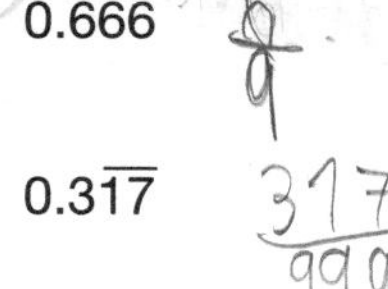

$0.3\overline{17}$ $\frac{317}{999}$

$2.1\overline{6}$ $\frac{214}{99}$

3. Andi converted the decimal $2.\overline{45}$ into a fraction. Analyze Andi's work and explain what mistake she made.

$$10x = 24.5454545...$$
$$- \quad x = 2.45454545...$$
$$99x = 21.\overline{09}$$
$$x = \frac{21.09}{99} = \frac{2109}{9900}$$

____

____

____

Convert the decimal correctly.

Test Tip Remember that a line over digits in a decimal indicates that those digits repeat.

4. Convert the decimal $1.5\overline{7}$ to a fraction.

$\frac{156}{99}$

5. What is the correct fraction form for the decimal $0.\overline{12}$?

Ⓐ $\frac{12}{100}$

Ⓑ $\frac{12}{10}$

Ⓒ $\frac{12}{99}$

Ⓓ $\frac{99}{12}$

Name ______________________________ Date ________________

Math

Approximate Irrational Numbers

The Number System

DIRECTIONS: Choose or write the correct answer.

Strategy Approximate irrational numbers by identifying where they are on the number line.

1. $\sqrt{11}$ is ...
   - (A) greater than 2, but less than 3
   - (B) greater than 3, but less than 4
   - (C) greater than 4, but less than 5
   - (D) greater than 5, but less than 6

2. **Between which two perfect squares does $\sqrt{27}$ fall?**

   ____

Test Tip

A perfect square is a number made by squaring a whole number.

3. **Place the following irrational numbers in their approximate locations on the number line.**

   $\sqrt{7}$, $\sqrt{2}$, $\sqrt{37}$, $\sqrt{17}$, $\sqrt{67}$

4. **Where is the best location on the number line for $\sqrt{137}$?**
   - (A) between 136 and 138
   - (B) between 127 and 147
   - (C) between 11 and 12
   - (D) between 10 and 11

5. **Put these numbers in order from least to greatest.**

   $\sqrt{2}$, 6, 2.1, $\sqrt{4}$, $\sqrt{6}$, 0.7, $\sqrt{8}$

   ____

Name ______________________________ Date ______________

Math

Simplify Expressions

Expressions and Equations

DIRECTIONS: Choose or write the correct answer.

Strategy Apply exponent rules to evaluate expressions.

Test Tip When multiplying powers with the same base, add the exponents. When dividing powers with the same base, subtract the exponents.

1. **$6^4 + 6^{12} =$**
   - Ⓐ 6^8
   - Ⓑ 6^{12}
   - Ⓒ 6^{48}
   - Ⓓ 6^{16}

2. **Which expressions have an answer of 3^2?**
   - Ⓐ $3^5 \div 3^3$
   - Ⓑ $3^{-2} \times 3^5$
   - Ⓒ $3^{-3} \times 3^5$
   - Ⓓ $3^1 + 3^1$

3. **Evaluate the expression. Show your work.**

   $$7^2 + \sqrt{9} - (5^9 \div 5^7)$$

   ____

4. **Choose all of the expressions that are equivalent. Choose all that apply.**
   - Ⓐ $4^3 \times 4^7$
   - Ⓑ $4^{12} \div 4^2$
   - Ⓒ $4^{-15} \times 4^{15}$
   - Ⓓ $4^{-2} \div 4^{-12}$

5. **Which expressions are equal to 1? Choose all that apply.**
   - Ⓐ 6^0
   - Ⓑ 1^5
   - Ⓒ 2^{-1}
   - Ⓓ $8^3 \times 8^{-3}$

6. **Write an expression with the solution 2^7.**

   ____

Name ______________________ Date ______________

Math

Evaluate Roots and Powers

Expressions and Equations

DIRECTIONS: Choose or write the correct answer.

Strategy Evaluate expressions by correctly applying rules and definitions of exponents, roots, and rational and irrational numbers.

Test Tip

Remember to isolate the variable by using addition, subtraction, multiplication, and division.

1. Which of the following roots is irrational?

(A) $\sqrt{4}$

(B) $\sqrt[3]{8}$

(C) $\sqrt{2}$

(D) $\sqrt[3]{8}$

2. Evaluate the roots.

$\sqrt{16}$ ______________________

$\sqrt[3]{27}$ ______________________

$\sqrt{81}$ ______________________

$\sqrt[3]{1}$ ______________________

3. Solve: $x^2 + 9 = 35$

____

4. A right triangle has side lengths of $a = 4$ and $b = 5$. What is the length of the hypotenuse?

(A) $c = 41$

(B) $c = 9$

(C) $c = \sqrt{41}$

(D) $c = 3$

5. Solve: $19 + p^3 = 36$

____

6. Solve: $m^3 - 8 = 10$

____

Name ______________________________ Date ______________

Math

Evaluate Roots and Powers

Expressions and Equations

DIRECTIONS: Choose or write the correct answer.

Strategy Combine knowledge of powers, roots, and rational and irrational numbers to evaluate and interpret expressions.

7. $\sqrt{81} - \sqrt{16} =$

(A) $\sqrt{65}$

(B) 5

(C) $\sqrt{5}$

(D) 2.5

Is the solution rational or irrational? Write how you know.

____

8. Which expression shows that $\sqrt[3]{64} = 4$?

(A) $64 \div 3$

(B) 4×3

(C) $3 \times 3 \times 3 \times 3$

(D) $4 \times 4 \times 4$

9. Evaluate the expression. Show your work.

$$\frac{x3 + 8}{3} = 25$$

How can you determine if the answer is rational or irrational?

____

____

10. List the first 5 perfect squares and perfect cubes in the table.

Perfect squares	Perfect cubes

Name ______________________________ Date ______________

Math

Evaluate Expressions with Powers of 10

Expressions and Equations

DIRECTIONS: Choose or write the correct answer.

Strategy Evaluate expressions by using powers of 10 and basic operations.

Test Tip In these problems, you will be estimating answers by using a single digit multiplied by a power of 10.

1. Evaluate each power.

10^4 _______

10^7 _______

10^3 _______

10^5 _______

Explain how the exponent in a power of 10 relates to the number of zeroes in the solution.

____

____

____

2. Write a decimal for each of the exponential expressions.

2×10^3 _______

4×10^1 _______

7×10^{-2} _______

1×10^{-5} _______

Explain how you evaluated these expressions.

____

____

____

____

____

3. Write an exponential expression using a power of 10 for each of the numbers.

0.0002 _______________

3,000,000 _______________

0.0000004 _______________

100,000,000,000 _______________

4. The Andromeda galaxy has at least 2×10^{11} stars. Write the number of stars as a decimal.

____

5. There are about 7,000,000,000 people on Earth. Write the number in exponential form using a power of 10.

____

Name ______________________________ Date ______________

Math

Evaluate Expressions with Powers of 10

Expressions and Equations

DIRECTIONS: Choose or write the correct answer.

Strategy Use a process to solve problems that have more than one step. First, express the powers of ten in standard notation. Then, compare the numbers.

1. Which statement is true?

Ⓐ $6 \times 10^8 > 5 \times 10^9$

Ⓑ $7 \times 10^9 > 6 \times 10^7$

Ⓒ $5 \times 10^9 < 5 \times 10^8$

Ⓓ $6 \times 10^7 < 3 \times 10^5$

2. The population of the United States is approximately 3×10^8. The population of the world is approximately 7×10^9. About how many times larger is the world population than the U.S.?

Ⓐ 10

Ⓑ 15

Ⓒ 20

Ⓓ 25

Write how you found your answer.

____

____

____

____

3. The two largest states by population are California and Texas. California's population is about 4×10^7. The population of Texas is about 3×10^7. About how much larger is California's population than Texas' population?

____

____

4. Tokyo, Japan has the highest population of any city in the world. About 4×10^7 people live in that city. Berne, the capital of Switzerland, has a population of about 1×10^5 people. About how many times more people live in Tokyo than in Berne?

____

____

Write how you found your answer.

____

____

____

____

Name ______________________________ Date ______________

Math

Perform Operations with Scientific Notation

Expressions and Equations

DIRECTIONS: Choose or write the correct answer.

Strategy Combine prior knowledge of measurement with learning about powers of ten to understand measurements expressed in scientific notation.

1. The distance from Earth to the moon is about 2.389×10^5 ________.

(A) inches
(B) feet
(C) yards
(D) miles

2. The volume of one water molecule is approximately 30×10^{-24} ________.

(A) $in.^3$
(B) cm^3
(C) $ft.^3$
(D) m^3

Explain why you chose your answer.

____

____

____

3. An adult mosquito usually grows to no larger than 16 ________.

(A) feet
(B) inches
(C) meters
(D) millimeters

4. Scientists have estimated the area of Antarctic ice to be about 1.2295×10^6 _____. What unit would make sense in this sentence?

____

5. A red blood cell is approximately 6×10^{-4} ________ in diameter. What unit best completes this sentence?

(A) meters
(B) centimeters
(C) kilometers
(D) decimeters

Name ______________________ Date ______________

Math

Perform Operations with Scientific Notation

Expressions and Equations

DIRECTIONS: Choose or write the correct answer.

Strategy Use scientific notation for expressing very large and very small numbers, such as distances in space and the sizes of atoms or molecules.

Test Tip When completing problems involving scientific notations, remember to write all of your answers in scientific notation.

1. $(6 \times 10^3) \times (5 \times 10^4)$

- (A) 30×10^{12}
- (B) 1.1×10^{13}
- (C) 3×10^{8}
- (D) 11×10^{7}

2. $(8 \times 10^{-4}) \div (2 \times 10^3)$

- (A) 4×10^{-7}
- (B) $4 \times 10^{-\frac{4}{3}}$
- (C) 4
- (D) 4^{-7}

3. The population of Wisconsin is 5.686986×10^6. The population of Minnesota is 5.303925×10^6. What is the combined population of these two states?

____

4. The two largest states in the United States are Alaska, with an area of 6.6326726×10^5 square miles, and Texas, with an area of 2.6858082×10^5 square miles. How much larger is the area of Alaska than the area of Texas?

____

5. In 2014, the highest paid football player received 2.24125×10^7 dollars per year. How much will he earn in 4 years at this salary? Write your answer in scientific notation.

____

Write your answer in standard form.

____

6. Scientists have estimated that there are about 7.77×10^6 animal species on Earth. Of those, only 953,434 have actually been discovered and cataloged. How many more animal species are left to be discovered?

____

Explain what you had to do to find your answer.

____

____

____

____

____

____

____

Name ______________________ Date ______________________

Math

Analyze Linear and Proportional Relationships

Expressions and Equations

DIRECTIONS: Choose or write the correct answer.

Strategy Use tables, graphs, or equations to understand linear and proportional relationships.

Test Tip A linear relationship can be shown by using an equation of the form $y = mx + c$. A proportional relationship can be shown by an equation of the form $y = mx$. Both are graphed as a straight line.

1. Which equation corresponds to this table?

X	0	1	2
y	1	4	7

Ⓐ $y = 3x + 1$

Ⓑ $y = x^3 + 1$

Ⓒ $y = 3x - 1$

Ⓓ $y = x^2 - 1$

2. Write the equation that corresponds to the graph.

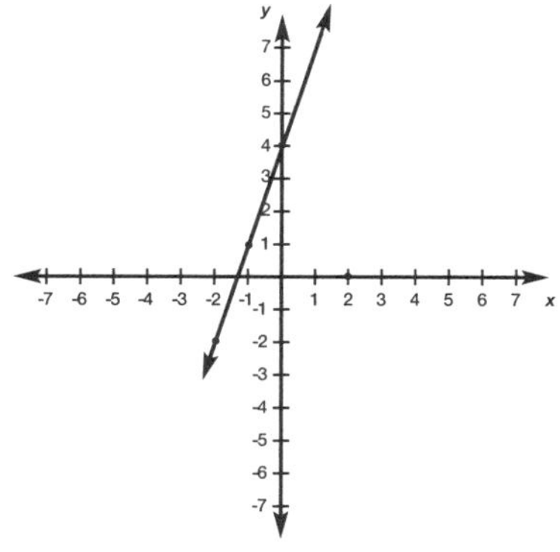

____

3. For the science fair, Aubrey wanted to know what kind of candle burned the longest. She tested two types of candles. For her experiment, Aubrey chose 3-inch candles and measured the length of the candle every 2 minutes. She recorded how much the candle had burned down in that time. For Candle A, Aubrey graphed the data. For candle B, she wrote an equation.

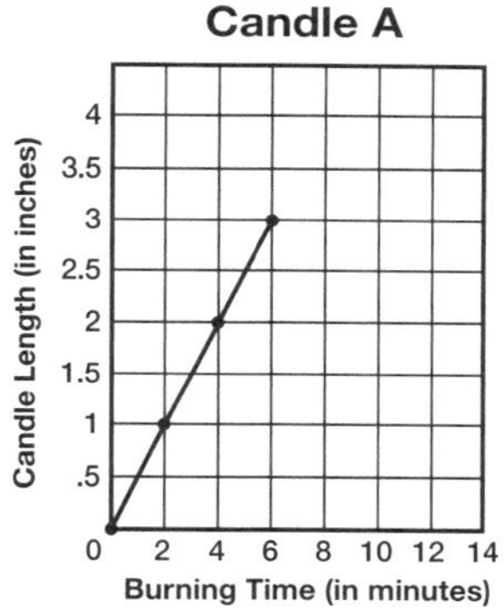

Candle B: $y = 0.25x$

Which candle lasted the longest?

____

Write how you know.

____

____

____

____

Name ______________________________ Date ______________

Math

Analyze Linear and Proportional Relationships

Expressions and Equations

DIRECTIONS: Choose or write the correct answer.

Strategy Graph and interpret equations to discover relationships between data sets.

4. For each equation, write if it is *linear* or *non-linear*.

$y = 5x - 2$ ______________

$y = 4x + 2$ ______________

$y = 3x^2$ ______________

$y = -x^2$ ______________

5. Analyze the equation $y = \frac{1}{2}x - 7$

Is this a linear equation? ________

What is the slope of the line? ________

What is the *y*-intercept? ________

Graph the equation below.

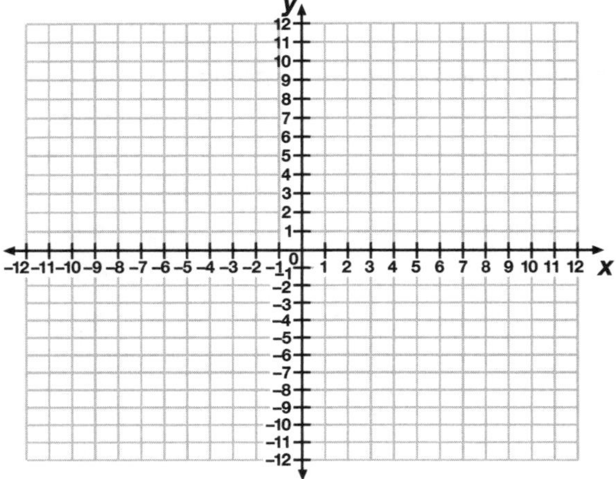

6. Which situation could be represented by the graph in item 7?

Ⓐ Marcee runs $\frac{1}{2}$ mile every day for 7 days. The following week, she increases her mileage to 1 mile each day.

Ⓑ A football team has lost 7 yards and loses the game 1 to 2.

Ⓒ Will owes his dad $7.00 for a book he wanted. He pays his dad back $0.50 each week until he has paid his debt off.

Ⓓ Half of the players on the Mustang's basketball team are under 7 feet tall.

7. A gallon of gas costs $3.59. If you were to graph this relationship, what would the slope be? How do you know?

____

____

____

8. Write a scenario for the equation $y = 2.50x - 0.75$.

____

____

____

Name ______________________ Date ______________
Math

Understand Slope

Expressions and Equations

DIRECTIONS: Choose or write the correct answer.

Strategy Use what you know about graphing points on a coordinate plane to find the slope of a line.

Test Tip The slope of a line is defined as $\frac{\text{rise}}{\text{run}}$. The rise can be found by finding the change in the y values. The run can be found by finding the change in the x values.

1. Use the triangle to explain why the slope between any two points on a line is the same.

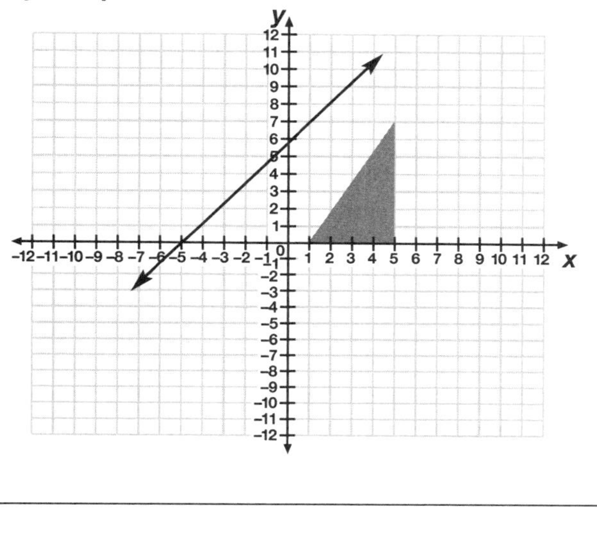

____
____
____
____

2. A linear equation is graphed and two points on the line are (2, 1) and (6, 3). What is the slope of the line? Show your work.

____

Find another point along the same line.

____

3. A line has the equation $y = \frac{2}{3}x - 7$. Find two points along the line.

____
____

4. Which equation represents the line?

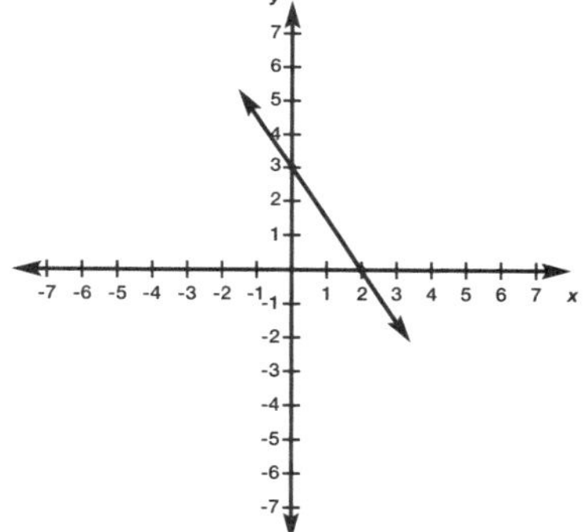

Ⓐ $y = \frac{3}{2}x + 3$
Ⓑ $y = -3x + 2$
Ⓒ $y = 2x + 3$
Ⓓ $y = -\frac{3}{2}x + 3$

Name ______________________________ Date ______________

Math

Understand Slope

Expressions and Equations

DIRECTIONS: Choose or write the correct answer.

Strategy Use or sketch visuals to understand and solve a problem.

5. Write the equation for the line shown below.

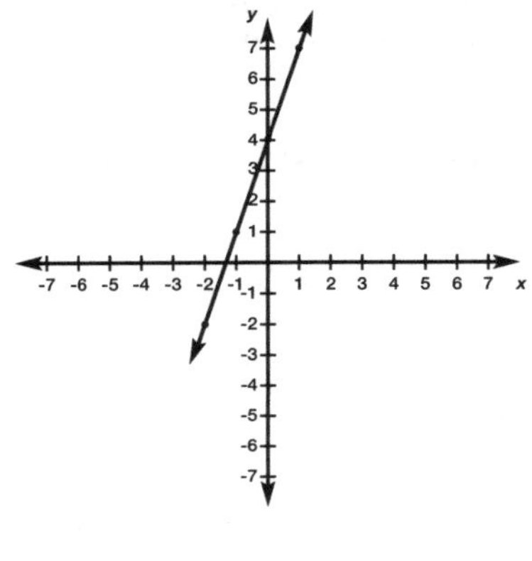

____

Write how you found the slope of the line.

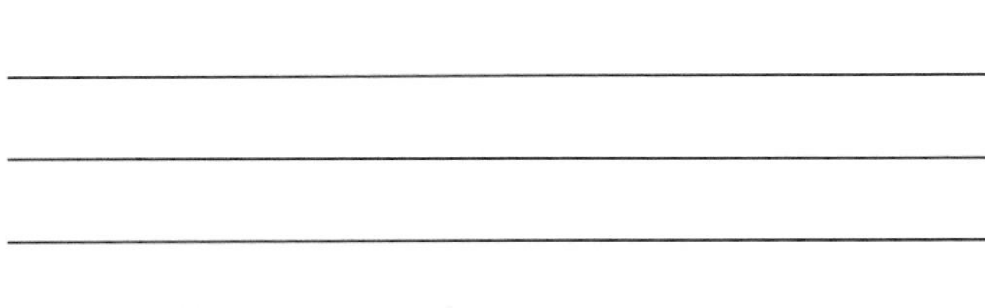

____

____

____

____

6. Write the equation for the line shown below.

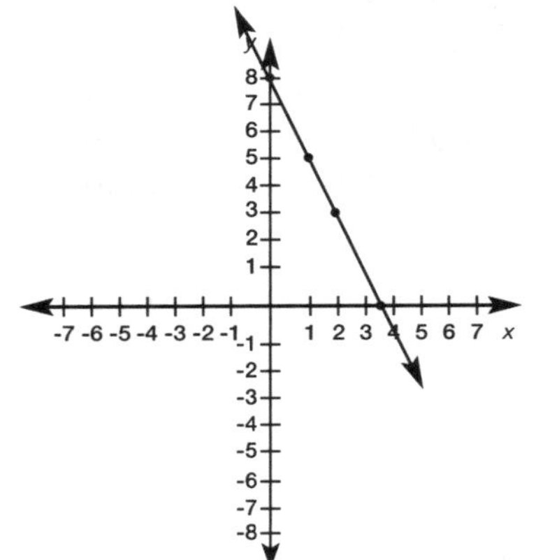

____

7. Describe the graph below. Use words, numbers, and symbols.

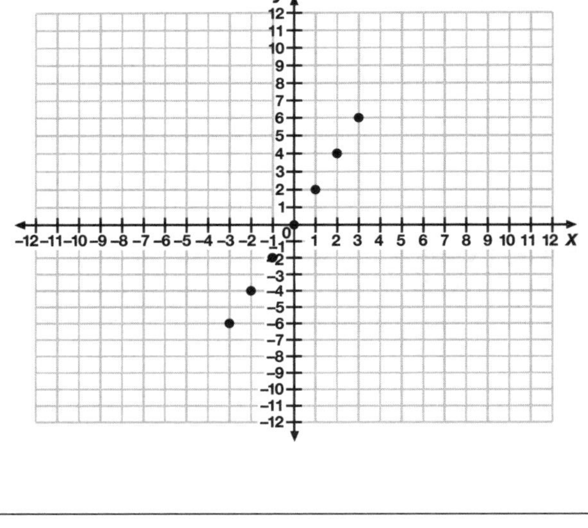

____

____

____

____

Name ______________________ Date ______________

Math

Simplify Linear Equations

Expressions and Equations

DIRECTIONS: Choose or write the correct answer.

Strategy Write and simplify equations to determine the number of solutions.

1. On each line, write if the equation has one solution, no solution, or infinite solutions.

$x + 7 = 23$ ______________

$3s = 3s$ ______________

$12 - v = 5 - v$ ______________

Test Tip

An equation has infinite solutions if it is always true no matter what the value of the variable is.

2. Write an equation that has only one solution.

____

3. Choose the two equations that have infinite solutions.

Ⓐ $2d = 2d$

Ⓑ $14 + p = 34$

Ⓒ $5b = 6b$

Ⓓ $u + 3 = u + 3$

4. You have 12 markers. Your friend has 3 markers and a box with an unknown number of markers in it. Write an equation that matches this scenario and has only one solution.

____

5. You have 4 game tokens and a bag with an unknown number of game tokens in it. Your friend also has 4 game tokens and a bag of tokens. Write an equation that matches this scenario and has an infinite number of solutions.

____

6. Write an equation that has no solutions.

____

Name ______________________ Date ______________

Math

Solve Linear Equations

Expressions and Equations

DIRECTIONS: Choose or write the correct answer.

Strategy Write and solve linear equations to solve real-world problems.

1. **Choose the solution to the equation $21 = 4x + 5$.**
   - (A) $x = 5$
   - (B) $x = -3$
   - (C) $x = 4$
   - (D) $x = -4$

2. **Solve for b.**

   $4(b + 2) = 20$

   ____

   Which property did you have to use to solve this equation?

   ____

3. **Brayden and Carter are selling pizzas for a school fundraiser. The school will triple their total amount of money collected. Brayden collected $30. The school donation was a total of $270. How much money did Carter collect? Write and solve an equation to find the answer.**

   ____

Test Tip

Think about what information you are given and what you need to find. Use a variable for the unknown value.

4. **Choose the solution to the equation $x + 5(x - 3) = 33$.**
   - (A) $x = 3$
   - (B) $x = 9$
   - (C) $x = 8$
   - (D) $x = \sqrt{12}$

5. **The temperature on Monday was 74°F. Over the next three days, the temperature rose the same amount each day. By the end of the week, the temperature was 86°F. Write and solve an equation to find out how much the temperature rose each day.**

   ____

6. **Harper swims every day. On Monday, she swam 5 laps. She swam again on Tuesday. On Wednesday she swam twice as many laps as Monday and Tuesday combined. All together, she swam 24 laps over the three days. How many laps did Harper swim on Tuesday?**
   - (A) 7
   - (B) 12
   - (C) 3
   - (D) 4.5

Name ____________________ Date ____________

Math

Solve Systems of Linear Equations

Expressions and Equations

DIRECTIONS: Choose or write the correct answer.

Strategy Graph equations to help you solve systems of equations.

Test Tip The solution to a system of equations is the point where their graphs intersect or overlap. If they will never intersect, there is no solution.

1. What is the solution for the system of equations?

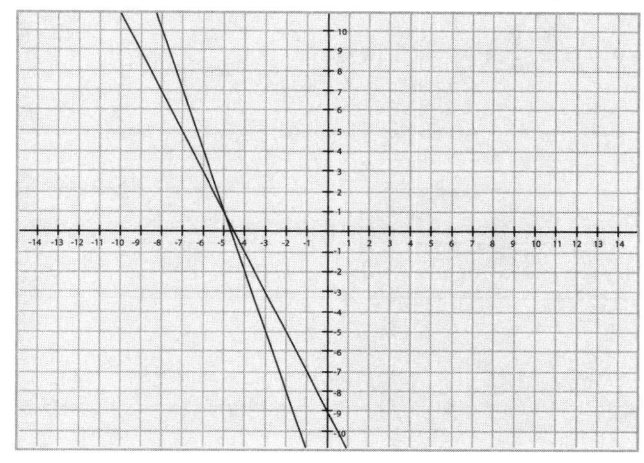

____

2. What is the solution for the system of equations?

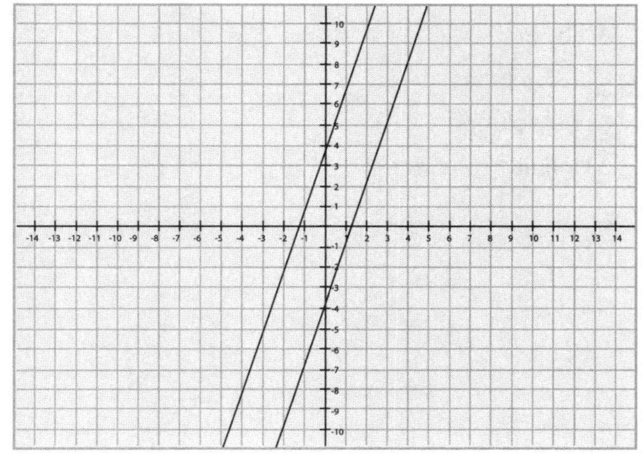

____

3. What is the solution for the system of equations?

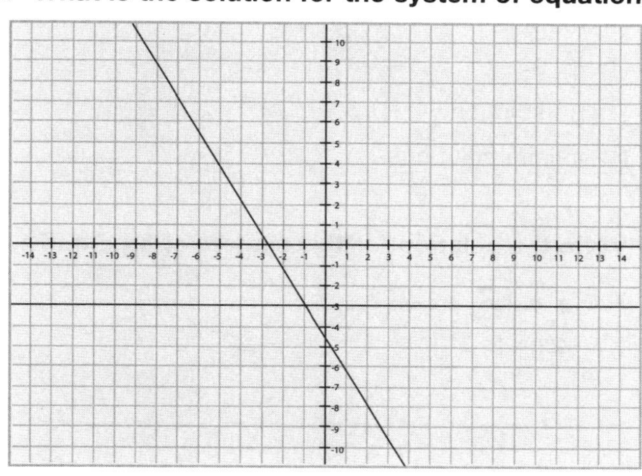

____

4. What is the solution for the system of equations?

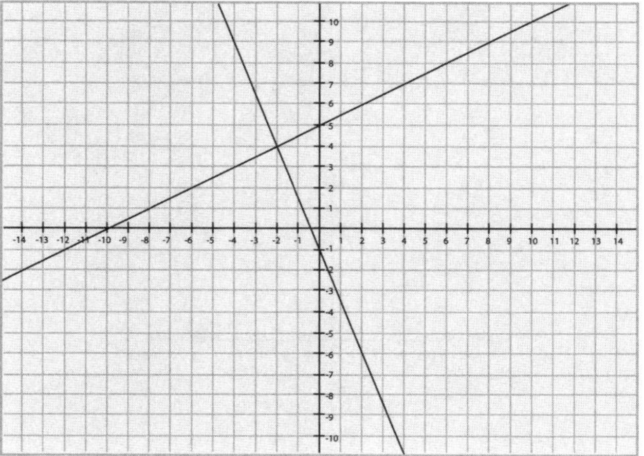

____

Name ______________________ Date ______________

Math

Solve Systems of Linear Equations

Expressions and Equations

DIRECTIONS: Choose or write the correct answer.

Strategy Solve systems of equations to evaluate if they have one solution, no solutions, or infinite solutions.

5. What is the solution for this system of equations?

$y = 3x + 5$

$y = 3x + 5$

(A) (3, 5)

(B) (5, 3)

(C) no solution

(D) infinite solutions

6. Write the solution for this system of equations.

$y = \frac{1}{2}x + 2$

$y = -2x + 2$

____

7. Find the solution to this system of equations. Then, graph the lines to check your work.

$2x + y = 11$

$7x = 14$

____

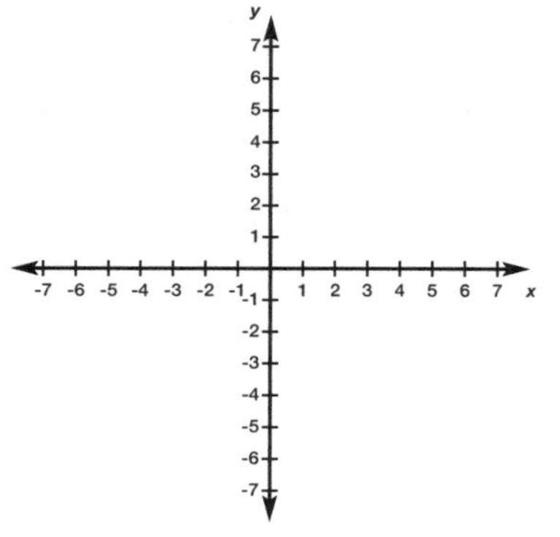

8. Explain how you know that there is no solution to this system of equations without graphing it.

$-\frac{2}{3}x + y = 6$

$y + 3 = \frac{2}{3}x$

____

____

____

____

____

____

____

9. What is the solution to this system of equations?

$x + 3y = 18$

$-x - 4y = -25$

(A) (3, –7)

(B) (–3, 7)

(C) no solution

(D) infinite solutions

ame ______________________ Date ______________________

lath

Solve Systems of Linear Equations

Expressions and Equations

Strategy Apply understanding of linear equations to recognize equations that form systems.

0. What is the solution to this system of equations?

$9x - 2y = 19$

$7x = 21$

Ⓐ (3, 4)

Ⓑ (–3, –4)

Ⓒ no solution

Ⓓ infinite solutions

1. Which two equations form a system that has one solution?

Ⓐ $y = -\frac{3}{4}x - 4$

Ⓑ $y = -\frac{3}{4}x + 4$

Ⓒ $y = -\frac{1}{2}x - 1$

Ⓓ $y = -\frac{3}{4}x + 2$

Vhat is the solution to the system of equations?

____

____

____

2. Which two equations form a system with a solution of (–4, –3)?

Ⓐ $y = \frac{3}{2}x - 3$

Ⓑ $y = \frac{3}{2}x + 3$

Ⓒ $y = \frac{3}{2}x + 3$

Ⓓ $y = -3$

13. Which two equations form a system with no solutions?

Ⓐ $y = \frac{7}{2}x - 5$

Ⓑ $y = \frac{7}{2}x + 3$

Ⓒ $y = -\frac{7}{2}x - 2$

Ⓓ $y = -5$

14. What is the solution for the system of equations?

$y = -\frac{2}{5}x - 4$

$y = \frac{9}{5}x + 7$

____

Name ______________________ Date ______________

Math

Solve Systems of Linear Equations

Expressions and Equations

Strategy Use systems of equations to express and solve problems based on real-world situations.

1. Ashley and her family went to the movies with their friends. Ashley's family bought 3 adult tickets and 2 children's tickets for a total price of \$52. Their friends bought 1 adult ticket and 3 children's tickets for a total price of \$36. Write and solve a system of equations to find the price of an adult ticket and the price of a child's ticket.

____

2. The Band Boosters set up a snack stand at the basketball games to raise money. At Friday night's game, they sold 32 boxes of popcorn and 50 cans of soda for a total profit of \$114. At Saturday's game, they sold 26 boxes of popcorn and 26 cans of soda for a total profit of \$78. Which two equations will give you the price per box of popcorn and the price per can of soda?

Ⓐ $32x + 50y = 114$

Ⓑ $114x - 32y = 50$

Ⓒ $78y + 26x = 26$

Ⓓ $26x + 26y = 78$

3. Kelle and Jen went shopping for new outfits. Kelle bought 4 shirts and 3 pairs of jeans. She paid \$320. Jen bought 3 shirts and 2 pairs of jeans and paid \$225. Write and solve a system of equations that will tell you the price for each shirt and each pair of jeans.

Shirts: \$ ____________

Jeans: \$ ____________

4. There are two cars traveling along different paths. Each path is represented by an equation. At what point will the two cars meet?

Car A: $10x + 7y = 1$

Car B: $-5x - 7y = 24$

____

5. Mrs. Hanson and Mrs. Florez are buying flowers for their gardens. Mrs. Hanson buys 4 peonies and 7 daylilies. Mrs. Florez buys 5 peonies and 3 daylilies. Mrs. Hanson's total comes to \$21.25 and Mrs. Florez's total is \$16.50. What is the cost for each type of flower?

Ⓐ Peonies: \$2.00; Daylilies: \$1.75

Ⓑ Peonies: \$2.25; Daylilies: \$1.75

Ⓒ Peonies: \$1.75; Daylilies: \$2.50

Ⓓ Peonies: \$21.25; Daylilies: \$16.50

6. When two numbers, *x* and *y*, are added, the sum is 37. When the same two numbers are multiplied, the sum is 336. Write and solve a system of equations to find the two numbers.

____

Name ______________________________ Date ______________

Math

Graph Functions

Functions

DIRECTIONS: Choose or write the correct answer.

Strategy Display data from a function table on a graph and interpret the graph.

Test Tip A function is an equation in which any value of *x* will result in exactly one value for *y*. A function table can be used to show the corresponding values of *x* and *y*. These pairs of *x* and *y* values can also be used to generate ordered pairs.

1. Create a function table and graph the function.

$y = 8x - 2$

x					
y					

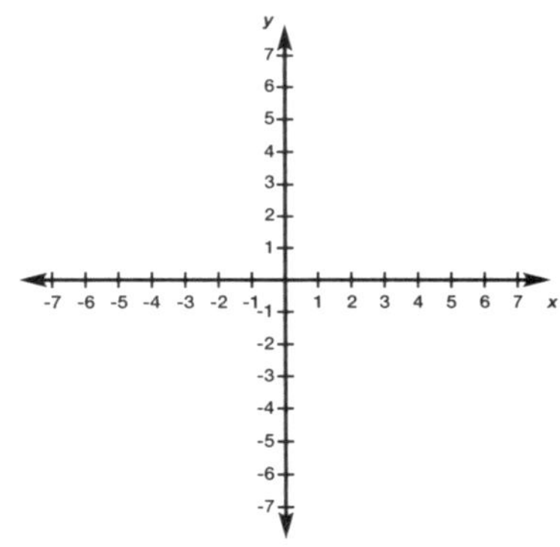

2. Create a function table and graph the function.

$y = -\frac{2}{3}x + 5$

x					
y					

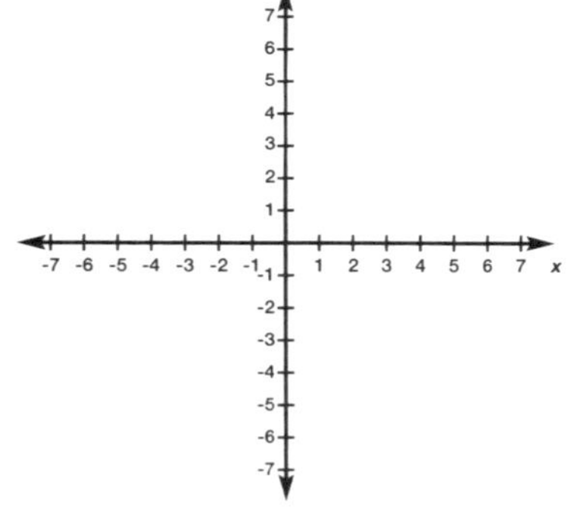

3. Create a function table to show why the equation $y = 3x^2 - 4$ is not a function.

x					
y					

____

____

____

____

____

____

Name ______________________________ Date ______________

Math

Compare Functions

Functions

DIRECTIONS: Choose or write the correct answer.

Strategy Compare functions by using graphs and data tables.

Test Tip The rate of change of a function is a rate that describes how one variable changes in relation to the other variable. On a graph, it can be observed as the slope of the line.

1. Look at the two functions below. Which function has the greater rate of change?

____

Function A: $y = \frac{2}{3}x + 7$

Function B:

x	–2	–1	0	1	2
y	–4	–2	0	2	4

Write how you know.

____

____

2. Look at the two functions below. What is the *y*-intercept for each function?

Function A: ______________

Function B: ______________

Function A:

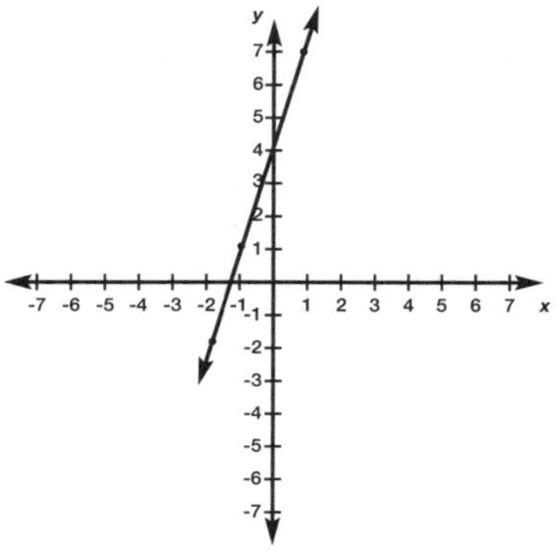

Function B:

x	–2	–1	0	1	2
y	–4	–2	0	2	4

3. Look at the two functions below. Which function has a negative slope?

____

Function A: For each magazine subscription Allen sells, he earns 15 points. Every 75 points earns him $500 for college.

Function B:

x	2	1	0	–1	–2
y	–5	–4	–3	–2	–1

4. Which function has the highest rate of change?

Ⓐ A workout claims to burn 10 calories per minute.

Ⓑ $3x + 2y = 54$

Ⓒ $y = 15x + 12$

Ⓓ

x	1	2	3	4	5
y	5	7	9	11	13

5. Write a function in algebraic form with a negative slope.

____

6. Make a function table that has a higher rate of change than the function $y = \frac{3}{4}x + 2$.

x					
y					

____

Name ______________________________ Date ______________

Math

Interpret Linear Functions

Functions

DIRECTIONS: Choose or write the correct answer.

Strategy Interpret linear functions by identifying characteristics of their graphs and equations.

Test Tip The word *linear* refers to a straight line or path.

1. Write the equations in the correct column of the chart.

$y = 5x - 3$ $y = 3x^2 - 4$ $y = 2x - 1$

$y = 4x + 2$ $y = -x^2$ $y = 7x^2 + 3x + 21$

Linear	Non-linear

2. Write three linear equations whose graphs will pass through the origin.

____

____

____

____

____

____

3. List three solutions of the function $A = s^2$ that prove it is not a linear function.

____

____

____

____

____

Explain why the three points you chose prove that this is not a linear function.

____

____

____

____

____

____

____

Name ______________________________ Date ______________

Math

Model Linear Relationships

Functions

DIRECTIONS: Choose or write the correct answer.

Strategy Graph lines in order to interpret data and solve problems.

Test Tip Recall that the *y*-intercept of a line is the value of *y* where the line crosses the *y*-axis. In the slope-intercept form of the equation of a line $y = mx + b$, *b* is the intercept.

1. Which equation represents the line that passes through (–2, –3) and (4, 6)?

(A) $y = -2x + 4$

(B) $y = -3x + 6$

(C) $y = \frac{3}{2}x + 3$

(D) $y = \frac{3}{2}x$

2. Sydney is plotting points on a coordinate grid. Sydney plots her first point 3 units down from the origin and 6 units to the left. She plots her second point 4 units to the right of the origin and 2 units up. What is the slope of the line between these two points?

____

Find the *y*-intercept of Sydney's line and write a linear equation that represents the line.

***y*-intercept:** ______________

Equation: ______________

DIRECTIONS: Use the graph below to answer the questions.

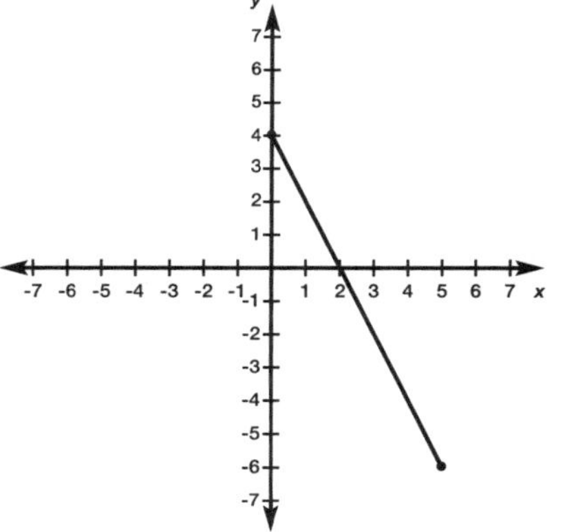

3. Describe the slope of this function.

____

4. Write an equation to describe the graph.

____

5. Which function table represents a line with a slope of 4 and a y-intercept of 5?

(A)

x	–2	–1	0	1	2
y	0	4	8	12	16

(B)

x	–2	–1	0	1	2
y	13	9	5	1	–3

(C)

x	–2	–1	0	1	2
y	–3	1	5	9	19

(D)

x	–2	–1	0	1	2
y	–6	–1	4	9	14

Name ______________________ Date ______________

Math

Describe Functional Relationships

Functions

DIRECTIONS: Choose or write the correct answer.

Strategy Predict characteristics of the graph of a function based on how given data are related.

Describe the graph of the function based on the information in the function table.

x	–2	–1	0	1	2
y	–13	–8	–3	2	7

1. Is the function linear? ______________

Write how you know.

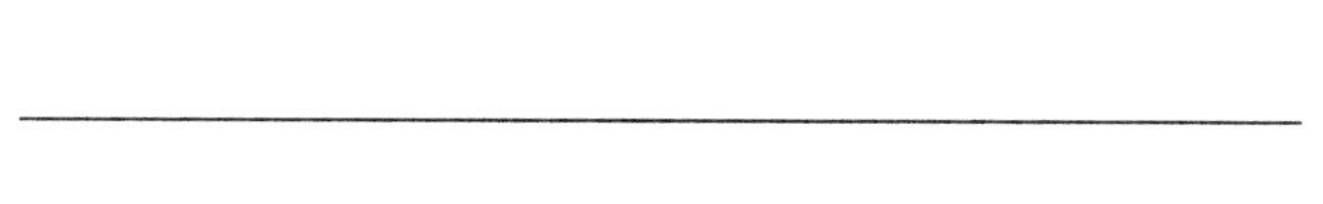

2. Does the graph increase or decrease?

____

Write how you know.

____

____

____

____

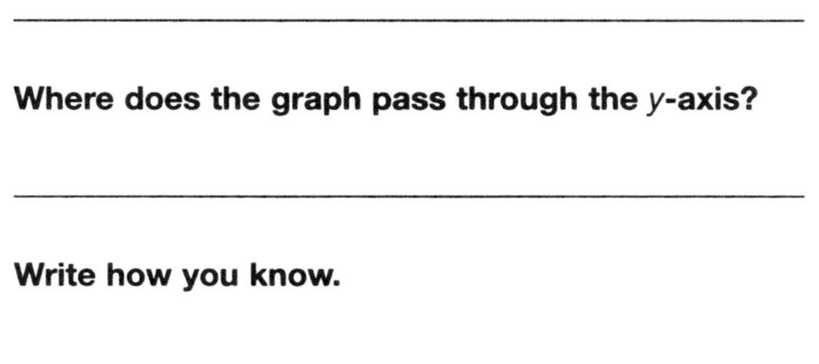

3. Where does the graph pass through the *y*-axis?

____

Write how you know.

____

____

4. Describe the graph of the function using at least four details.

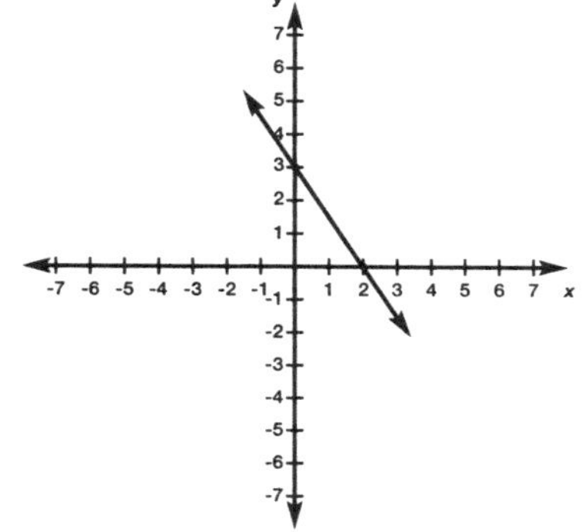

____

____

____

____

____

Name ________________________________ Date ____________________

Math

Draw a Graph Based on Its Description

Functions

DIRECTIONS: Draw each graph.

Strategy Draw a graph based on the description of a function.

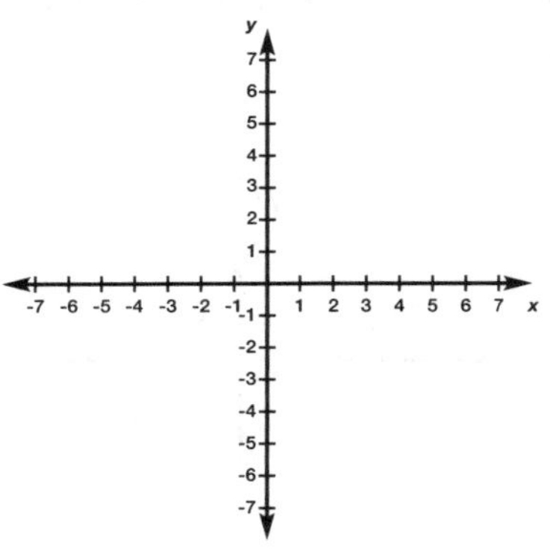

1. **This is a graph of a linear function.**
2. **The graph increases.**
3. **The graph has a *y*-intercept of (0, –3)**
4. **For each unit the graph moves to the right, it rises 3 units.**

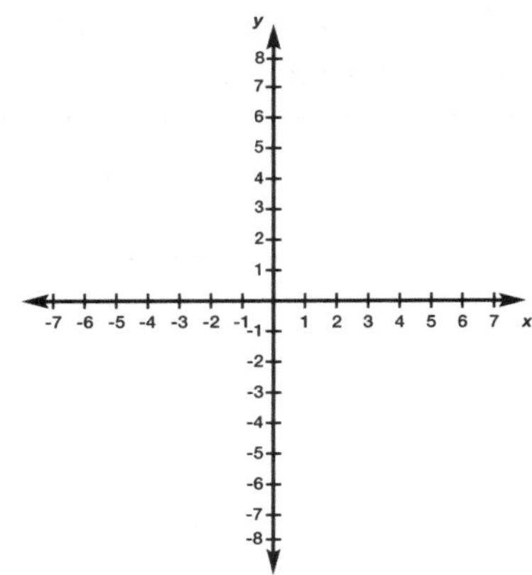

5. **This is not a graph of a linear function.**
6. **The graph increases between (–6, –5) and (–4, 0). Then, it decreases to (0, –2).**
7. **The section of the graph starting at (0, –2) has a slope of $\frac{5}{2}$.**
8. **This graph ends at (4, 8).**

Test Tip

Recall that slope is $\frac{\text{rise}}{\text{run}}$.

Name ______________________________ Date ______________
Math

Understand Rotations, Reflections, and Translations

Geometry

DIRECTIONS: Choose or write the correct answer.

Strategy Translate, rotate, and reflect figures on the coordinate plane.

Test Tip Rotations, reflections, and translations are all types of transformations that do not change the size of the figure.

1. Parallelogram QRST translated to a new position on the grid as shown. Which moves describe the translation?

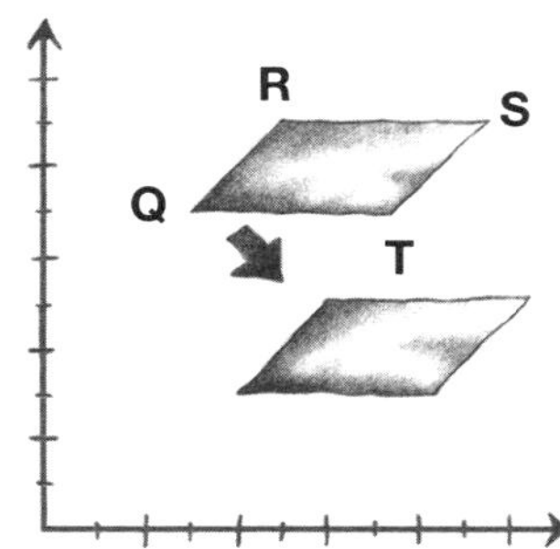

(A) translated 1 right, 4 down

(B) translated 1 right, 5 down

(C) translated 2 right, 4 down

(D) translated 1 right, 3 down

DIRECTIONS: Compare the following images to their transformation images. What type of transformation was performed? Be as specific as possible.

2.

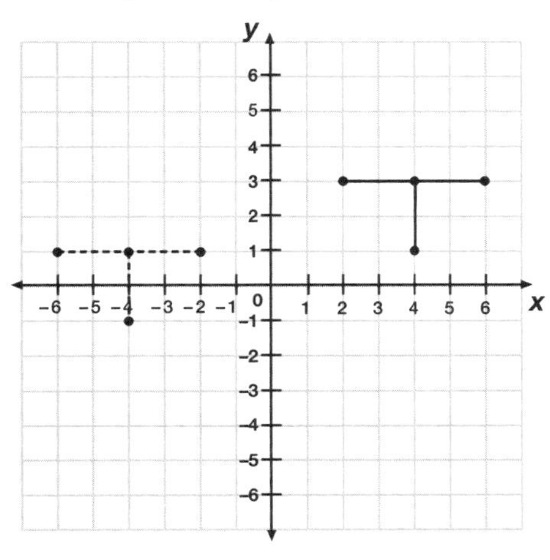

____

____

3.

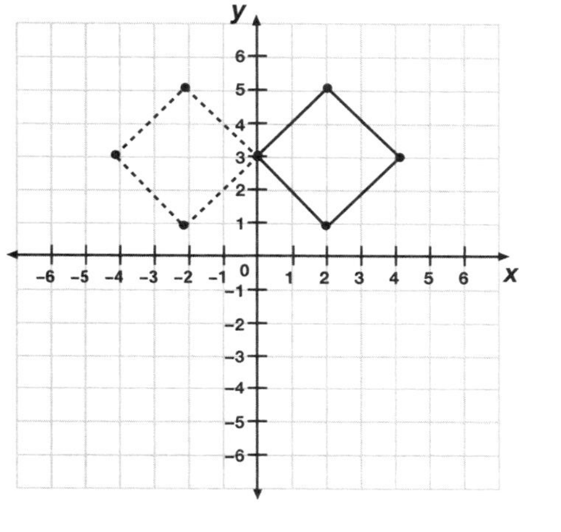

____

____

4.

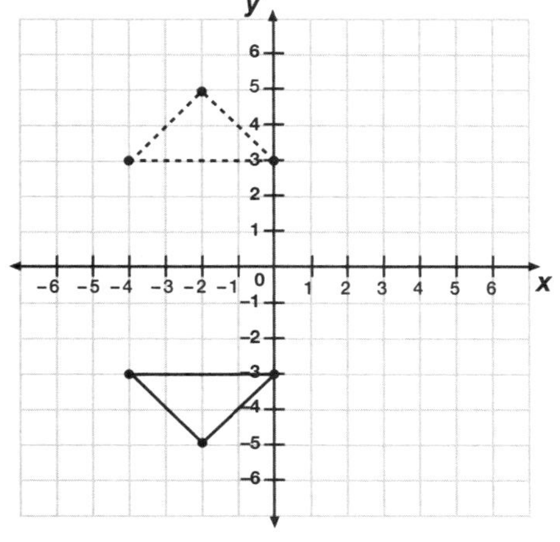

____

____

Name ______________________________ Date ______________

Math

Understand Congruence

Geometry

DIRECTIONS: For each pair of polygons, tell if the two shapes are congruent. Describe the transformations that were made to draw your conclusion.

Strategy Use drawings to help determine if figures are congruent.

Test Tip Congruent shapes are exactly the same size. Rotations, translations, and reflections all result in congruent figures.

1.

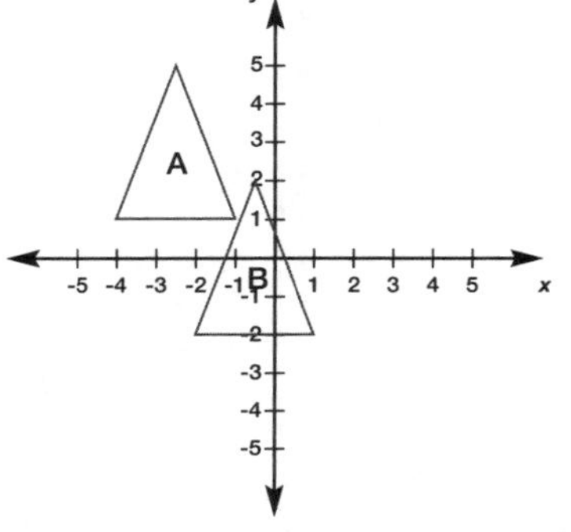

Are the shapes congruent? ___________

What transformations were performed?

____

____

____

2.

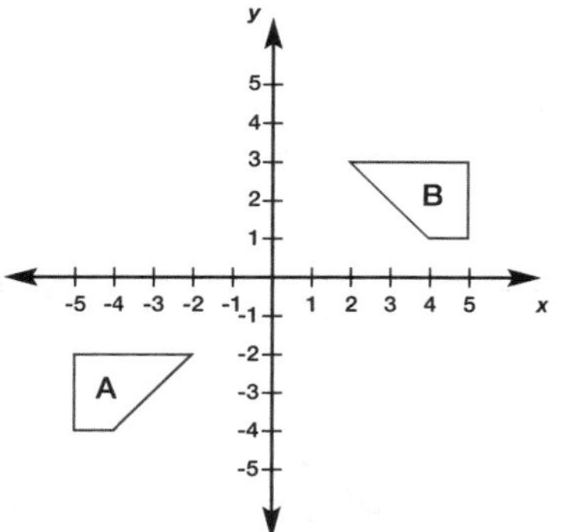

Are the shapes congruent? ___________

What transformations were performed?

____

____

3.

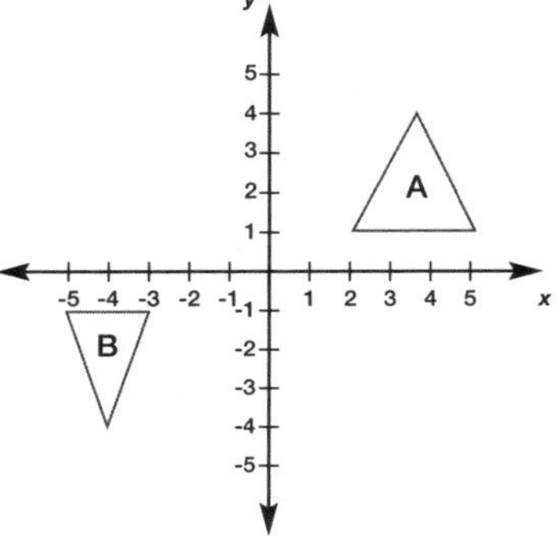

Are the shapes congruent? ___________

What transformations were performed?

____

____

____

4.

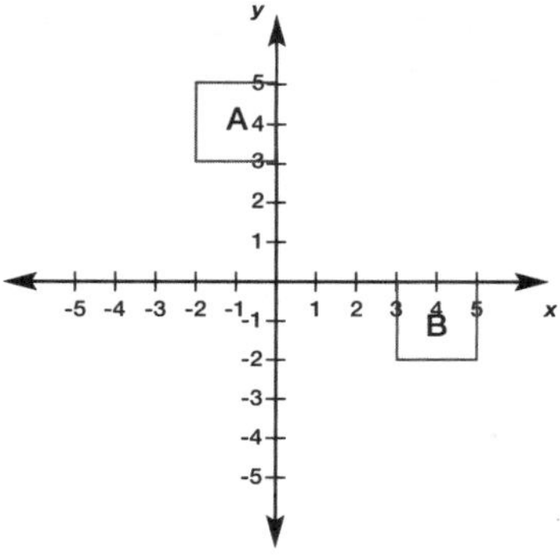

Are the shapes congruent? ___________

What transformations were performed?

____

____

____

Name ______________________________ Date ______________
Math

Draw Congruent Polygons

Geometry

Strategy Use drawings to draw and understand congruence.

1. Draw a congruent polygon by following these steps.

Translate 2 right, 3 down

Rotate clockwise 90°

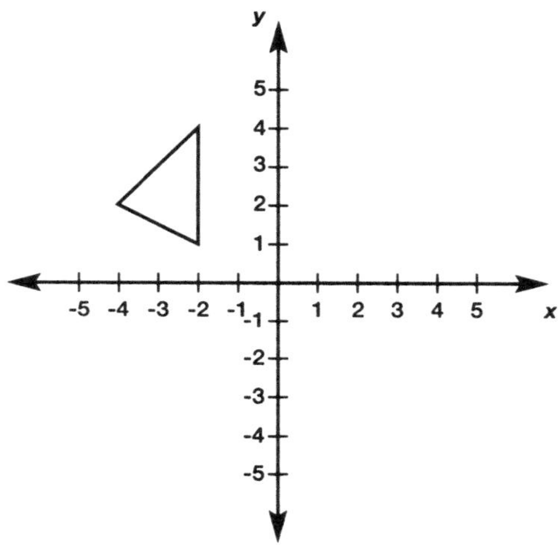

2. Draw a congruent polygon by following these steps.

Reflect over *y*-axis

Translate 2 up

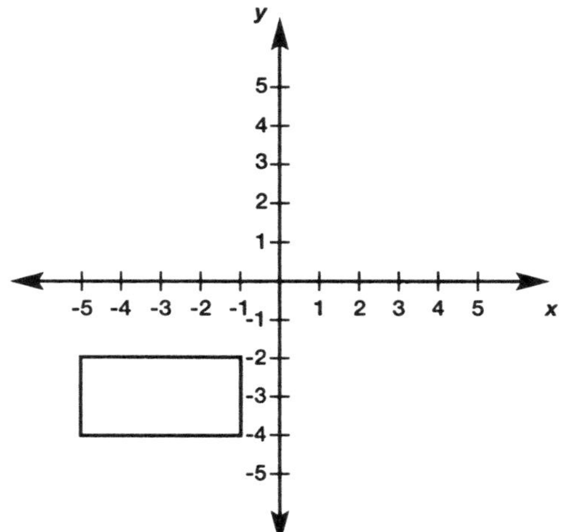

3. Draw a congruent polygon by following these steps.

Rotate 180° around the axis

Translate 2 left

Reflect over *x*-axis

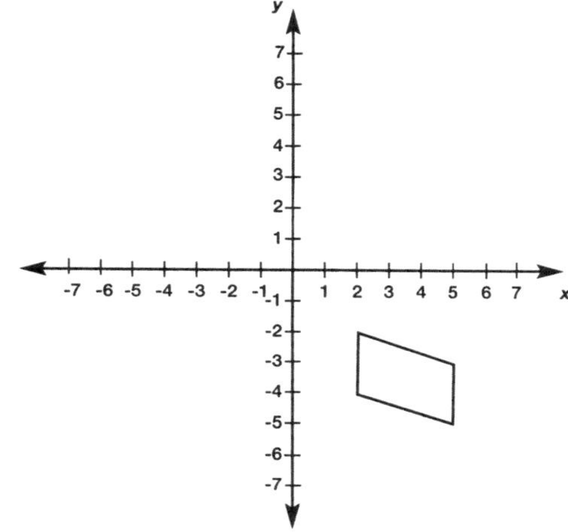

4. Draw a congruent polygon by following these steps.

Reflect over *x*-axis

Translate 2 left

Rotate clockwise 90°

Translate up 6

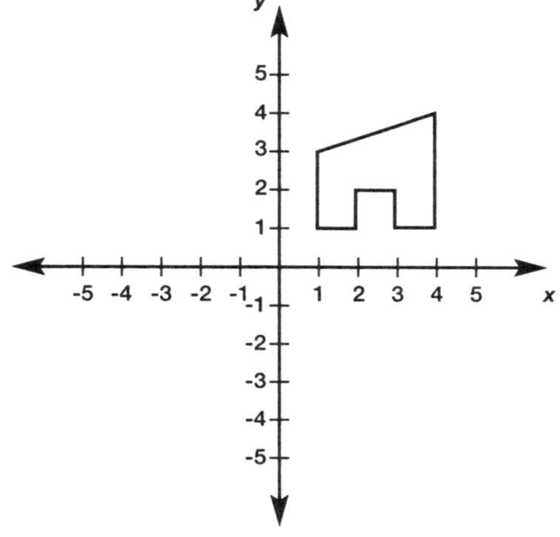

Name ______________________ Date ______________

Math

Use Coordinates to Describe Transformations

Geometry

DIRECTIONS: Choose or write the correct answer.

Strategy Transform figures by graphing the original figures and their transformations on a coordinate grid.

Test Tip A dilation is a type of transformation that changes the size of the figure. A dilation can make a figure smaller or larger. If a figure is dilated, it is similar but no longer congruent to the original figure.

1.

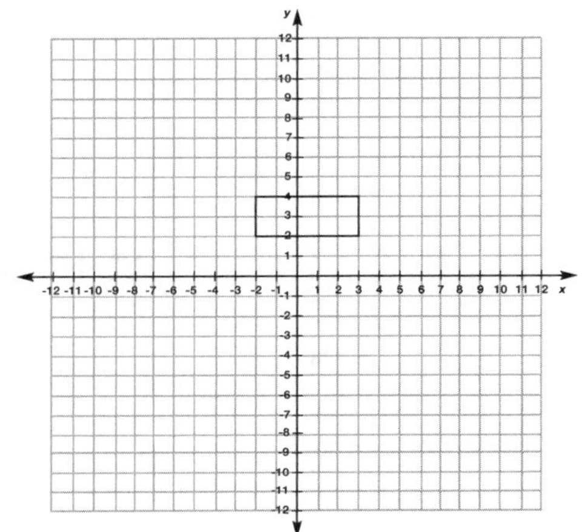

Write the coordinates for each point if the shape is reflected across the *x*-axis.

A' ______________

B' ______________

C' ______________

D' ______________

2.

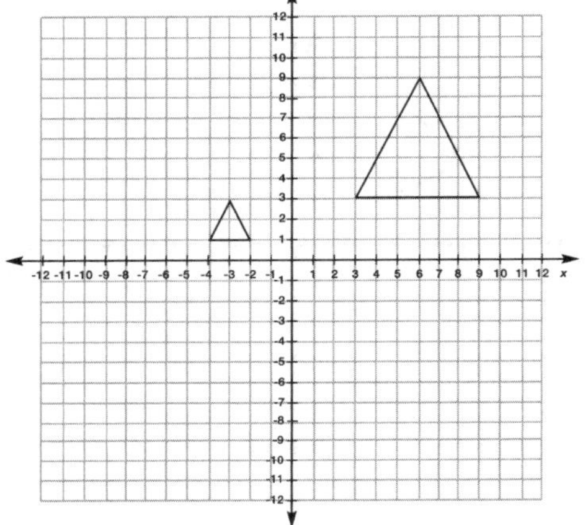

Write the coordinates for each point if the shape is dilated by a factor of 3.

A' ______________

B' ______________

C' ______________

3. A triangle has the points A (–2, 1), B (2, 3), and C (4, 1). Write the coordinates for each point if the shape is dilated by a factor of $\frac{1}{2}$.

A' ______________

B' ______________

C' ______________

Name ________________________________ Date ________________

Math

Understand Similarity

Geometry

DIRECTIONS: Choose or write the correct answer.

Strategy Use the rules of transformations to draw similar figures.

1.

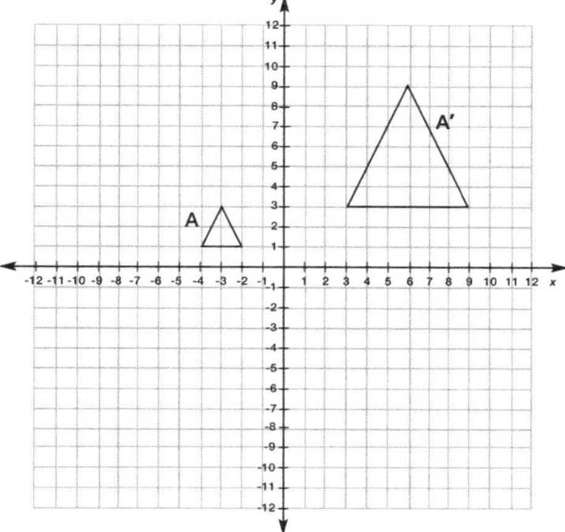

Write the sequence transformations that were performed to obtain the similar figure.

____

____

____

2.

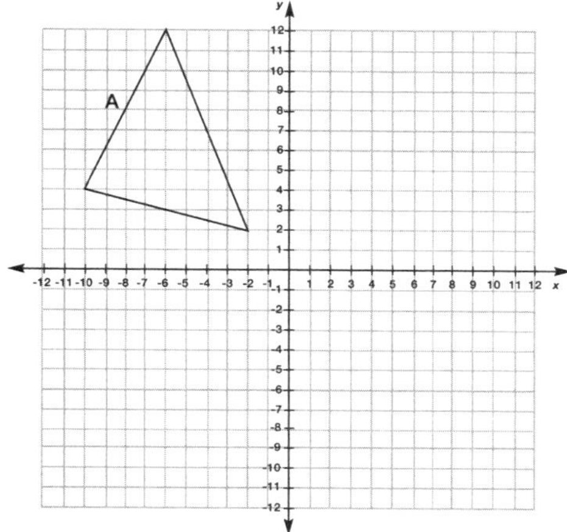

Write the sequence of transformations that were performed to obtain the similar figure.

____

____

3.

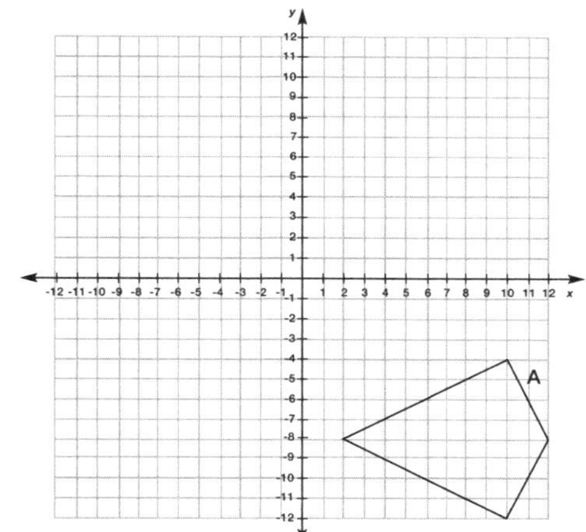

Follow the sequence of transformations to obtain a similar figure.

Reflect across the *x*–axis.

Dilate by a factor of $\frac{1}{2}$.

Name ______________________ Date ____________

Math

Understand Angle Properties

Geometry

DIRECTIONS: Choose or write the correct answer.

Strategy Use drawings to understand properties of angles.

1. Examine the figure below. Use what you know about angles to prove that ∠1 = ∠ 2. Do not measure the angles. Complete the table below to help you find your answers. Fill in the missing formulas under the Statement column and the missing justifications under the Reason column. Some of the entries have been completed for you.

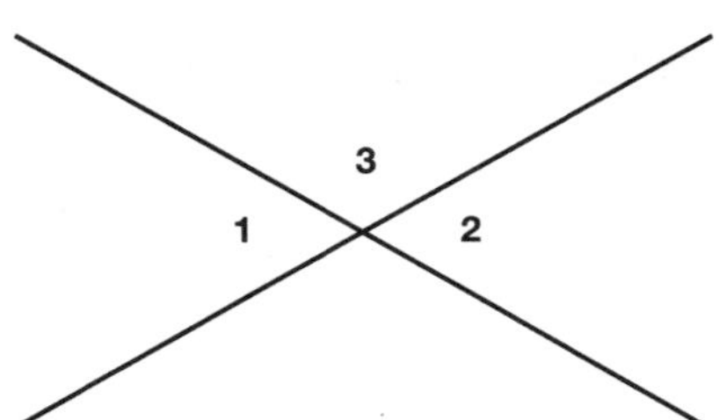

Statement	Reason
∠1 + ∠3 = 180° ∠ 2 + ∠3 = 180°	
If the above statements are true, then:	Substitution
If the above statements are true, then:	Algebra

2. Look at the equilateral triangles below. What do they prove about the measure of a straight angle? Explain your answer.

____

____

Test Tip

Review the characteristics of complementary and supplementary angles before taking your test. The sum of complementary angles is 90°. The sum of supplementary angles is 180°.

3. Which two statements about the exterior angles of triangles are true?

Ⓐ They form a supplementary angle with the adjacent interior angle.

Ⓑ The sum of the exterior angles is 180°.

Ⓒ They form a complementary angle with the adjacent interior angle.

Ⓓ The sum of the exterior angles is 360°.

Use the diagram below to answer the questions.

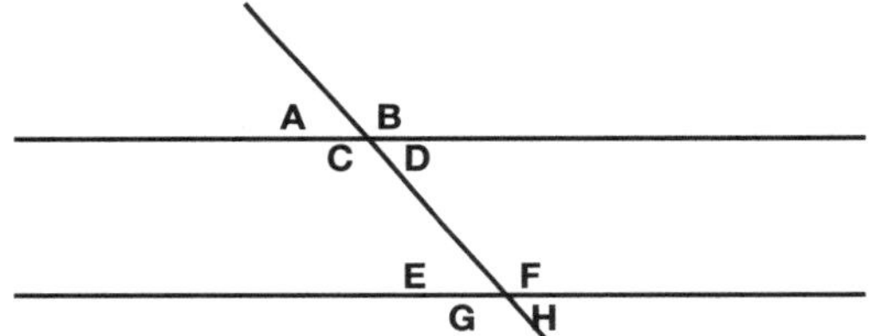

4. Name two pairs of angles that form supplementary angles.

____

____

5. How do you know that ∠H and ∠D are congruent angles?

____

____

____

Name ______________________ Date ______________
Math

Explain the Pythagorean Theorem

Geometry

DIRECTIONS: Choose or write the correct answer.

Strategy Use angle properties to understand the Pythagorean Theorem.

Test Tip The Pythagorean Theorem can be written $a^2 + b^2 = c^2$. It only applies to right triangles.

1. Use the picture below to explain the Pythagorean Theorem.

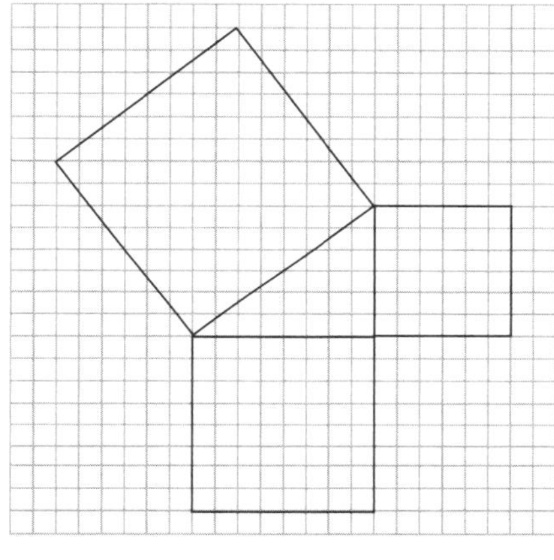

____
____
____
____
____
____

2. Can a triangle have the following measurements: 4, 9, and 8? Support your answer using the Pythagorean Theorem.

____
____
____

3. Which three side lengths can be used to form a right triangle?

Ⓐ 5
Ⓑ 7
Ⓒ 12
Ⓓ 13

4. Is a triangle with side lengths 7, 24, and 25 a right triangle? Support your answer with the Pythagorean Theorem.

____
____

Name ______________________ Date ______________

Math

Use the Pythagorean Theorem to Solve Problems

Geometry

DIRECTIONS: Choose or write the correct answer.

Strategy Use the Pythagorean Theorem to solve real-world problems.

Test Tip The hypotenuse of a right triangle is the side opposite the right angle.

1. Aniyah walks home from school. She walks 6 blocks north and 8 blocks east. How far is her house from the school?

(A) 10 blocks
(B) 40 blocks
(C) 48 blocks
(D) 12 blocks

2. A 25-foot ladder is placed 7 feet from the base of a wall. How far up the wall will the ladder reach?

____

Write how you found your answer.

____

____

____

3. A tablet has a diagonal length of 17 inches. It is 15 inches wide. How tall is the tablet?

(A) 10 inches
(B) 9 inches
(C) 8 inches
(D) 7 inches

4. Write a scenario that uses the Pythagorean triple 3, 4, 5.

____

____

____

____

____

5. To make sure his planter box has right angles, M Munding runs a string from one corner to the opposite corner. If the planter box is 40 feet long and 9 feet wide, how long must his string be to prove that the angles are square?

____

____

____

ame ______________________________ Date ______________

lath

se the Pythagorean Theorem to Find Distance

Geometry

IRECTIONS: Choose or write the correct answer.

Strategy Use the Pythagorean Theorem to find the distance between points.

1. What is the distance between the two points?

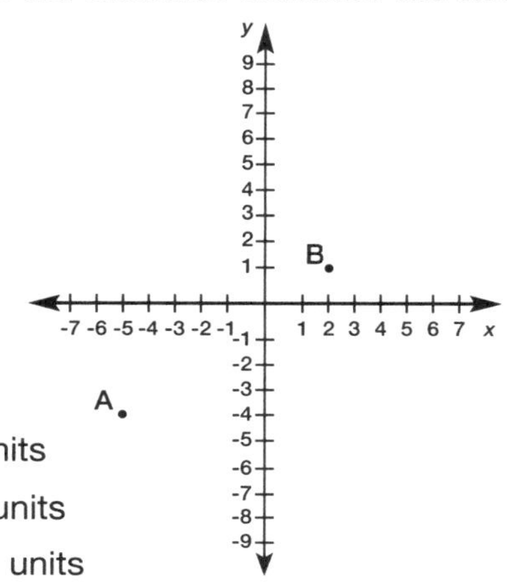

(A) 6 units

(B) 12 units

(C) $\sqrt{12}$ units

(D) $\sqrt{74}$ units

Write how you found your answer.

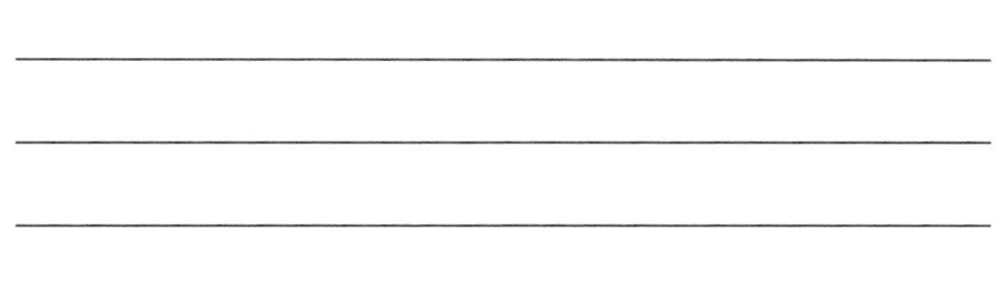

2. What is the distance between the two points?

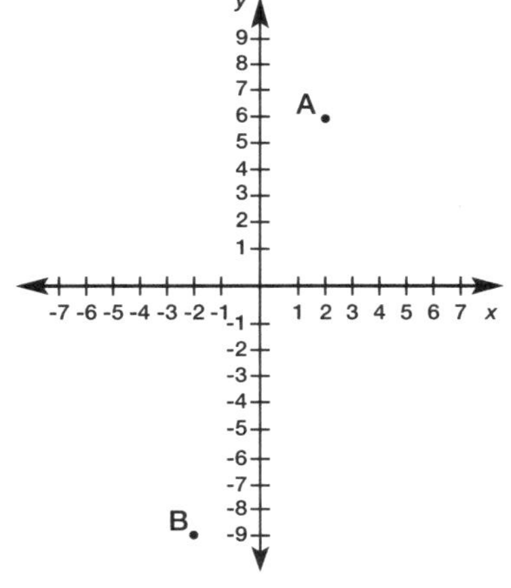

3. What is the distance between the two points?

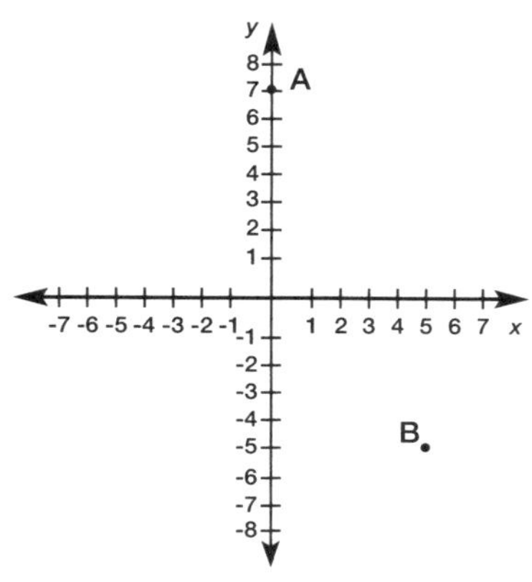

4. Plot a second point that would make the distance between the points 17 units.

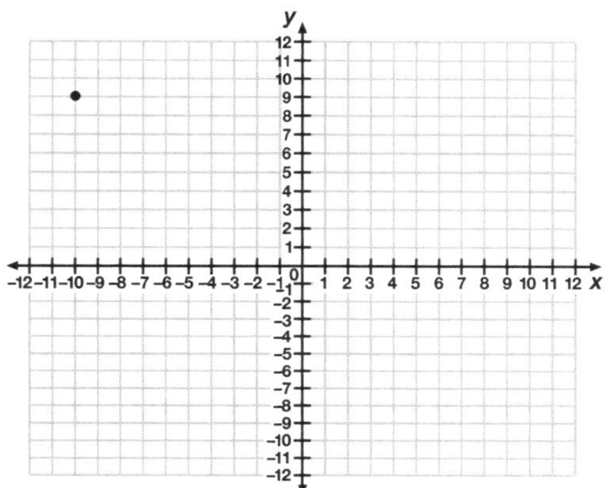

Explain how you decided where to plot the point.

Name ______________________ Date ______________

Math

Find Volume

Geometry

DIRECTIONS: Choose or write the correct answer.

Strategy Use the formula for volume to solve problems.

Test Tip Remember these formulas: volume of a cylinder: $\pi r^2 \bullet h$. volume of a cone: $\frac{1}{3}\pi r^2 \bullet h$ volume of a sphere: $\frac{4}{3}\pi r^3$

1. Find the volume of the cylinder below. Show your work.

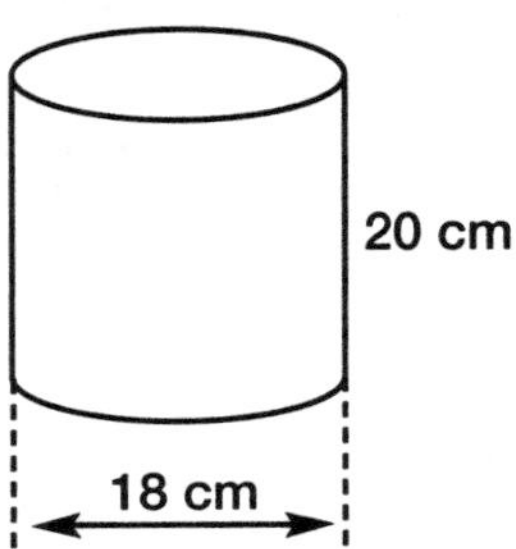

____

2. How many cubic inches of air are needed to fill a basketball with a radius of 6 inches?

(A) 904.78

(B) 108

(C) 339.12

(D) 113.12

Write how you found your answer.

____

____

____

3. Tim wants to put the basketball in question 2 into a cylindrical case that has a diameter of 13 inches and a height of 7 inches. Will it fit? Show your work and explain your answer.

____

____

4. A party hat is shaped like a cone. The radius is 4 inches, and it is 6 inches tall. What is the volume of the hat? Show your work.

____

____

5. Arielle has 65 one-inch cube-shaped beads. She wants to put them into a cylindrical jar with a diameter of 4 inches and a height of 6 inches. Will the beads fit? Show your work and explain your answer.

____

____

me ______________________________ Date ____________________

ath

Interpret Scatter Plots

Statistics and Probability

ECTIONS: Choose or write the correct answer.

Strategy Interpret scatter plots to draw conclusions about a data set.

Test Tip Use a line of best fit to interpret the relationship between the two variables.

. The scatter plot below shows the relationship between the number of hours a player practices and her success rate in shooting free-throws.

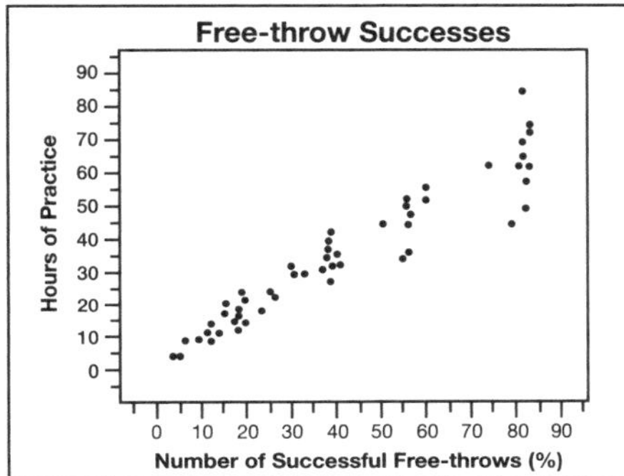

Complete the sentence to interpret the data.

The ______________ a player practices, the ______________ her success rate is.

. The scatter plot below shows the relationship between students' math and reading scores on a recent test. Describe the relationship shown in the graph.

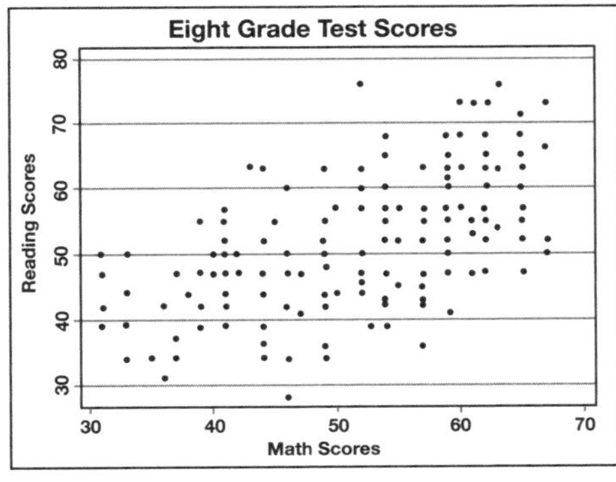

____

____

3. The scatter plot below shows the relationship between smoking and a person's ability to run on a treadmill. Describe the relationship shown in the graph.

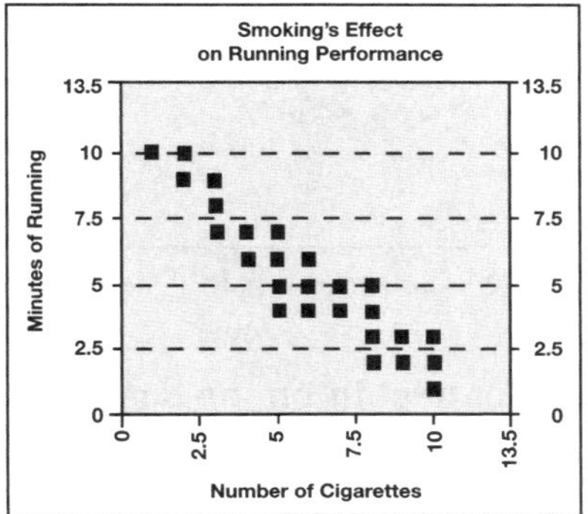

____

____

4. The scatter plot below shows the relationship between exercise and a person's cholesterol level. Describe the relationship shown in the graph.

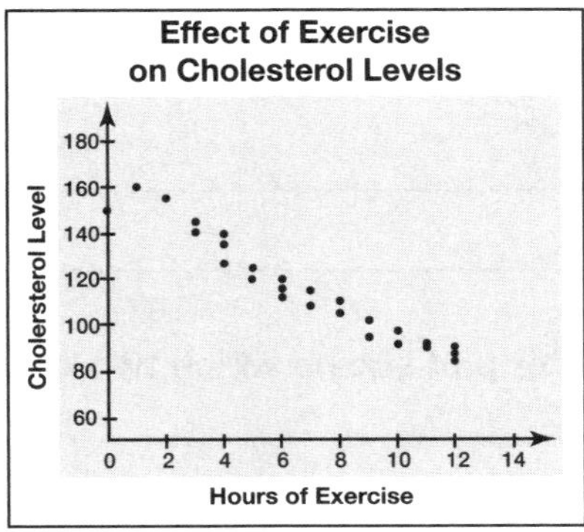

____

____

____

Name ______________________ Date ______________

Math

Construct and Interpret Scatter Plots

Statistics and Probability

Strategy Create scatter plots to understand and interpret data.

Test Tip A line of best fit is a straight line that best represents the data on a scatter plot. This line may pass through some of the points, none of the points, or all of the points.

DIRECTIONS: Use the scatter plot to answer questions 1–4.

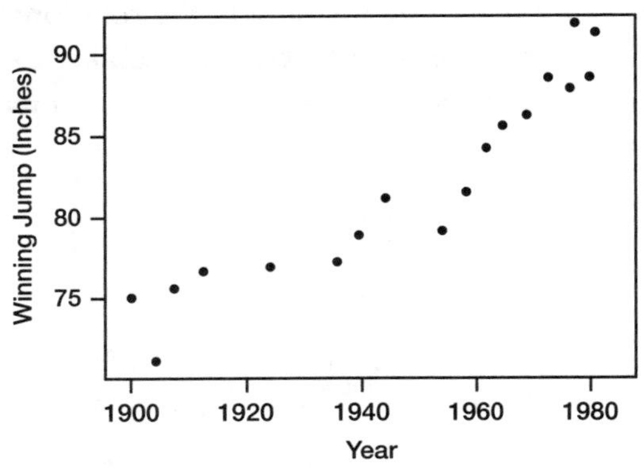

1. **Draw a line of best fit on the scatter plot.**

2. **What trend is illustrated by the data in the scatter plot?**

____

____

____

3. **What prediction can you make for the winning high jump for the 1988 Olympics?**

____

____

4. **This scatter plot shows which two of the following?**

   Ⓐ positive association between variables

   Ⓑ negative association between variables

   Ⓒ linear association between variables

   Ⓓ nonlinear association between variables

DIRECTIONS: Use the scatter plot and table to answer questions 5–7.

North Coast California: Number of Earthquakes per Year

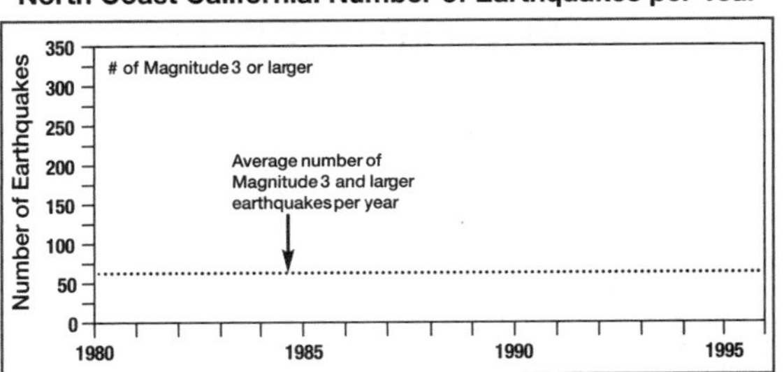

Year	Number of Earthquakes
1980	130
1981	125
1982	65
1983	90
1984	75
1985	50
1986	75
1987	90
1988	60
1989	60
1990	55
1991	75
1992	300
1993	75
1994	90
1995	95
1996	50

Construct and Interpret Scatter Plots

Statistics and Probability

5. **Plot the data from the table on the graph.**

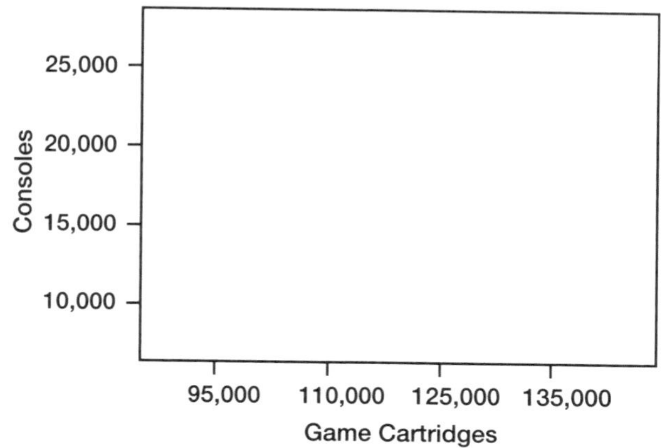

6. **Is there a relationship between the two variables? Explain your answer.**

____

____

____

____

7. **Is there anything unusual in the graph? Explain your answer.**

____

____

____

____

____

____

RECTIONS: Plot the data from the table in the scatter plot d draw a line of best fit to answer the questions.

Strategy

Use a ruler or the straight edge of a sheet of paper to line your data points up on the graph.

Video Game Company	Consoles	Game Cartridges
VideoMod	20,000	125,000
GamePlay	15,000	110,000
SuperSport	25,000	135,000
Standard Games	10,000	95,000

8. **Is there any relationship between game console sales and game cartridge sales? Describe the relationship.**

____

____

How does the line of best fit help you to know that?

____

____

____

____

Name ____________________ Date ____________

Math

Use Graphed Data to Explain Real-World Scenarios

Statistics and Probability

DIRECTIONS: Choose or write the correct answer.

Strategy Look for key words in word problems that help you know which operation to use in an equation.

Test Tip Remember that the change in one variable depends on the change in the other. Think about which variable is dependent and which is independent.

1. Devin performed a science experiment comparing plant growth to hours of sunlight. She graphed her data and found a slope of 1.5 cm/hr. What does this mean?

Ⓐ for every 1.5 cm of growth, there was an additional hour of sunlight

Ⓑ for every hour of sunlight, there was an additional 1.5 cm of growth

Ⓒ for every 1.5 cm of sunlight, there was an additional hour of growth

Ⓓ for every centimeter of growth there was an additional 1.5 hours of sunlight

2. When Aaron graphed the gas mileage of his hew car, he discovered a negative slope of 0.125 gal/mi. What does this mean?

____

____

3. Kendra wants to save up for a new bike. She graphed her savings and her hourly babysitting income and found the equation $y = 25 + 3.25x$. What does this tell you?

____

____

____

____

Use the equation to find out how many hours Kendra needs to babysit to earn enough money for a bike that costs $175.99. Show your work.

4. A scatter plot shows a negative linear associatio[n] between number of hours training and a runner's time in minutes in a half marathon. The slope of the line is –1.25. What does this mean?

____

____

____

____

____

Name _______________________________ Date _______________

Math

Use Graphed Data to Solve Problems

Statistics and Probability

Strategy Apply rules of scatter plots, lines of best fit, and equations to solve problems.

Test Tip Remember that a line of best fit is a straight line. Don't try to curve the line to meet all of the points.

DIRECTIONS: The scatter plot below shows the association between the number of hours students spend online and the number of hours they spend studying each week. Use the graph to answer the questions.

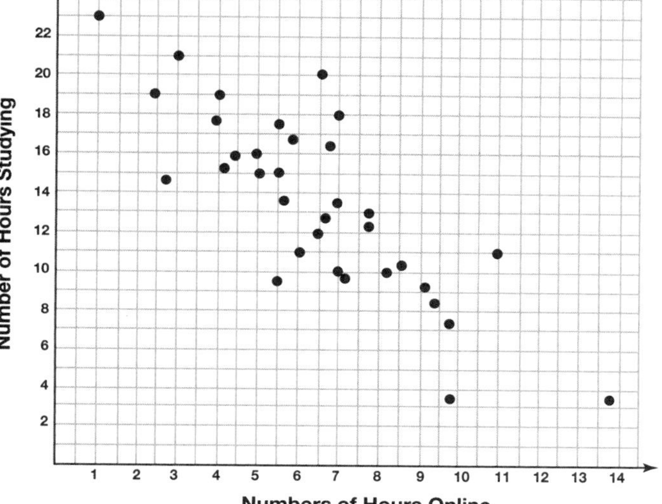

1. Draw a line of best fit and find its slope.

____

____

____

2. What does the line of best fit tell you about the relationship between studying and online habits?

Ⓐ for every hour studying, online time goes down about $\frac{4}{3}$ hours

Ⓑ for every hour of studying, online time goes up about $\frac{4}{3}$ hours

Ⓒ for every hour online, study time goes down by about $\frac{4}{3}$ hours

Ⓓ for every hour online, study time goes up by about $\frac{4}{3}$ hours

3. Jamal spends about 6 hours a week online. Based on the scatter plot, how many hours of studying does Jamal probably do per week?

____

4. If you were to make a scatter plot comparing students' test scores to the hours spent online, how do you think it would compare to the plot above?

____

____

____

____

Name ______________________________ Date ______________

Math

Interpret Bivariate Frequency Tables

Statistics and Probability

Strategy Organize and display data in frequency tables in order to interpret it.

Test Tip When answering the questions, decide whether the tally chart or the frequency table is going to give you the best information.

DIRECTIONS: Mrs. Weinstein asked her students if they play a sport or a musical instrument. She collected the data below. Use the data to answer the questions.

Student	1	2	3	4	5	6	7	8	9	10	11	12	13	14	15	16	17	18	19	20	21	22	23	24	25
Sport	X				X				X		X		X		X	X	X			X		X			X
Instrument	X	X			X		X		X		X		X		X		X	X		X		X		X	

1. Use the data to create a frequency table.

2. Of the students who play a sport, what ratio also plays a musical instrument?

____

3. Of the students who do not play a sport, what ratio also plays a musical instrument?

____

4. Based on this data, what correlation do you see between playing a sport and playing a musical instrument?

____

____

____

____

____

____

____

Name ______________________________ Date ______________

Math

Interpret Bivariate Frequency Tables

Statistics and Probability

Strategy Double check to make sure the numbers in your frequency table match the number of tallies in the tally chart.

DIRECTIONS: Eighth graders in one class were asked if they had chores or a curfew. Use the data to answer the questions.

Student	1	2	3	4	5	6	7	8	9	10	11	12	13	14	15	16	17	18	19	20	21	22	23	24	25
Curfew	X			X	X			X	X		X		X		X	X	X		X	X	X	X		X	X
Chores	X	X		X	X		X		X		X	X	X		X		X	X	X	X	X	X		X	

5. Use the data to create a frequency table.

6. Of students who have curfews, what ratio also has chores?

(A) $\frac{16}{25}$

(B) $\frac{16}{17}$

(C) $\frac{13}{16}$

(D) $\frac{13}{17}$

7. Of students who do not have curfews, what ratio has chores?

____

8. What correlation can you make between having a curfew and having chores?

____

____

____

____

Name ______________________________ Date ______________

Math

Strategy Review

DIRECTIONS: Choose or write the correct answer.

Strategy Review the strategies you learned and apply them to practice the skills.

EXAMPLE

Josie spent $185 at the mall. She bought 5 shirts and 2 pairs of jeans. The jeans cost $30 each. How much did one shirt cost if they were all the same price?

First, write an equation using a variable for the price of the shirts.

$185 = 5s + (2 \times 30)$

Next, compute the value in the parentheses.

$185 = 5s + 60$

Use inverse relationships to isolate the variable.

$185 - 60 = 5s$

$125 = 5s$

Use division to isolate the variable.

$125 \div 5 = 25$

Each shirt cost $25.

1. **Glenn is trying to maintain his weight for wrestling season. He limits himself to 1,600 calories per day. He has used 1,050 of his calories for the day. How many servings of pasta can he have if each serving is 180 calories? Show your work.**

____

2. **Jessica runs the same distance every Monday, Wednesday, and Friday. Her total distance for the three days is 6.75 miles. How far does she run each day?**

   Ⓐ 3.25 miles

   Ⓑ 1.75 miles

   Ⓒ 2.25 miles

   Ⓓ 2.5 miles

How did the strategy help you answer these questions?

____

____

Strategy

Apply prior knowledge and basic operations to solve problems.

EXAMPLE

Mr. Hale has a 25-foot ladder. How far from the wall does the foot of the ladder need to be to reach 24 feet up?

First, use the Pythagorean Theorem to represent the situation.

$252 = 242 + b^2$

Evaluate the powers.

$625 = 576 + b^2$

Solve the equation.

$625 - 576 = b^2$

$49 = b^2$

$7 = b$

The ladder needs to be 7 feet from the wall.

3. **Barb walks 4 blocks north and 3 blocks west to get to her best friend's house. What is the distance between Barb's house and her friend's house? Show your work.**

____

Strategy Review

Strategy Read word problems carefully to identify the given information and what you are being asked to find.

EXAMPLE

During the school's first social, the Honor Society sold raffle tickets and game tickets. Helena bought 10 raffle tickets and 15 game tickets for a total cost of $65. Megan bought 10 game tickets for a cost of $30. How much did each type of ticket cost?

First, think about what you are trying to find and how you can do that.

I need to find the price of two different types of tickets. I can use a system of equations to solve this problem.

Next, write a system of equations to represent the problem.

$10r + 15g = 65$

$10g = 30$

Solve for *g*.

$g = \$3$

Substitute $3 for *g*.

$10r + 45 = 65$

Solve for *r*.

$r = 2$

Raffle tickets cost $2.00 each and game tickets cost $3.00 each.

Strategy

Use drawings, graphs, or number lines to understand and solve a problem.

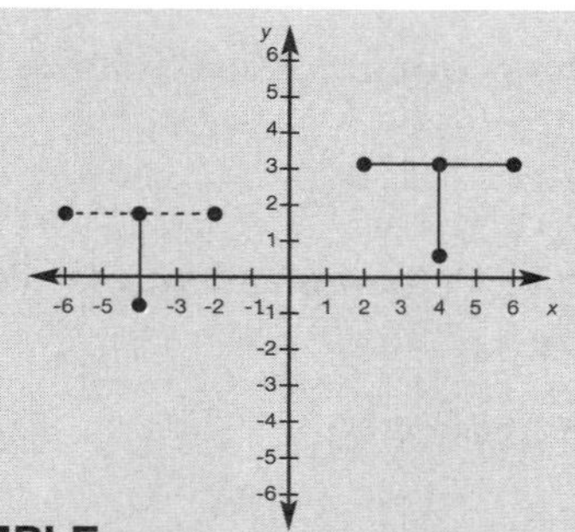

EXAMPLE

Describe the transformation that has taken place.

First, determine if the transformation was a translation, a reflection, or a rotation.

The transformation looks like it was a translation.

Next, find the relationship between the first and second images.

To get the second image, it looks like the first image was moved down 2 units and to the left 8.

The image was translated down 2, left 8.

1. Andy and Alex went out to lunch. Andy had 3 slices of pizza for a total bill of $9.75. Alex had 2 slices of pizza and a large drink for a total of $9.00. How much did Alex's drink cost? Show your work.

______

2. What transformation was performed?

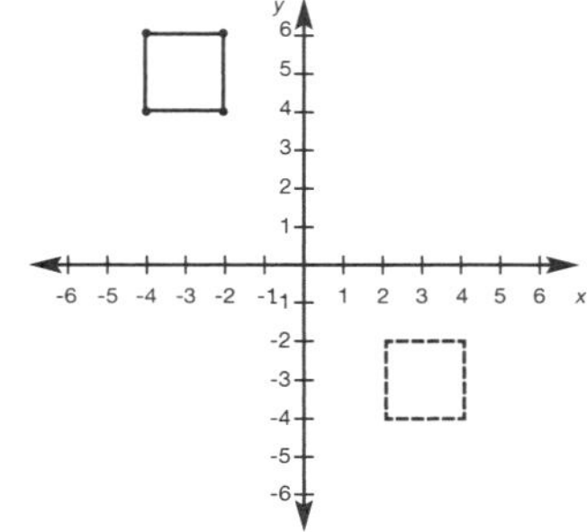

______

Name ______________________ Date ______________

Math

Strategy Review

Strategy

Use rules, properties, or formulas to solve problems.

EXAMPLE

Sophie bought an aquarium in the shape of a cylinder. It has a diameter of 18 inches and a height of 24 inches. How many cubic inches of water will the aquarium hold?

First, write the formula for the volume of a cylinder.

$V = \pi r^2 \cdot h$

Next, substitute in the values you know.

$V = 3.14 \cdot 81 \cdot 24$

Solve the equation.

6,104.16

The aquarium will hold 6,104.16 cubic inches of water.

1. What is the volume of a cone with a radius of 10 cm and a height of 20 cm?

Ⓐ 209.3 cm^3

Ⓑ 6,280 cm^3

Ⓒ 200 cm^3

Ⓓ 2,093.3 cm^3

2. A baseball has a diameter of about 3 inches. What is the volume of a baseball? Show your work.

____

Strategy

Organize and display data in order to interpret it.

EXAMPLE

A local restaurant took a survey of its customers to see what they were ordering. The data is in the table below.

Chicken Nuggets	X			X	X				X	X			X		
Hamburger	X	X	X			X	X	X			X	X		X	X

First, make a frequency table of the data to observe any correlations.

Chicken Nuggets	6
Hamburger	10

Next, Consider the context of the data.

There were 15 people surveyed.

6 people ordered chicken nuggets.

10 people ordered hamburgers.

One person ordered both.

Draw a conclusion about the correlation between the two variables.

No correlation

There is no correlation between ordering a hamburger and ordering chicken nuggets.

3. Ms. Cortez found that, of her 62 students, 35 of them used the online videos she made available to them. Of those 35 students, 26 of them had a grade of B or higher. Of the students who did not use the online videos, only 8 had a grade of B or higher. Put this data into a frequency table and analyze it.

Students who use online videos	
Students with a grade of B or higher	

____

____

____

ame ______________________ Date ______________

Strategy Review

Strategy Look for key words in word problems that help you know which operation to use.

EXAMPLE

A cellular company offers a family plan for a \$150 start-up fee and \$50 per month for four lines. What will the bill be for the first 3-month cycle?

First, think about the context and look for key words to decide what operations to perform.

\$150 start-up fee: tells me that I have to add this one time

\$50 per month: tells me that I have to add \$50 multiple times

3-month cycle: tells me that I have to find the monthly bill 3 times

Write an equation.

$b = 150 + 3 \bullet 50$

Use order of operations when solving the equation.

$(3 \bullet 50) = 150$

$b = 150 + 150$

$b = \$300$

The bill for the first 3-month cycle will be \$300.

1. **Brenda is not sure how far she travels to work each day, but wants to find out. She knows she drives at a constant speed of 35 miles per hour, and it takes her 45 minutes to get to work. Write and solve an equation to find out the distance to Brenda's work.**

2. **George bought 6 pounds of ground beef for \$21.54 and 6 pounds of ground turkey. His total bill was \$47.28. How much did the ground turkey cost per pound?**

   (A) \$4.29

   (B) \$25.74

   (C) \$23.64

   (D) \$11.82

3. **In the game Kerboperfluven, you can earn points by scoring plavins and storins. Sadie scored 11 plavins and 5 storins for a total score of 57 points. Samantha scored 14 plavins and 8 storins for a total score of 84 points. How many points is each plavin and storin worth?**

   (A) plavin: 1; storin: 11

   (B) plavin: 2; storin: 7

   (C) plavin: 3; storin: 9

   (D) plavin: 5; storin: 15

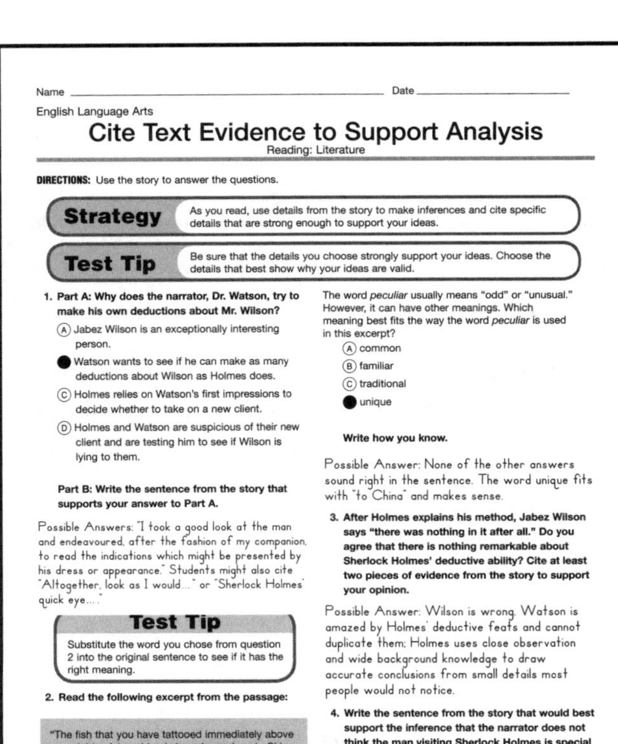

Name ______________________ Date ____________

English Language Arts

Cite Text Evidence to Support Analysis

Reading: Literature

DIRECTIONS: Use the story to answer the questions.

Strategy As you read, use details from the story to make inferences and cite specific details that are strong enough to support your ideas.

Test Tip Be sure that the details you choose strongly support your ideas. Choose the details that best show why your ideas are valid.

1. Part A: Why does the narrator, Dr. Watson, try to make his own deductions about Mr. Wilson?

Ⓐ Jabez Wilson is an exceptionally interesting person.
● Watson wants to see if he can make as many deductions about Wilson as Holmes does.
Ⓒ Holmes relies on Watson's first impressions to decide whether to take on a new client.
Ⓓ Holmes and Watson are suspicious of their new client and are testing him to see if Wilson is lying to them.

Part B: Write the sentence from the story that supports your answer to Part A.

Possible Answers: "I took a good look at the man and endeavoured, after the fashion of my companion, to read the indications which might be presented by his dress or appearance." Students might also cite "Altogether, look as I would…" or "Sherlock Holmes' quick eye…."

Test Tip Substitute the word you chose from question 2 into the original sentence to see if it has the right meaning.

2. Read the following excerpt from the passage:

"The fish that you have tattooed immediately above your right wrist could only have been done in China. . . . That trick of staining the fishes' scales a delicate pink is quite peculiar to China."

The word *peculiar* usually means "odd" or "unusual." However, it can have other meanings. Which meaning best fits the way the word *peculiar* is used in this excerpt?

Ⓐ common
Ⓑ familiar
Ⓒ traditional
● unique

Write how you know.

Possible Answer: None of the other answers sound right in the sentence. The word unique fits with "to China" and makes sense.

3. After Holmes explains his method, Jabez Wilson says "there was nothing in it after all." Do you agree that there is nothing remarkable about Sherlock Holmes' deductive ability? Cite at least two pieces of evidence from the story to support your opinion.

Possible Answer: Wilson is wrong. Watson is amazed by Holmes' deductive feats and cannot duplicate them; Holmes uses close observation and wide background knowledge to draw accurate conclusions from small details most people would not notice.

4. Write the sentence from the story that would best support the inference that the narrator does not think the man visiting Sherlock Holmes is special or interesting.

"Altogether, look as I would, there was nothing remarkable about the man save his blazing red head, and the expression of extreme chagrin and discontent upon his features."

English Language Arts 8 Spectrum Test Prep Grade 8

8

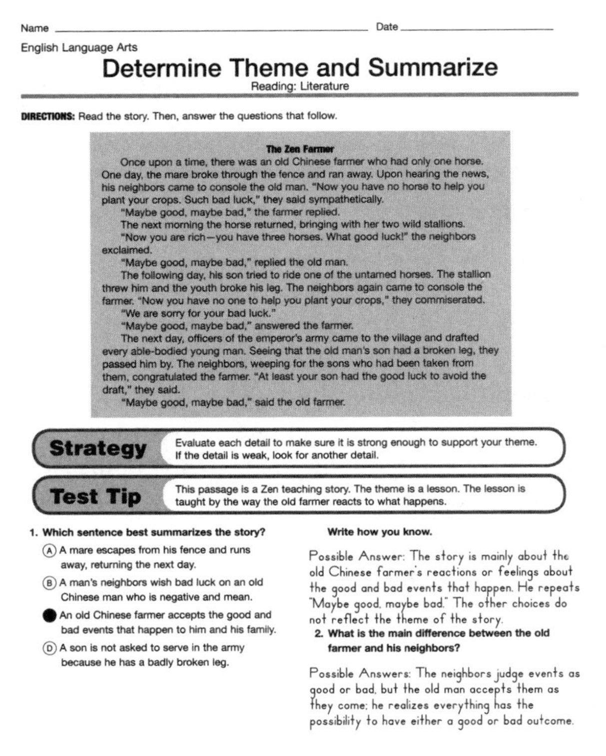

Name ______________________ Date ____________

English Language Arts

Determine Theme and Summarize

Reading: Literature

DIRECTIONS: Read the story. Then, answer the questions that follow.

The Zen Farmer

Once upon a time, there was an old Chinese farmer who had only one horse. One day, the mare broke through the fence and ran away. Upon hearing the news, his neighbors came to console the old man. "Now you have no horse to help you plant your crops. Such bad luck," they said sympathetically.

"Maybe good, maybe bad," the farmer replied.

The next morning the horse returned, bringing with her two wild stallions.

"Now you are rich—you have three horses. What good luck!" the neighbors exclaimed.

"Maybe good, maybe bad," replied the old man.

The following day, his son tried to ride one of the untamed horses. The stallion threw him and the youth broke his leg. The neighbors again came to console the farmer. "Now you have no one to help you plant your crops," they commiserated. "We are sorry for your bad luck."

"Maybe good, maybe bad," answered the farmer.

The next day, officers of the emperor's army came to the village and drafted every able-bodied young man. Seeing that the old man's son had a broken leg, they passed him by. The neighbors, weeping for the sons who had been taken from them, congratulated the farmer. "At least your son had the good luck to avoid the draft," they said.

"Maybe good, maybe bad," said the old farmer.

Strategy Evaluate each detail to make sure it is strong enough to support your theme. If the detail is weak, look for another detail.

Test Tip This passage is a Zen teaching story. The theme is a lesson. The lesson is taught by the way the old farmer reacts to what happens.

1. Which sentence best summarizes the story?

Ⓐ A mare escapes from his fence and runs away, returning the next day.
Ⓑ A man's neighbors wish bad luck on an old Chinese man who is negative and mean.
● An old Chinese farmer accepts the good and bad events that happen to him and his family.
Ⓓ A son is not asked to serve in the army because he has a badly broken leg.

Write how you know.

Possible Answer: The story is mainly about the old Chinese farmer's reactions or feelings about the good and bad events that happen. He repeats "Maybe good, maybe bad." The other choices do not reflect the theme of the story.

2. What is the main difference between the old farmer and his neighbors?

Possible Answers: The neighbors judge events as good or bad, but the old man accepts them as they come; he realizes everything has the possibility to have either a good or bad outcome.

Spectrum Test Prep Grade 8 English Language Arts 9

9

Name ______________________ Date ____________

English Language Arts

Determine Theme and Summarize

Reading: Literature

DIRECTIONS: Read the story. Then, answer the questions using details from the story.

Strategy When you determine a theme, find at least two details in the story that supports it. If you can't find any details, look for a new theme.

Test Tip Remember that the theme is the overall message or lesson in a story. It is not the topic, or what the story is about. It is also not the plot, or what happens in the story.

3. If the story continued, what would you expect to happen next?

● an event that seems to be bad luck
Ⓑ an event that seems to be good luck
Ⓒ another visit from the army officers
Ⓓ a shift from the farmer's point of view to his son's

Write how you know.

Possible Answer: The theme is developed through a repetitive pattern. First something happens that seems like good luck; the farmer knows it can have negative consequences. Then, something happens that seems like bad luck; the farmer knows it can have a good outcome. The good luck-bad luck pattern repeats. Since the last event seems like good luck, the next event will seem like bad luck.

4. What detail tells you the story is set in China?

Ⓐ Wild horses live near the village.
Ⓑ Farmers do not use tractors to plant crops.
● Young men are drafted into the emperor's army.
Ⓓ Someone with three horses is considered wealthy.

5. State the main lesson, or theme, of the story in your own words.

Possible Answers: Accept whatever comes; luck is random; events are not good or bad in themselves—the way we think about them makes them seem good or bad.

Write two details from the story that supports the theme you wrote above.

Students should choose sentences that support their theme. Possible Answers: The farmer repeats "Maybe good, maybe bad," to show that luck is random. The farmer gets three horses, and then his son breaks his leg, showing that fortunes can change.

English Language Arts 10 Spectrum Test Prep Grade 8

10

Name ______________________ Date ____________

English Language Arts

Interpret Figurative and Connotative Language

Reading: Literature

DIRECTIONS: Read the poem. Then, answer the questions that follow.

O Captain! My Captain! *by Walt Whitman*

O Captain! my Captain! our fearful trip is done,
The ship has weather'd every rack, the prize we sought is won,
The port is near, the bells I hear, the people all exulting,
While follow eyes the steady keel, the vessel grim and daring;
But O heart! heart! heart!
O the bleeding drops of red,
Where on the deck my Captain lies,
Fallen cold and dead.

O Captain! my Captain! rise up and hear the bells;
Rise up—for you the flag is flung—for you the bugle trills,
For you bouquets and ribbon'd wreaths—for you the shores a-crowding,
For you they call, the swaying mass, their eager faces turning;
Here Captain! dear father!
The arm beneath your head!
It is some dream that on the deck,
You've fallen cold and dead.

My Captain does not answer, his lips are pale and still,
My father does not feel my arm, he has no pulse nor will,
The ship is anchor'd safe and sound, its voyage closed and done,
From fearful trip the victor ship comes in with object won;
Exult O shores, and ring O bells!
But I with mournful tread,
Walk the deck my Captain lies,
Fallen cold and dead.

Strategy To gain a deeper understanding of poetry, reread a poem and identify the nonliteral meanings of figurative language. Then, determine the connotative meaning of words and phrases.

Test Tip Historical events may be part of a poem or story's theme. This poem was written to mark the death of Abraham Lincoln, shortly after the Civil War ended. As you read, connect words in the poem to what you know about Lincoln.

1. The author uses the word *exulting* to describe the people waiting for the ship to arrive. Use the context to choose the phrase that best explains the connotative meaning of *exulting*.

Ⓐ negative: amazed surprise
Ⓑ positive: nervous excitement
Ⓒ negative: deep sorrow and grief
● positive: great happiness and joy

Would the word *cheering* have the same meaning? Write how you know.

Possible Answer: No. Cheering is something people do when they are happy about an event. It won't work here because the ship is returning from a "fearful" trip. The people are not just happy, they are relieved.

Spectrum Test Prep Grade 8 English Language Arts 11

11

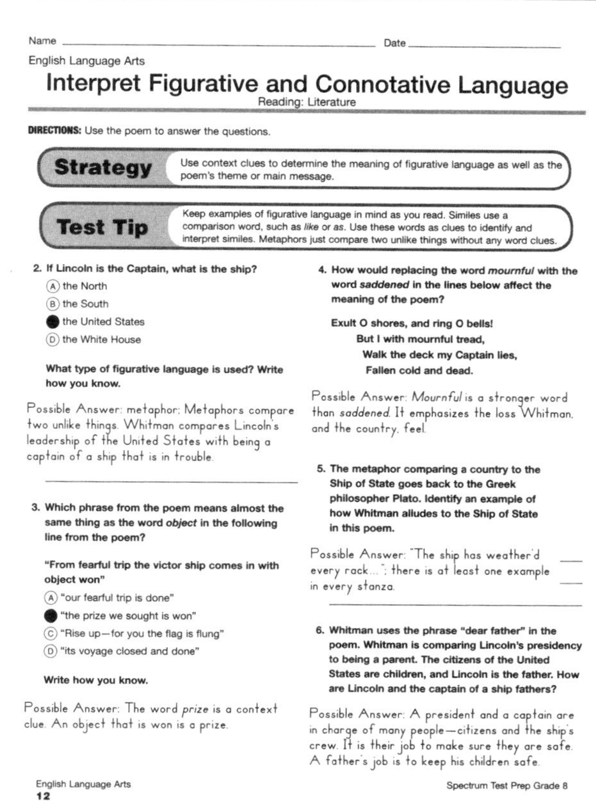
Name ______________________ Date ______________

English Language Arts

Interpret Figurative and Connotative Language

Reading: Literature

DIRECTIONS: Use the poem to answer the questions.

Strategy Use context clues to determine the meaning of figurative language as well as the poem's theme or main message.

Test Tip Keep examples of figurative language in mind as you read. Similes use a comparison word, such as *like* or *as*. Use these words as clues to identify and interpret similes. Metaphors just compare two unlike things without any word clues.

2. If Lincoln is the Captain, what is the ship?

Ⓐ the North
Ⓑ the South
● the United States
Ⓓ the White House

What type of figurative language is used? Write how you know.

Possible Answer: metaphor; Metaphors compare two unlike things. Whitman compares Lincoln's leadership of the United States with being a captain of a ship that is in trouble.

3. Which phrase from the poem means almost the same thing as the word *object* in the following line from the poem?

"From fearful trip the victor ship comes in with object won"

Ⓐ "our fearful trip is done"
● "the prize we sought is won"
Ⓒ "Rise up—for you the flag is flung"
Ⓓ "its voyage closed and done"

Write how you know.

Possible Answer: The word *prize* is a context clue. An object that is won is a prize.

4. How would replacing the word *mournful* with the word *saddened* in the lines below affect the meaning of the poem?

Exult O shores, and ring O bells!
But I with mournful tread,
Walk the deck my Captain lies,
Fallen cold and dead.

Possible Answer: *Mournful* is a stronger word than *saddened*. It emphasizes the loss Whitman, and the country, feel.

5. The metaphor comparing a country to the Ship of State goes back to the Greek philosopher Plato. Identify an example of how Whitman alludes to the Ship of State in this poem.

Possible Answer: "The ship has weather'd every rack..."; there is at least one example in every stanza.

6. Whitman uses the phrase "dear father" in the poem. Whitman is comparing Lincoln's presidency to being a parent. The citizens of the United States are children, and Lincoln is the father. How are Lincoln and the captain of a ship fathers?

Possible Answer: A president and a captain are in charge of many people—citizens and the ship's crew. It is their job to make sure they are safe. A father's job is to keep his children safe.

English Language Arts 12   Spectrum Test Prep Grade 8

12

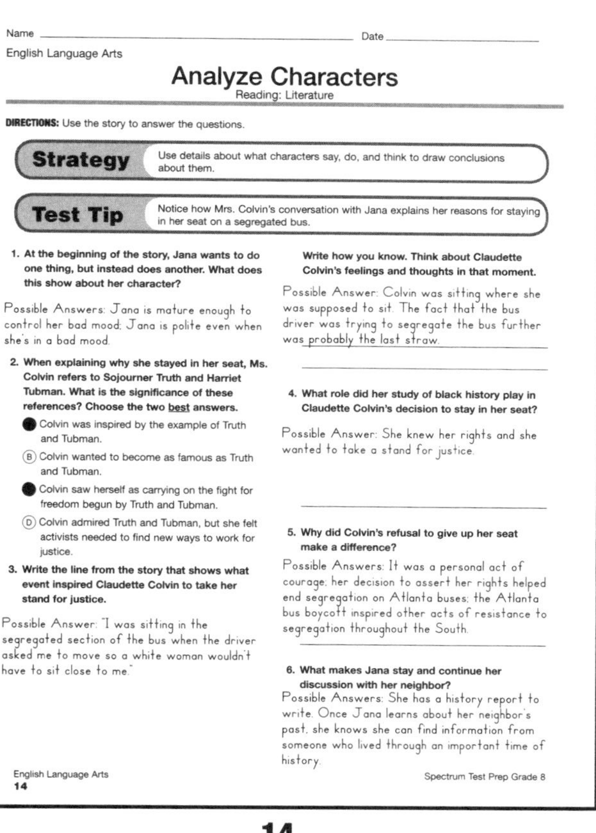
Name ______________________ Date ______________

English Language Arts

Analyze Characters

Reading: Literature

DIRECTIONS: Use the story to answer the questions.

Strategy Use details about what characters say, do, and think to draw conclusions about them.

Test Tip Notice how Mrs. Colvin's conversation with Jana explains her reasons for staying in her seat on a segregated bus.

1. At the beginning of the story, Jana wants to do one thing, but instead does another. What does this show about her character?

Possible Answers: Jana is mature enough to control her bad mood; Jana is polite even when she's in a bad mood.

2. When explaining why she stayed in her seat, Ms. Colvin refers to Sojourner Truth and Harriet Tubman. What is the significance of these references? Choose the two best answers.

● Colvin was inspired by the example of Truth and Tubman.
Ⓑ Colvin wanted to become as famous as Truth and Tubman.
● Colvin saw herself as carrying on the fight for freedom begun by Truth and Tubman.
Ⓓ Colvin admired Truth and Tubman, but she felt activists needed to find new ways to work for justice.

3. Write the line from the story that shows what event inspired Claudette Colvin to take her stand for justice.

Possible Answer: "I was sitting in the segregated section of the bus when the driver asked me to move so a white woman wouldn't have to sit close to me."

Write how you know. Think about Claudette Colvin's feelings and thoughts in that moment.

Possible Answer: Colvin was sitting where she was supposed to sit. The fact that the bus driver was trying to segregate the bus further was probably the last straw.

4. What role did her study of black history play in Claudette Colvin's decision to stay in her seat?

Possible Answer: She knew her rights and she wanted to take a stand for justice.

5. Why did Colvin's refusal to give up her seat make a difference?

Possible Answers: It was a personal act of courage; her decision to assert her rights helped end segregation on Atlanta buses; the Atlanta bus boycott inspired other acts of resistance to segregation throughout the South.

6. What makes Jana stay and continue her discussion with her neighbor?

Possible Answers: She has a history report to write. Once Jana learns about her neighbor's past, she knows she can find information from someone who lived through an important time of history.

English Language Arts 14   Spectrum Test Prep Grade 8

14

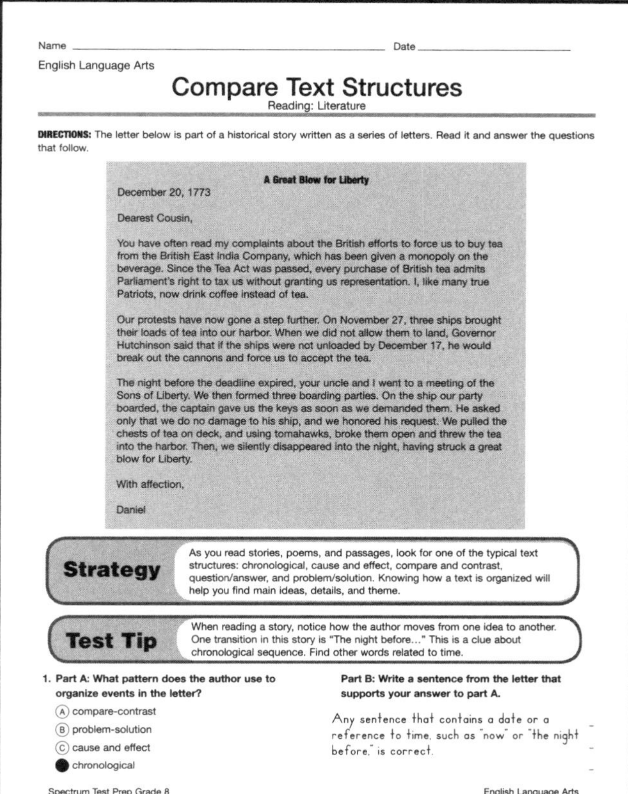
Name ______________________ Date ______________

English Language Arts

Compare Text Structures

Reading: Literature

DIRECTIONS: The letter below is part of a historical story written as a series of letters. Read it and answer the questions that follow.

A Great Blow for Liberty

December 20, 1773

Dearest Cousin,

You have often read my complaints about the British efforts to force us to buy tea from the British East India Company, which has been given a monopoly on the beverage. Since the Tea Act was passed, every purchase of British tea admits Parliament's right to tax us without granting us representation. I, like many true Patriots, now drink coffee instead of tea.

Our protests have now gone a step further. On November 27, three ships brought their loads of tea into our harbor. When we did not allow them to land, Governor Hutchinson said that if the ships were not unloaded by December 17, he would break out the cannons and force us to accept the tea.

The night before the deadline expired, your uncle and I went to a meeting of the Sons of Liberty. We then formed three boarding parties. On the ship our party boarded, the captain gave us the keys as soon as we demanded them. He asked only that we do no damage to his ship, and we honored his request. We pulled the chests of tea on deck, and using tomahawks, broke them open and threw the tea into the harbor. Then, we silently disappeared into the night, having struck a great blow for Liberty.

With affection,

Daniel

Strategy As you read stories, poems, and passages, look for one of the typical text structures: chronological, cause and effect, compare and contrast, question/answer, and problem/solution. Knowing how a text is organized will help you find main ideas, details, and theme.

Test Tip When reading a story, notice how the author moves from one idea to another. One transition in this story is "The night before..." This is a clue about chronological sequence. Find other words related to time.

1. Part A: What pattern does the author use to organize events in the letter?

Ⓐ compare-contrast
Ⓑ problem-solution
Ⓒ cause and effect
● chronological

Part B: Write a sentence from the letter that supports your answer to part A.

Any sentence that contains a date or a reference to time, such as "now" or "the night before," is correct.

Spectrum Test Prep Grade 8   English Language Arts 15

15

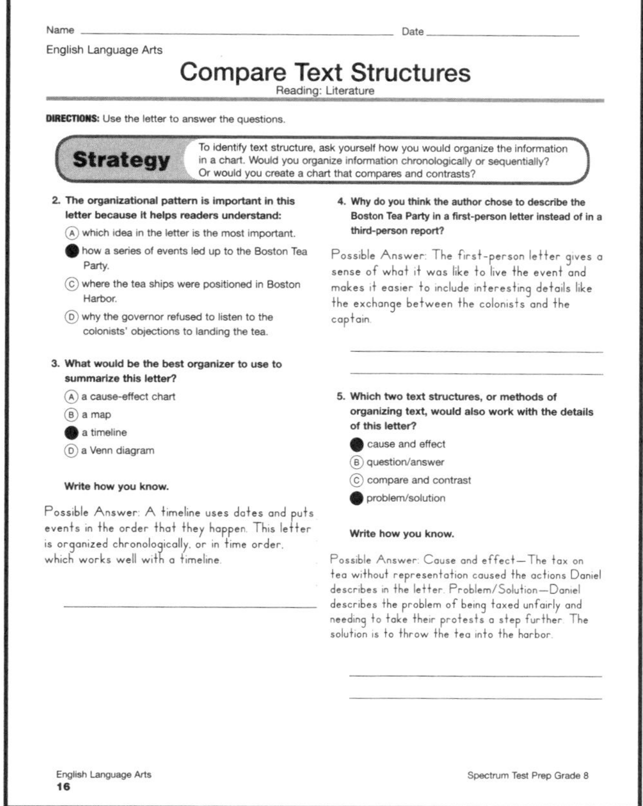
Name ______________________ Date ______________

English Language Arts

Compare Text Structures

Reading: Literature

DIRECTIONS: Use the letter to answer the questions.

Strategy To identify text structure, ask yourself how you would organize the information in a chart. Would you organize information chronologically or sequentially? Or would you create a chart that compares and contrasts?

2. The organizational pattern is important in this letter because it helps readers understand:

Ⓐ which idea in the letter is the most important.
● how a series of events led up to the Boston Tea Party.
Ⓒ where the tea ships were positioned in Boston Harbor.
Ⓓ why the governor refused to listen to the colonists' objections to landing the tea.

3. What would be the best organizer to use to summarize this letter?

Ⓐ a cause-effect chart
Ⓑ a map
● a timeline
Ⓓ a Venn diagram

Write how you know.

Possible Answer: A timeline uses dates and puts events in the order that they happen. This letter is organized chronologically, or in time order, which works well with a timeline.

4. Why do you think the author chose to describe the Boston Tea Party in a first-person letter instead of in a third-person report?

Possible Answer: The first-person letter gives a sense of what it was like to live the event and makes it easier to include interesting details like the exchange between the colonists and the captain.

5. Which two text structures, or methods of organizing text, would also work with the details of this letter?

● cause and effect
Ⓑ question/answer
Ⓒ compare and contrast
● problem/solution

Write how you know.

Possible Answer: Cause and effect—The tax on tea without representation caused the actions Daniel describes in the letter. Problem/Solution—Daniel describes the problem of being taxed unfairly and needing to take their protests a step further. The solution is to throw the tea into the harbor.

English Language Arts 16   Spectrum Test Prep Grade 8

16

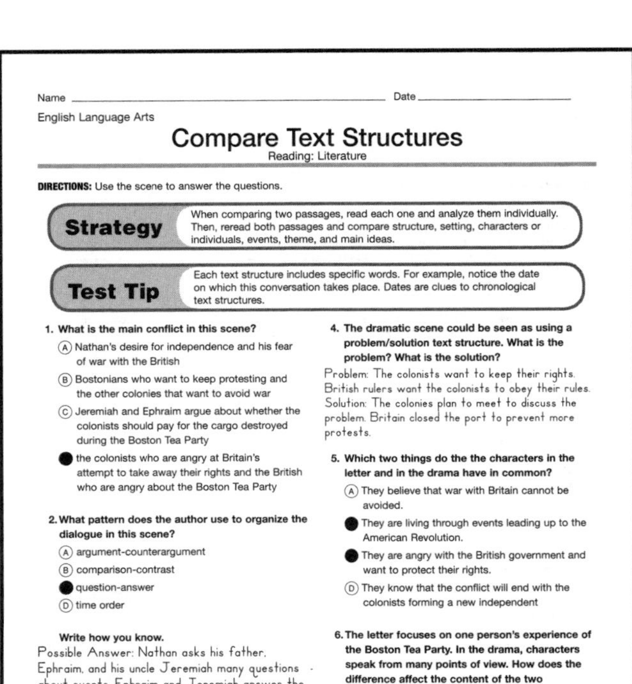

Name ______________________ Date ____________

English Language Arts

Compare Text Structures

Reading: Literature

DIRECTIONS: Use the scene to answer the questions.

Strategy When comparing two passages, read each one and analyze them individually. Then, reread both passages and compare structure, setting, characters or individuals, events, theme, and main ideas.

Test Tip Each text structure includes specific words. For example, notice the date on which this conversation takes place. Dates are clues to chronological text structures.

1. What is the main conflict in this scene?

Ⓐ Nathan's desire for independence and his fear of war with the British
Ⓑ Bostonians who want to keep protesting and the other colonies that want to avoid war
Ⓒ Jeremiah and Ephraim argue about whether the colonists should pay for the cargo destroyed during the Boston Tea Party
● the colonists who are angry at Britain's attempt to take away their rights and the British who are angry about the Boston Tea Party

2. What pattern does the author use to organize the dialogue in this scene?

Ⓐ argument-counterargument
Ⓑ comparison-contrast
● question-answer
Ⓓ time order

Write how you know.

Possible Answer: Nathan asks his father, Ephraim, and his uncle Jeremiah many questions about events. Ephraim and Jeremiah answer the questions.

3. Why do you think the author chose to describe the British reaction to the Boston Tea Party in a dramatic scene rather than in an objective report?

Possible Answers: to show how ordinary people felt and thought about the Intolerable Acts; to make history come to life

4. The dramatic scene could be seen as using a problem/solution text structure. What is the problem? What is the solution?

Problem: The colonists want to keep their rights. British rulers want the colonists to obey their rules. Solution: The colonies plan to meet to discuss the problem. Britain closed the port to prevent more protests.

5. Which two things do the the characters in the letter and in the drama have in common?

Ⓐ They believe that war with Britain cannot be avoided.
● They are living through events leading up to the American Revolution.
● They are angry with the British government and want to protect their rights.
Ⓓ They know that the conflict will end with the colonists forming a new independent

6. The letter focuses on one person's experience of the Boston Tea Party. In the drama, characters speak from many points of view. How does the difference affect the content of the two passages?

Possible Answer: The letter focuses on one person's experience in depth and gives only one person's opinion about why the Tea Party was a justified protest; the drama includes many points of view and so can give a sense of different opinions among the colonists and also why tensions kept escalating between the colonists and the British.

English Language Arts
18

18

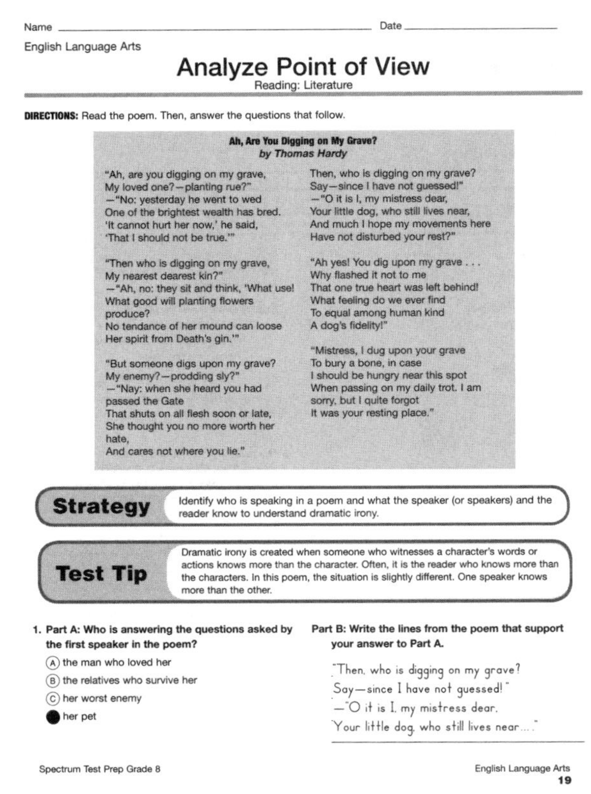

Name ______________________ Date ____________

English Language Arts

Analyze Point of View

Reading: Literature

DIRECTIONS: Read the poem. Then, answer the questions that follow.

Ah, Are You Digging on My Grave?
by Thomas Hardy

"Ah, are you digging on my grave,
My loved one?—planting rue?"
—"No: yesterday he went to wed
One of the brightest wealth has bred.
'It cannot hurt her now,' he said,
'That I should not be true.'"

"Then who is digging on my grave,
My nearest dearest kin?"
—"Ah, no: they sit and think, 'What use!
What good will planting flowers
produce?
No tendance of her mound can loose
Her spirit from Death's gin.'"

"But someone digs upon my grave?
My enemy?—prodding sly?"
—"Nay: when she heard you had
passed the Gate
That shuts on all flesh soon or late,
She thought you no more worth her
hate,
And cares not where you lie."

Then, who is digging on my grave?
Say—since I have not guessed!"
—"O it is I, my mistress dear,
Your little dog, who still lives near,
And much I hope my movements here
Have not disturbed your rest?"

"Ah yes! You dig upon my grave . . .
Why flashed it not to me
That one true heart was left behind!
What feeling do we ever find
To equal among human kind
A dog's fidelity!"

"Mistress, I dug upon your grave
To bury a bone, in case
I should be hungry near this spot
When passing on my daily trot. I am
sorry, but I quite forgot
It was your resting place."

Strategy Identify who is speaking in a poem and what the speaker (or speakers) and the reader know to understand dramatic irony.

Test Tip Dramatic irony is created when someone who witnesses a character's words or actions knows more than the character. Often, it is the reader who knows more than the characters. In this poem, the situation is slightly different. One speaker knows more than the other.

1. Part A: Who is answering the questions asked by the first speaker in the poem?

Ⓐ the man who loved her
Ⓑ the relatives who survive her
Ⓒ her worst enemy
● her pet

Part B: Write the lines from the poem that support your answer to Part A.

"Then, who is digging on my grave?
Say—since I have not guessed!"
—"O it is I, my mistress dear,
Your little dog, who still lives near . . ."

Spectrum Test Prep Grade 8 English Language Arts
19

19

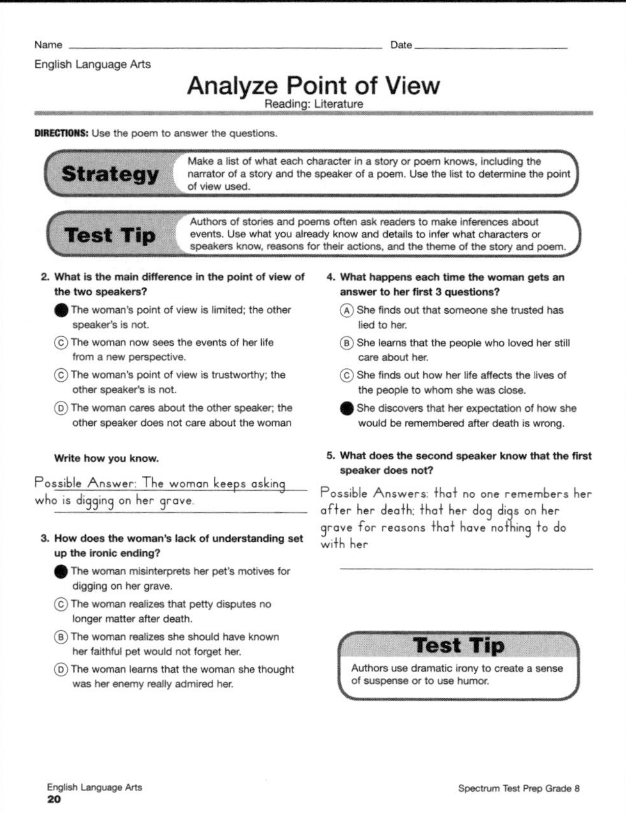

Name ______________________ Date ____________

English Language Arts

Analyze Point of View

Reading: Literature

DIRECTIONS: Use the poem to answer the questions.

Strategy Make a list of what each character in a story or poem knows, including the narrator of a story and the speaker of a poem. Use the list to determine the point of view used.

Test Tip Authors of stories and poems often ask readers to make inferences about events. Use what you already know and details to infer what characters or speakers know, reasons for their actions, and the theme of the story and poem.

2. What is the main difference in the point of view of the two speakers?

● The woman's point of view is limited; the other speaker's is not.
Ⓒ The woman now sees the events of her life from a new perspective.
Ⓒ The woman's point of view is trustworthy; the other speaker's is not.
Ⓓ The woman cares about the other speaker; the other speaker does not care about the woman

Write how you know.

Possible Answer: The woman keeps asking who is digging on her grave.

3. How does the woman's lack of understanding set up the ironic ending?

● The woman misinterprets her pet's motives for digging on her grave.
Ⓒ The woman realizes that petty disputes no longer matter after death.
Ⓑ The woman realizes she should have known her faithful pet would not forget her.
Ⓓ The woman learns that the woman she thought was her enemy really admired her.

4. What happens each time the woman gets an answer to her first 3 questions?

Ⓐ She finds out that someone she trusted has lied to her.
Ⓑ She learns that the people who loved her still care about her.
Ⓒ She finds out how her life affects the lives of the people to whom she was close.
● She discovers that her expectation of how she would be remembered after death is wrong.

5. What does the second speaker know that the first speaker does not?

Possible Answers: that no one remembers her after her death; that her dog digs on her grave for reasons that have nothing to do with her

Test Tip Authors use dramatic irony to create a sense of suspense or to use humor.

English Language Arts
20 Spectrum Test Prep Grade 8

20

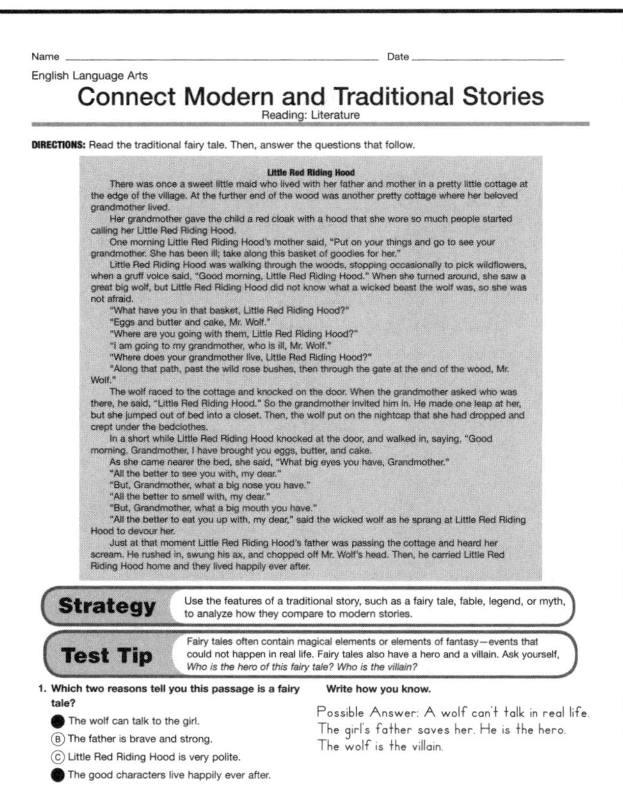

Name ______________________ Date ____________

English Language Arts

Connect Modern and Traditional Stories

Reading: Literature

DIRECTIONS: Read the traditional fairy tale. Then, answer the questions that follow.

Little Red Riding Hood

There was once a sweet little maid who lived with her father and mother in a pretty little cottage at the edge of the village. At the further end of the wood was another pretty cottage where her beloved grandmother lived.

Her grandmother gave the child a red cloak with a hood that she wore so much people started calling her Little Red Riding Hood.

One morning Little Red Riding Hood's mother said, "Put on your things and go to see your grandmother. She has been ill; take along this basket of goodies for her."

Little Red Riding Hood was walking through the woods, stopping occasionally to pick wildflowers, when a gruff voice said, "Good morning, Little Red Riding Hood." When she turned around, she saw a great big wolf, but Little Red Riding Hood did not know what a wicked beast the wolf was, so she was not afraid.

"What have you in that basket, Little Red Riding Hood?"

"Eggs and butter and cake, Mr. Wolf."

"Where are you going with them, Little Red Riding Hood?"

"I am going to my grandmother, who is ill, Mr. Wolf."

"Where does your grandmother live, Little Red Riding Hood?"

"Along that path, past the wild rose bushes, then through the gate at the end of the wood, Mr. Wolf."

The wolf raced to the cottage and knocked on the door. When the grandmother asked who was there, he said, "Little Red Riding Hood." So the grandmother invited him in. He made one leap at her, but she jumped out of bed into a closet. Then, the wolf put on the nightcap that she had dropped and crept under the bedclothes.

In a short while Little Red Riding Hood knocked at the door, and walked in, saying, "Good morning, Grandmother, I have brought you eggs, butter, and cake.

As she came nearer the bed, she said, "What big eyes you have, Grandmother."

"All the better to see you with, my dear."

"But, Grandmother, what a big nose you have."

"All the better to smell with, my dear."

"But, Grandmother, what a big mouth you have."

"All the better to eat you up with, my dear," said the wicked wolf as he sprang at Little Red Riding Hood to devour her.

Just at that moment Little Red Riding Hood's father was passing the cottage and heard her scream. He rushed in, swung his ax, and chopped off Mr. Wolf's head. Then, he carried Little Red Riding Hood home and they lived happily ever after.

Strategy Use the features of a traditional story, such as a fairy tale, fable, legend, or myth, to analyze how they compare to modern stories.

Test Tip Fairy tales often contain magical elements or elements of fantasy—events that could not happen in real life. Fairy tales also have a hero and a villain. Ask yourself, *Who is the hero of this fairy tale? Who is the villain?*

1. Which two reasons tell you this passage is a fairy tale?

● The wolf can talk to the girl.
Ⓑ The father is brave and strong.
Ⓒ Little Red Riding Hood is very polite.
● The good characters live happily ever after.

Write how you know.

Possible Answer: A wolf can't talk in real life. The girl's father saves her. He is the hero. The wolf is the villain.

Spectrum Test Prep Grade 8 English Language Arts
21

21

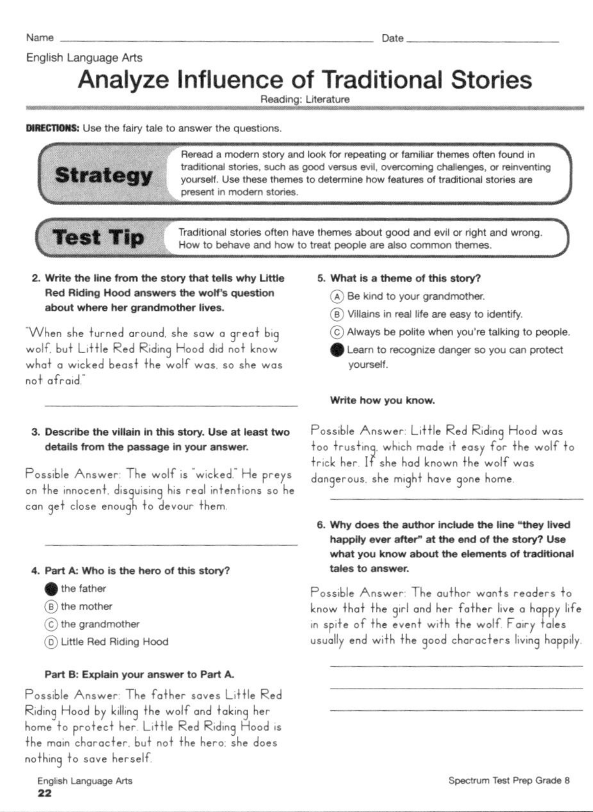

Name ______________________ Date ____________

English Language Arts

Analyze Influence of Traditional Stories

Reading: Literature

DIRECTIONS: Use the fairy tale to answer the questions.

Strategy Reread a modern story and look for repeating or familiar themes often found in traditional stories, such as good versus evil, overcoming challenges, or reinventing yourself. Use these themes to determine how features of traditional stories are present in modern stories.

Test Tip Traditional stories often have themes about good and evil or right and wrong. How to behave and how to treat people are also common themes.

2. Write the line from the story that tells why Little Red Riding Hood answers the wolf's question about where her grandmother lives.

"When she turned around, she saw a great big wolf, but Little Red Riding Hood did not know what a wicked beast the wolf was, so she was not afraid."

3. Describe the villain in this story. Use at least two details from the passage in your answer.

Possible Answer: The wolf is "wicked." He preys on the innocent, disguising his real intentions so he can get close enough to devour them.

4. Part A: Who is the hero of this story?

- ● the father
- Ⓑ the mother
- Ⓒ the grandmother
- Ⓓ Little Red Riding Hood

Part B: Explain your answer to Part A.

Possible Answer: The father saves Little Red Riding Hood by killing the wolf and taking her home to protect her. Little Red Riding Hood is the main character, but not the hero; she does nothing to save herself.

5. What is a theme of this story?

- Ⓐ Be kind to your grandmother.
- Ⓑ Villains in real life are easy to identify.
- Ⓒ Always be polite when you're talking to people.
- ● Learn to recognize danger so you can protect yourself.

Write how you know.

Possible Answer: Little Red Riding Hood was too trusting, which made it easy for the wolf to trick her. If she had known the wolf was dangerous, she might have gone home.

6. Why does the author include the line "they lived happily ever after" at the end of the story? Use what you know about the elements of traditional tales to answer.

Possible Answer: The author wants readers to know that the girl and her father live a happy life in spite of the event with the wolf. Fairy tales usually end with the good characters living happily.

English Language Arts 22 Spectrum Test Prep Grade 8

22

Name ______________________ Date ____________

English Language Arts

Connect Modern and Traditional Stories

Reading: Literature

DIRECTIONS: Use the fairy tale to answer the questions.

Strategy To determine if a story is a traditional story or a modern story that retells a tale, identify the setting. Ask yourself if this story could happen today.

Test Tip A traditional story is one that has been shared for many years, such as a fairy tale, a fable, or a folktale. Consider how the characters, setting, tone, point of view, and plot events in the two stories compare.

1. Contrast the way Little Red Riding Hood and Red react the first time they meet the wolf. What does this show about their characters?

Little Red Riding Hood is too innocent to recognize the wolf is a threat, so she is polite to him and gives him the information he needs to set his trap for her. In contrast, Red knows the wolf is dangerous and takes action to protect her grandmother and herself.

2. Modern fairy tales often have a twist, or an unexpected turn, to the ending. What is the twist in this tale?

Possible Answer: Red and her grandmother turn the tables on the wolf.

3. Write a line from the modern version that reminds you of the original version.

Possible Answers: "What big, sensitive ears you have," I say" or "Why don't you use your big, long legs and run away?"

4. Part A: According to "Little Red Riding Hood," what two qualities were young women expected to have at the time the tale was written?

- Ⓐ courage
- ● innocence
- Ⓒ intelligence
- ● politeness

Part B: How does Red differ from a typical female character in a traditional fairy tale? Use your response to Part A to explain.

Possible Answer: She has many of the choices in Part A that I did not choose; she is courageous, intelligent, and strong. Red is smart enough to recognize danger and she doesn't wait for someone to rescue her. She sees through the wolf's sneaky tactics and works with her grandmother to stand up for herself. She is a heroine, not a victim waiting for rescue.

5. Which statement best expresses the message, or theme, of the modern version of the story?

- Ⓐ People only live happily ever after in fairy tales.
- Ⓑ Young girls cannot learn to recognize signs of danger.
- ● You can be kind and polite without letting others take advantage of you.
- Ⓓ If you are good and sweet, someone will always come along to rescue you from danger.

English Language Arts 24 Spectrum Test Prep Grade 8

24

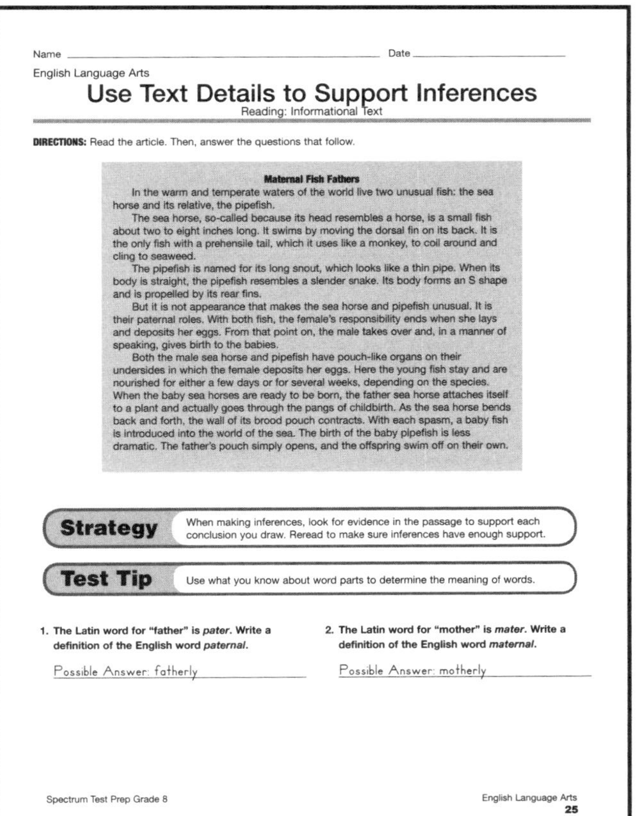

Name ______________________ Date ____________

English Language Arts

Use Text Details to Support Inferences

Reading: Informational Text

DIRECTIONS: Read the article. Then, answer the questions that follow.

Maternal Fish Fathers

In the warm and temperate waters of the world live two unusual fish: the sea horse and its relative, the pipefish.

The sea horse, so-called because its head resembles a horse, is a small fish about two to eight inches long. It swims by moving the dorsal fin on its back. It is the only fish with a prehensile tail, which it uses like a monkey, to coil around and cling to seaweed.

The pipefish is named for its long snout, which looks like a thin pipe. When its body is straight, the pipefish resembles a slender snake. Its body forms an S shape and is propelled by its rear fins.

But it is not appearance that makes the sea horse and pipefish unusual. It is their paternal roles. With both fish, the female's responsibility ends when she lays and deposits her eggs. From that point on, the male takes over and, in a manner of speaking, gives birth to the babies.

Both the male sea horse and pipefish have pouch-like organs on their undersides in which the female deposits her eggs. Here the young fish stay and are nourished for either a few days or for several weeks, depending on the species. When the baby sea horses are ready to be born, the father sea horse attaches itself to a plant and actually goes through the pangs of childbirth. As the sea horse bends back and forth, the wall of its brood pouch contracts. With each spasm, a baby fish is introduced into the world of the sea. The birth of the baby pipefish is less dramatic. The father's pouch simply opens, and the offspring swim off on their own.

Strategy When making inferences, look for evidence in the passage to support each conclusion you draw. Reread to make sure inferences have enough support.

Test Tip Use what you know about word parts to determine the meaning of words.

1. The Latin word for "father" is *pater*. Write a definition of the English word *paternal*.

Possible Answer: fatherly

2. The Latin word for "mother" is *mater*. Write a definition of the English word *maternal*.

Possible Answer: motherly

Spectrum Test Prep Grade 8 English Language Arts 25

25

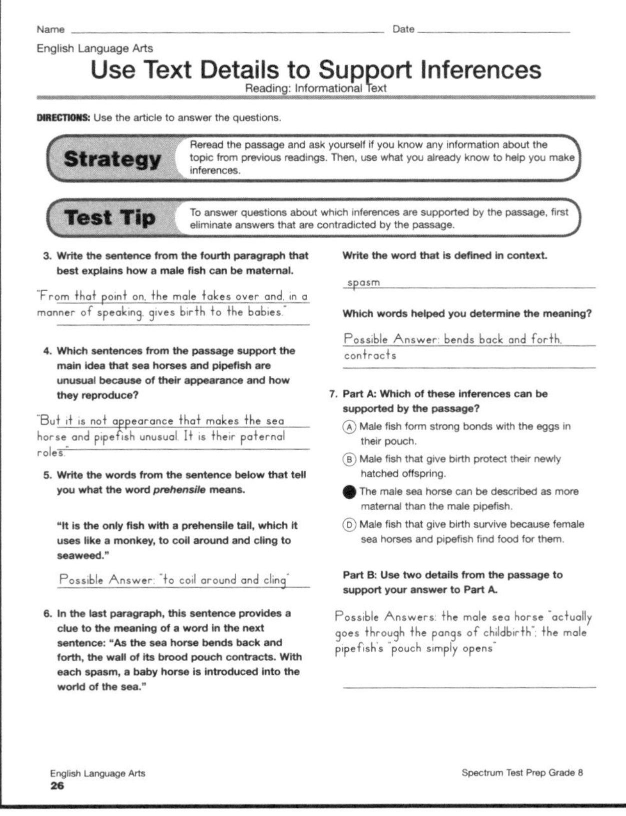

Name ______________________ Date ____________

English Language Arts

Use Text Details to Support Inferences

Reading: Informational Text

DIRECTIONS: Use the article to answer the questions.

Strategy Reread the passage and ask yourself if you know any information about the topic from previous readings. Then, use what you already know to help you make inferences.

Test Tip To answer questions about which inferences are supported by the passage, first eliminate answers that are contradicted by the passage.

3. Write the sentence from the fourth paragraph that best explains how a male fish can be maternal.

"From that point on, the male takes over and, in a manner of speaking, gives birth to the babies."

4. Which sentences from the passage support the main idea that sea horses and pipefish are unusual because of their appearance and how they reproduce?

"But it is not appearance that makes the sea horse and pipefish unusual. It is their paternal roles."

5. Write the words from the sentence below that tell you what the word *prehensile* means.

"It is the only fish with a prehensile tail, which it uses like a monkey, to coil around and cling to seaweed."

Possible Answer: "to coil around and cling"

6. In the last paragraph, this sentence provides a clue to the meaning of a word in the next sentence: "As the sea horse bends back and forth, the wall of its brood pouch contracts. With each spasm, a baby horse is introduced into the world of the sea."

Write the word that is defined in context.

spasm

Which words helped you determine the meaning?

Possible Answer: bends back and forth, contracts

7. Part A: Which of these inferences can be supported by the passage?

- Ⓐ Male fish form strong bonds with the eggs in their pouch.
- Ⓑ Male fish that give birth protect their newly hatched offspring.
- ● The male sea horse can be described as more maternal than the male pipefish.
- Ⓓ Male fish that give birth survive because female sea horses and pipefish find food for them.

Part B: Use two details from the passage to support your answer to Part A.

Possible Answers: the male sea horse "actually goes through the pangs of childbirth"; the male pipefish's "pouch simply opens"

English Language Arts 26 Spectrum Test Prep Grade 8

26

Name ______________________ Date ______________

English Language Arts

Use Main Ideas and Details to Summarize

Reading: Informational Text

DIRECTIONS: Read the passages. Then, answer the questions using details from the passages.

Mathew Brady: The Father of Photojournalism

Mathew B. Brady opened his first photography studio in 1844. The images he produced were daguerreotypes, recorded images on sheets of copper, coated with silver. They required long exposures to produce the image, so a person being photographed would have to stay perfectly still for three to fifteen minutes. That made daguerreotypes impractical for portraits. By 1855, though, Brady was advertising a new type of image that had just been invented: a photograph made on paper.

From the beginning of his career, Brady thought that photography could serve an important purpose. His images could create a record of national life. When the Civil War broke out, he wanted to create a photographic record of the war. Although his costs were prohibitive and his friends discouraged him, he assembled a corps of photographers to take photos of the battlefield and surgeons' tents. He also bought photographs from others returning from the field. Near the end of his life, he reflected, "No one will ever know what [those photographs] cost me; some of them almost cost me my life."

At the time, photographs could not be reproduced in newspapers, so Brady displayed them in his gallery in New York City. His efforts culminated in an 1862 display of photographs made after the Battle of Antietam. The bloodshed shocked the exhibit's visitors, most of whom had never known what warfare was like. A reviewer for *The New York Times* wrote, "These pictures have a terrible distinctness. By the aid of the magnifying glass, the very features of the slain may be distinguished. We would scarce choose to be in the gallery, when one of the women bending over them should recognize a husband, a son, or a brother in the still, lifeless lines of bodies, that lie ready for the gaping trenches."

Brady's goal was to use powerful photos to end all war. Brady did not stop warfare, of course. He did not even earn enough money to pay for his venture. Still, Brady recorded one of the most important episodes in American history, the Civil War. In doing so, he created the first photodocumentation of a war and achieved his lifelong goal: to make photography "a great and truthful medium of history."

Strategy Identify the central idea and key supporting details, and use these to summarize a passage.

Test Tip Read the title and use it to help you identify the central idea. Remember that the central idea is the most important idea of the passage.

1. Part A: What is the central idea of this passage?

● Brady used photography to create a truthful record of history.

Ⓑ Brady did not let his friends discourage him from taking battlefield photographs.

Ⓒ Brady exhibited photographs of Antietam that were more realistic than any New Yorkers had ever seen.

Ⓓ Brady took photos on Civil War battlefields because he believed there was little danger to people who weren't actually fighting.

Part B: Write a sentence from the story that supports your answer to Part A.

". . . [he] achieved his lifelong goal: to make photography 'a great and truthful medium of history.'"

27

Name ______________________ Date ______________

English Language Arts

Use Main Ideas and Details to Summarize

Reading: Informational Text

DIRECTIONS: Use the passage to answer the questions.

Strategy When you summarize, make sure to only include the most important ideas. Any details that you use should relate only to the central idea. Avoid adding your personal opinions.

2. What is the most likely reason the author included the quotation from *The New York Times* reviewer?

Ⓐ to show the amazing technical quality of Brady's photographs

Ⓑ to explain why so many New Yorkers came to Brady's exhibits

● to emphasize the emotional impact of Brady's battlefield photographs

Ⓓ to show that people recognized the importance of Brady's innovative photojournalism

3. Write the sentence in the second paragraph that supports the idea that using photography to capture history was Brady's "lifelong goal."

"From the beginning of his career, Brady thought that photography could serve an important purpose."

4. Part A: Which definition of the word *medium* best fits the way the word is used in the last sentence of the passage?

● a way of communication

Ⓑ the midpoint between extremes

Ⓒ material used in a work of art, such as acrylic

Ⓓ substance in which scientists grow bacteria

Write how you know.

Possible Answer: The word *photodocumentation* contains the word *document*. Documents communicate ideas. None of the other answers sound right in the sentence.

5. Use the central idea and key supporting details to summarize how Brady's photography achieved historical importance.

Possible Answer: Mathew Brady is considered the "Father of Photojournalism" because he realized that photographs could be an important way to study history. His ambition was to create a photographic record of the Civil War. He achieved his goal by taking photos on the battlefield and by paying other photographers for their images. Because he understood that photographs could be "a great and truthful medium of history," Brady inspired others to use their cameras to document important events in photographs.

28

Name ______________________ Date ______________

English Language Arts

Analyze Text Structure

Reading: Informational Text

DIRECTIONS: Read the passage. Then, answer the questions that follow.

"Yankee Doodle": From Insult to Anthem

Singing a song in Revolutionary America could get you in trouble. At the time, almost everyone sang in public on occasion. People might sing hymns in church or entertain themselves by singing popular songs. However, songs were also important instruments of satire. People used them to make fun of public figures, to pass ugly rumors, or to playfully insult their enemies.

As opposition to British rule in the American colonies heated up, satirical songs took on a new edge. Rebellious colonists sang songs insulting Britain's king, George III, as a drunken tyrant. British soldiers answered with songs ridiculing the Americans as ignorant backwoods yokels.

One of these songs told the story of a poorly dressed Yankee simpleton, or doodle. An early version used the insulting term *Yankee* to refer to the colonists:

Yankee Doodle came to town
Riding on a pony,
Stuck a feather in his hat
And called him Macaroni.

The song was so popular with British troops that they played it as they marched to battle on the first day of the Revolutionary War. However, the rebels quickly claimed the song as their own. They created dozens of new verses that mocked the British, praised the new Continental Army, and hailed its commander, George Washington. One anti-British version declared

Yankee Doodle is the tune,
That we all delight in;
It suits for feasts, it suits for fun,
And just as well for fighting!

By 1781, when the British surrendered at Yorktown, the colonists no longer considered being called a Yankee Doodle an insult. The song had become the unofficial national anthem of their new country.

Strategy Analyze the structure of the passage and use it to understand the central idea of a passage.

Test Tip Look for ways that the meaning of "Yankee Doodle" changes.

1. How is the passage structured?

Ⓐ cause-effect

● comparison-contrast

Ⓒ least important to most important

Ⓓ time order

Write how you know.

Possible Answer: Two songs are compared in the passage. The passage uses the words "one of the songs" and "version" which suggests two songs.

29

Name ______________________ Date ______________

English Language Arts

Analyze Text Structure

Reading: Informational Text

DIRECTIONS: Use the passage to answer the questions.

Strategy Determine how information is organized to identify which text structure is used.

Test Tip Use text structure to find information. Problem–solution passages introduce a problem and then describe a solution; compare-and-contrast passages organize information into how things are alike and how they are different.

2. The structure helps you understand the passage because it

Ⓐ establishes the order in which events took place.

Ⓑ signals that the most important information will be at the end of the passage

● alerts readers to pay attention to the difference between the two versions of the song.

Ⓓ explains the reason that the rebels began singing anti-British verses to "Yankee Doodle."

3. What other text structures would work for the passage? Write two other structures and explain how they would work to organize the information.

Possible Answers: Question/Answer—The author could list questions about each version of the song and then supply answers. Cause and Effect—The author could explain the reasons each song was created and the effect each song had.

4. Where in the passage does the author shift from writing about the British version of "Yankee Doodle" to the colonial version of the song?

Ⓐ the last sentence of the first paragraph

Ⓑ the entire third paragraph

● the first two lines of the fourth paragraph

Ⓓ the first sentence of the last paragraph

5. What claim does the author support by including a verse from "Yankee Doodle" in the fourth paragraph?

Possible Answers: "The rebels quickly claimed the song for their own"; the colonists sang anti-British verses of "Yankee Doodle."

6. Below is an incomplete outline of the passage. Fill in the blank.

I. Introduction
  - A. Singing in Colonial America
  - B. Satirical Songs

II. Example of a Satirical Song: "Yankee Doodle"
  - A. ____
  - B. Colonial version

III. Conclusion
  - A. New meaning
  - B. "Unofficial national anthem

British version

30

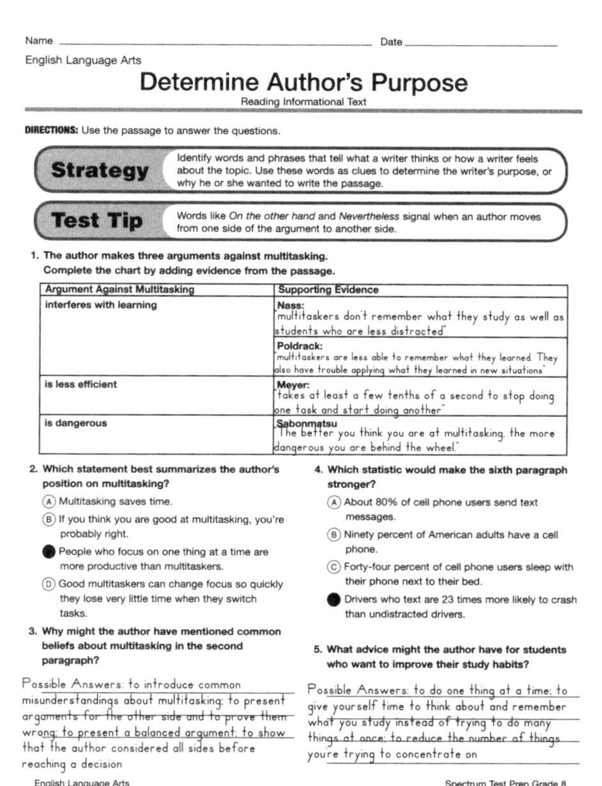

Name ______________________ Date ____________

English Language Arts

Determine Author's Purpose

Reading Informational Text

DIRECTIONS: Use the passage to answer the questions.

Strategy Identify words and phrases that tell what a writer thinks or how a writer feels about the topic. Use these words as clues to determine the writer's purpose, or why he or she wanted to write the passage.

Test Tip Words like *On the other hand* and *Nevertheless* signal when an author moves from one side of the argument to another side.

1. The author makes three arguments against multitasking. Complete the chart by adding evidence from the passage.

Argument Against Multitasking	Supporting Evidence
interferes with learning	**Nass:** multitaskers don't remember what they study as well as students who are less distracted
	Poldrack: multitaskers are less able to remember what they learned. They also have trouble applying what they learned in new situations
is less efficient	**Meyer:** "takes at least a few tenths of a second to stop doing one task and start doing another"
is dangerous	**Sabonmatsu** "The better you think you are at multitasking, the more dangerous you are behind the wheel."

2. Which statement best summarizes the author's position on multitasking?

- Ⓐ Multitasking saves time.
- Ⓑ If you think you are good at multitasking, you're probably right.
- ● People who focus on one thing at a time are more productive than multitaskers.
- Ⓓ Good multitaskers can change focus so quickly they lose very little time when they switch tasks.

3. Why might the author have mentioned common beliefs about multitasking in the second paragraph?

Possible Answers: to introduce common misunderstandings about multitasking; ~~to present arguments for the other side and to prove them wrong~~; to present a balanced argument; to show that the author considered all sides before reaching a decision

4. Which statistic would make the sixth paragraph stronger?

- Ⓐ About 80% of cell phone users send text messages.
- Ⓑ Ninety percent of American adults have a cell phone.
- Ⓒ Forty-four percent of cell phone users sleep with their phone next to their bed.
- ● Drivers who text are 23 times more likely to crash than undistracted drivers.

5. What advice might the author have for students who want to improve their study habits?

Possible Answers: to do one thing at a time; to give yourself time to think about and remember what you study instead of trying to do many things at once; to reduce the number of things you're trying to concentrate on

English Language Arts 32 — Spectrum Test Prep Grade 8

32

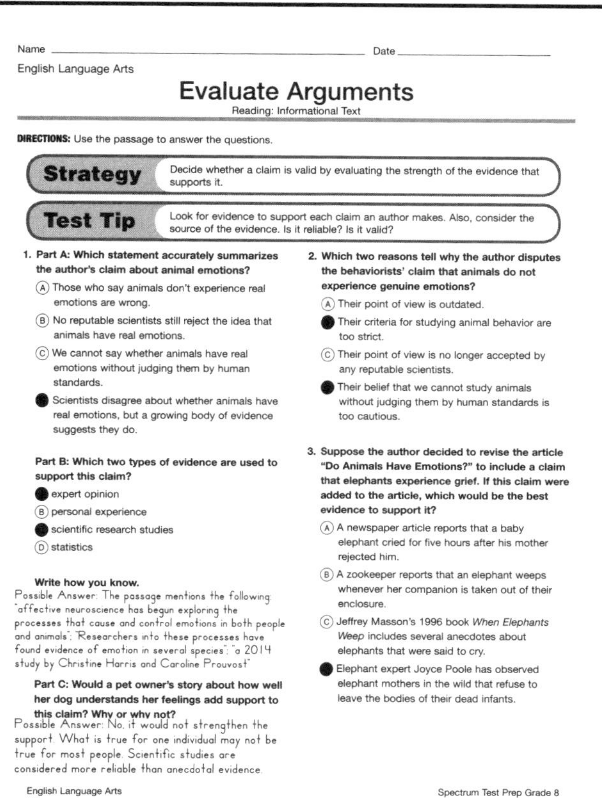

Name ______________________ Date ____________

English Language Arts

Evaluate Arguments

Reading: Informational Text

DIRECTIONS: Use the passage to answer the questions.

Strategy Decide whether a claim is valid by evaluating the strength of the evidence that supports it.

Test Tip Look for evidence to support each claim an author makes. Also, consider the source of the evidence. Is it reliable? Is it valid?

1. Part A: Which statement accurately summarizes the author's claim about animal emotions?

- Ⓐ Those who say animals don't experience real emotions are wrong.
- Ⓑ No reputable scientists still reject the idea that animals have real emotions.
- Ⓒ We cannot say whether animals have real emotions without judging them by human standards.
- ● Scientists disagree about whether animals have real emotions, but a growing body of evidence suggests they do.

Part B: Which two types of evidence are used to support this claim?

- ● expert opinion
- Ⓑ personal experience
- ● scientific research studies
- Ⓓ statistics

Write how you know.

Possible Answer: The passage mentions the following: "affective neuroscience has begun exploring the processes that cause and control emotions in both people and animals"; "Researchers into these processes have found evidence of emotion in several species"; "a 2014 study by Christine Harris and Caroline Prouvost"

Part C: Would a pet owner's story about how well her dog understands her feelings add support to this claim? Why or why not?

Possible Answer: No, it would not strengthen the support. What is true for one individual may not be true for most people. Scientific studies are considered more reliable than anecdotal evidence.

2. Which two reasons tell why the author disputes the behaviorists' claim that animals do not experience genuine emotions?

- Ⓐ Their point of view is outdated.
- ● Their criteria for studying animal behavior are too strict.
- Ⓒ Their point of view is no longer accepted by any reputable scientists.
- ● Their belief that we cannot study animals without judging them by human standards is too cautious.

3. Suppose the author decided to revise the article "Do Animals Have Emotions?" to include a claim that elephants experience grief. If this claim were added to the article, which would be the best evidence to support it?

- Ⓐ A newspaper article reports that a baby elephant cried for five hours after his mother rejected him.
- Ⓑ A zookeeper reports that an elephant weeps whenever her companion is taken out of their enclosure.
- Ⓒ Jeffrey Masson's 1996 book *When Elephants Weep* includes several anecdotes about elephants that were said to cry.
- ● Elephant expert Joyce Poole has observed elephant mothers in the wild that refuse to leave the bodies of their dead infants.

English Language Arts 34 — Spectrum Test Prep Grade 8

34

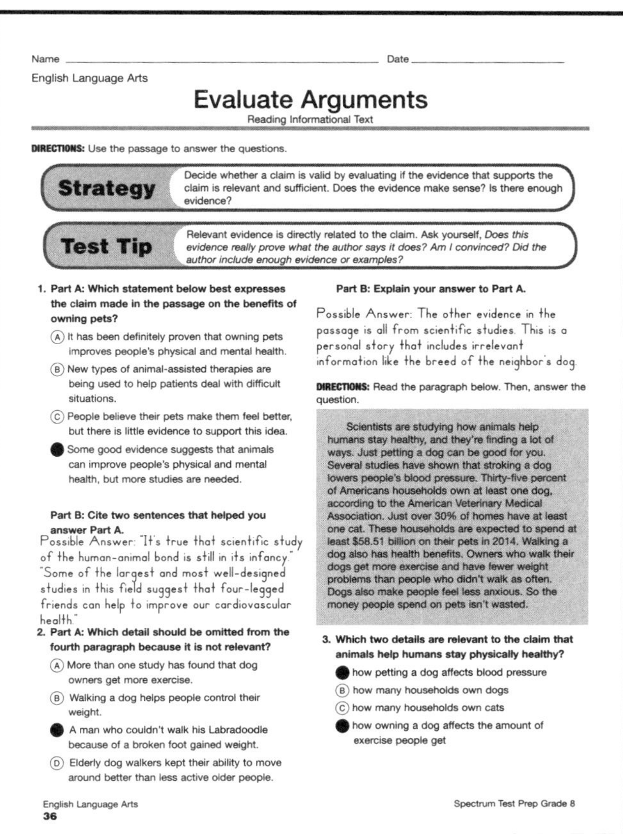

Name ______________________ Date ____________

English Language Arts

Evaluate Arguments

Reading Informational Text

DIRECTIONS: Use the passage to answer the questions.

Strategy Decide whether a claim is valid by evaluating if the evidence that supports the claim is relevant and sufficient. Does the evidence make sense? Is there enough evidence?

Test Tip Relevant evidence is directly related to the claim. Ask yourself, *Does this evidence really prove what the author says it does? Am I convinced? Did the author include enough evidence or examples?*

1. Part A: Which statement below best expresses the claim made in the passage on the benefits of owning pets?

- Ⓐ It has been definitely proven that owning pets improves people's physical and mental health.
- Ⓑ New types of animal-assisted therapies are being used to help patients deal with difficult situations.
- Ⓒ People believe their pets make them feel better, but there is little evidence to support this idea.
- ● Some good evidence suggests that animals can improve people's physical and mental health, but more studies are needed.

Part B: Cite two sentences that helped you answer Part A.

Possible Answer: "It's true that scientific study of the human-animal bond is still in its infancy." "Some of the largest and most well-designed studies in this field suggest that four-legged friends can help to improve our cardiovascular health."

2. Part A: Which detail should be omitted from the fourth paragraph because it is not relevant?

- Ⓐ More than one study has found that dog owners get more exercise.
- Ⓑ Walking a dog helps people control their weight.
- ● A man who couldn't walk his Labradoodle because of a broken foot gained weight.
- Ⓓ Elderly dog walkers kept their ability to move around better than less active older people.

Part B: Explain your answer to Part A.

Possible Answer: The other evidence in the passage is all from scientific studies. This is a personal story that includes irrelevant information like the breed of the neighbor's dog.

DIRECTIONS: Read the paragraph below. Then, answer the question.

> Scientists are studying how animals help humans stay healthy, and they're finding a lot of ways. Just petting a dog can be good for you. Several studies have shown that stroking a dog lowers people's blood pressure. Thirty-five percent of Americans households own at least one dog, according to the American Veterinary Medical Association. Just over 30% of homes have at least one cat. These households are expected to spend at least $58.51 billion on their pets in 2014. Walking a dog also has health benefits. Owners who walk their dogs get more exercise and have fewer weight problems than people who didn't walk as often. Dogs also make people feel less anxious. So the money people spend on pets isn't wasted.

3. Which two details are relevant to the claim that animals help humans stay physically healthy?

- ● how petting a dog affects blood pressure
- Ⓑ how many households own dogs
- Ⓒ how many households own cats
- ● how owning a dog affects the amount of exercise people get

English Language Arts 36 — Spectrum Test Prep Grade 8

36

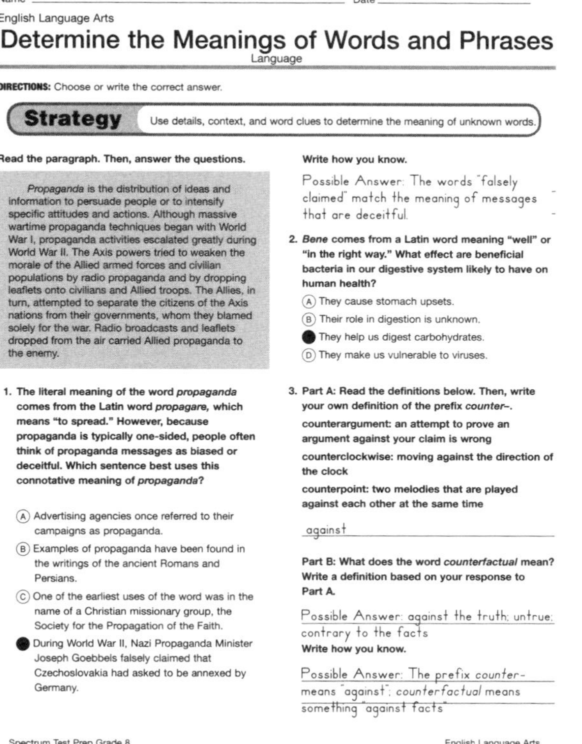

Name ______________________ Date ____________

English Language Arts

Determine the Meanings of Words and Phrases

Language

DIRECTIONS: Choose or write the correct answer.

Strategy Use details, context, and word clues to determine the meaning of unknown words.

Read the paragraph. Then, answer the questions.

> *Propaganda* is the distribution of ideas and information to persuade people or to intensify specific attitudes and actions. Although massive wartime propaganda techniques began with World War I, propaganda activities escalated greatly during World War II. The Axis powers tried to weaken the morale of the Allied armed forces and civilian populations by radio propaganda and by dropping leaflets onto civilians and Allied troops. The Allies, in turn, attempted to separate the citizens of the Axis nations from their governments, whom they blamed solely for the war. Radio broadcasts and leaflets dropped from the air carried Allied propaganda to the enemy.

1. The literal meaning of the word *propaganda* comes from the Latin word *propagare*, which means "to spread." However, because propaganda is typically one-sided, people often think of propaganda messages as biased or deceitful. Which sentence best uses this connotative meaning of *propaganda*?

- Ⓐ Advertising agencies once referred to their campaigns as propaganda.
- Ⓑ Examples of propaganda have been found in the writings of the ancient Romans and Persians.
- Ⓒ One of the earliest uses of the word was in the name of a Christian missionary group, the Society for the Propagation of the Faith.
- ● During World War II, Nazi Propaganda Minister Joseph Goebbels falsely claimed that Czechoslovakia had asked to be annexed by Germany.

Write how you know.

Possible Answer: The words "falsely claimed" match the meaning of messages that are deceitful.

2. *Bene* comes from a Latin word meaning "well" or "in the right way." What effect are beneficial bacteria in our digestive system likely to have on human health?

- Ⓐ They cause stomach upsets.
- Ⓑ Their role in digestion is unknown.
- ● They help us digest carbohydrates.
- Ⓓ They make us vulnerable to viruses.

3. Part A: Read the definitions below. Then, write your own definition of the prefix *counter–*.

counterargument: an attempt to prove an argument against your claim is wrong

counterclockwise: moving against the direction of the clock

counterpoint: two melodies that are played against each other at the same time

against

Part B: What does the word *counterfactual* mean? Write a definition based on your response to Part A.

Possible Answer: against the truth; untrue; contrary to the facts

Write how you know.

Possible Answer: The prefix *counter–* means "against"; *counterfactual* means something "against facts"

Spectrum Test Prep Grade 8 — English Language Arts 37

37

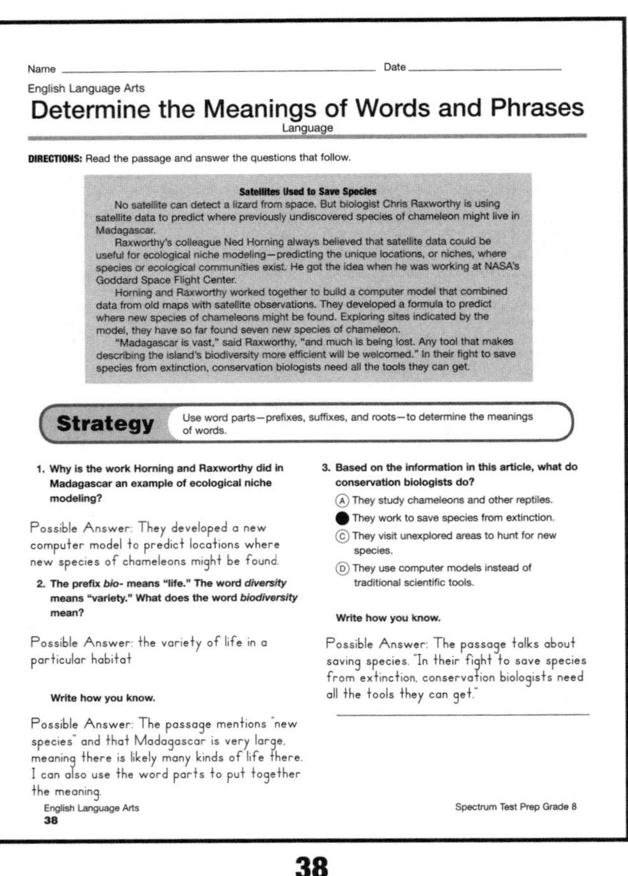

Name ______________________ Date ____________

English Language Arts

Determine the Meanings of Words and Phrases

Language

DIRECTIONS: Read the passage and answer the questions that follow.

Satellites Used to Save Species

No satellite can detect a lizard from space. But biologist Chris Raxworthy is using satellite data to predict where previously undiscovered species of chameleon might live in Madagascar.

Raxworthy's colleague Ned Horning always believed that satellite data could be useful for ecological niche modeling—predicting the unique locations, or niches, where species or ecological communities exist. He got the idea when he was working at NASA's Goddard Space Flight Center.

Horning and Raxworthy worked together to build a computer model that combined data from old maps with satellite observations. They developed a formula to predict where new species of chameleons might be found. Exploring sites indicated by the model, they have so far found seven new species of chameleon.

"Madagascar is vast," said Raxworthy, "and much is being lost. Any tool that makes describing the island's biodiversity more efficient will be welcomed." In their fight to save species from extinction, conservation biologists need all the tools they can get.

Strategy Use word parts—prefixes, suffixes, and roots—to determine the meanings of words.

1. Why is the work Horning and Raxworthy did in Madagascar an example of ecological niche modeling?

Possible Answer: They developed a new computer model to predict locations where new species of chameleons might be found.

2. The prefix *bio-* means "life." The word *diversity* means "variety." What does the word *biodiversity* mean?

Possible Answer: the variety of life in a particular habitat

Write how you know.

Possible Answer: The passage mentions "new species" and that Madagascar is very large, meaning there is likely many kinds of life there. I can also use the word parts to put together the meaning.

3. Based on the information in this article, what do conservation biologists do?

Ⓐ They study chameleons and other reptiles.
● They work to save species from extinction.
Ⓒ They visit unexplored areas to hunt for new species.
Ⓓ They use computer models instead of traditional scientific tools.

Write how you know.

Possible Answer: The passage talks about saving species. "In their fight to save species from extinction, conservation biologists need all the tools they can get."

English Language Arts 38 Spectrum Test Prep Grade 8

38

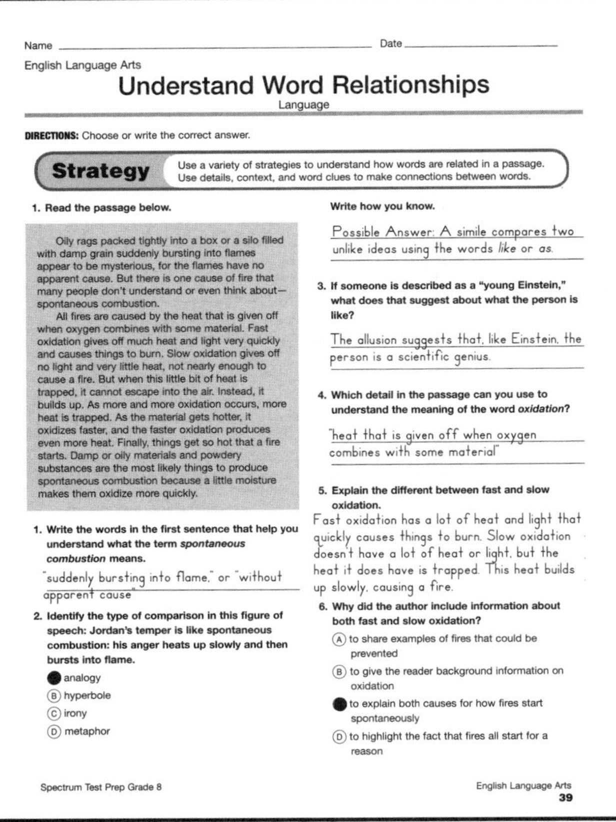

Name ______________________ Date ____________

English Language Arts

Understand Word Relationships

Language

DIRECTIONS: Choose or write the correct answer.

Strategy Use a variety of strategies to understand how words are related in a passage. Use details, context, and word clues to make connections between words.

1. Read the passage below.

Oily rags packed tightly into a box or a silo filled with damp grain suddenly bursting into flames appear to be mysterious, for the flames have no apparent cause. But there is one cause of fire that many people don't understand or even think about—spontaneous combustion.

All fires are caused by the heat that is given off when oxygen combines with some material. Fast oxidation gives off much heat and light very quickly and causes things to burn. Slow oxidation gives off no light and very little heat, not nearly enough to cause a fire. But when this little bit of heat is trapped, it cannot escape into the air. Instead, it builds up. As more and more oxidation occurs, more heat is trapped. As the material gets hotter, it oxidizes faster, and the faster oxidation produces even more heat. Finally, things get so hot that a fire starts. Damp or oily materials and powdery substances are the most likely things to produce spontaneous combustion because a little moisture makes them oxidize more quickly.

1. Write the words in the first sentence that help you understand what the term *spontaneous combustion* means.

"suddenly bursting into flame," or "without apparent cause"

2. Identify the type of comparison in this figure of speech: Jordan's temper is like spontaneous combustion: his anger heats up slowly and then bursts into flame.

● analogy
Ⓑ hyperbole
Ⓒ irony
Ⓓ metaphor

Write how you know.

Possible Answer: A simile compares two unlike ideas using the words *like* or *as*.

3. If someone is described as a "young Einstein," what does that suggest about what the person is like?

The allusion suggests that, like Einstein, the person is a scientific genius.

4. Which detail in the passage can you use to understand the meaning of the word *oxidation*?

"heat that is given off when oxygen combines with some material"

5. Explain the different between fast and slow oxidation.

Fast oxidation has a lot of heat and light that quickly causes things to burn. Slow oxidation doesn't have a lot of heat or light, but the heat it does have is trapped. This heat builds up slowly, causing a fire.

6. Why did the author include information about both fast and slow oxidation?

Ⓐ to share examples of fires that could be prevented
Ⓑ to give the reader background information on oxidation
● to explain both causes for how fires start spontaneously
Ⓓ to highlight the fact that fires all start for a reason

Spectrum Test Prep Grade 8 English Language Arts 39

39

Name ______________________ Date ____________

English Language Arts

Understand Word Relationships

Language

DIRECTIONS: Choose or write the correct answer.

Strategy Identify figurative language and ask yourself why the author included it in the sentence. Does it add a new meaning? Does it help explain an idea through comparisons

1. Part A: A pun is a joke based on the different possible meanings of a word. They often rely on homophones—words that sound the same but have different meanings. Which of the following is an example of a pun?

Ⓐ I think of you a million times a day.
● Seven days without laughter makes one weak.
Ⓒ My sister has a mind like a computer.
Ⓓ My dad is so tall, Sir Edmund Hillary tried to climb him!

Part B: In this excerpt from Shakespeare's *Romeo and Juliet*, Mercutio and Romeo are at a ball. Romeo is feeling sad about a woman, but Mercutio encourages him to dance anyway. Identify the homophones used in the passage. Then, explain how Romeo uses the pun to explain to Mercutio why he doesn't want to dance.

Mercutio: Nay, gentle Romeo, we must have you dance.
Romeo: Not I, believe me. You have dancing shoes
With nimble soles; I have a soul of lead
So stakes me to the ground I cannot move.
Mercutio: You are a lover. Borrow Cupid's wings
And soar with them above a common bound.
—*Romeo and Juliet*, Act I, Scene IV

Possible Answer: The homophones are *sole* and *soul*. Mercutio's feet, or his "nimble *soles*," are light because he is not weighed down by longing for his beloved; in contrast, Romeo's "soul" is heavy as lead.

2. Which of these synonyms for the word *untruth* has the most negative connotation?

Ⓐ bluff
Ⓑ fib
● lie
Ⓓ whopper

3. Part A: Read the excerpt from "The Cloud" below. Identify the figure of speech that creates the most vivid picture of the cloud in your mind.

I bring fresh showers for the thirsting flowers,
From the seas and the streams;
I bear light shade for the leaves when laid
In their noonday dreams.
From my wings are shaken the dews that waken
The sweet buds every one,
When rocked to rest on their mother's breast,
As she dances about the sun.
I wield the flail of the lashing hail,
And whiten the green plains under,
And then again I dissolve it in rain,
And laugh as I pass in thunder.
—from "The Cloud,"
by Percy Bysshe Shelley

Any image of the cloud is acceptable.

Part B: Based on your answer to Part A, describe what you would draw if you were to illustrate this poem.

Any image of the cloud that is consistent with the answer to Part A is acceptable.

English Language Arts 40 Spectrum Test Prep Grade 8

40

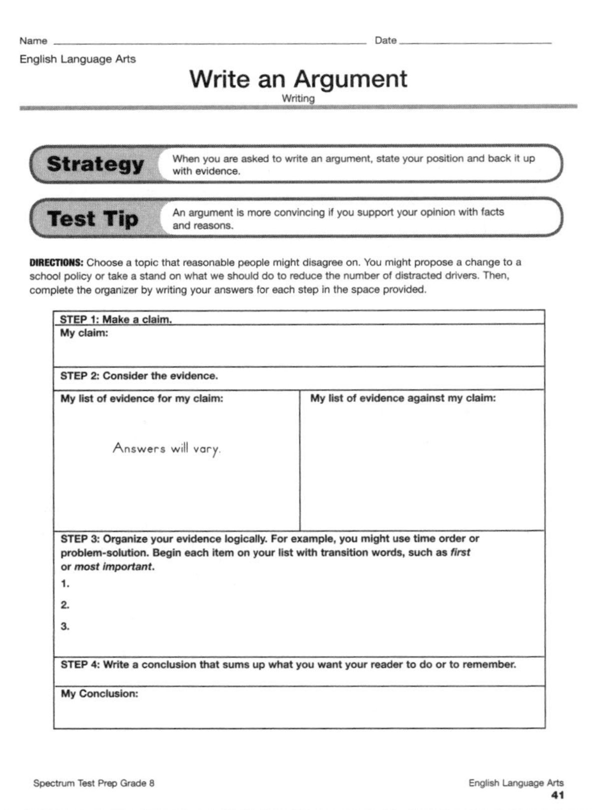

Name ______________________ Date ____________

English Language Arts

Write an Argument

Writing

Strategy When you are asked to write an argument, state your position and back it up with evidence.

Test Tip An argument is more convincing if you support your opinion with facts and reasons.

DIRECTIONS: Choose a topic that reasonable people might disagree on. You might propose a change to a school policy or take a stand on what we should do to reduce the number of distracted drivers. Then, complete the organizer by writing your answers for each step in the space provided.

STEP 1: Make a claim.	
My claim:	
STEP 2: Consider the evidence.	
My list of evidence for my claim: Answers will vary.	My list of evidence against my claim:
STEP 3: Organize your evidence logically. For example, you might use time order or problem-solution. Begin each item on your list with transition words, such as *first* or *most important*. 1. 2. 3.	
STEP 4: Write a conclusion that sums up what you want your reader to do or to remember.	
My Conclusion:	

Spectrum Test Prep Grade 8 English Language Arts 41

41

Name ______________________ Date ______________

English Language Arts

Write an Argument

Writing

DIRECTIONS: Read the passage. Then, answer the questions that follow.

> [1] All but six states have laws banning texting while driving, but laws and fines aren't the best way to end distracted driving. [2] There is no doubt that texting while behind the wheel is dangerous, especially for teenagers. [3] Teens who text while driving are four times more likely to be involved in an accident than undistracted drivers. [4] So the laws against distracted driving should stay on the books, but states should do one more thing. [5] States should send a message that other drivers disapprove of texting while driving. [6] Psychologist Robert Cialdini found that people are more likely to break rules when they think other people are breaking them. [7] People are more likely to litter in areas where others have left trash and stuff lying around.

1. The first sentence is an example of how to

Ⓐ use scientific data as evidence.
● state your claim in one sentence.
Ⓒ preview each main point of your argument.
Ⓓ acknowledge arguments that can be made against your claim.

2. Which of the words or phrases below could be added to sentence 7 to connect it more smoothly to sentence 6?

Ⓐ Although
● For example,
Ⓒ On the other hand,
Ⓓ Then,

3. Rewrite sentence 7 so it matches the formal tone of the rest of the passage.

Possible Answer: People are more likely to litter in areas where others have already deposited litter.

4. Write a conclusion to the passage on distracted driving. If you support bans on cell phone use and texting while driving, you may write a conclusion for the passage. If you do not support the bans, write a conclusion that expresses your point of view on what to do about distracted driving.

Conclusions should restate the claim without introducing new ideas.

English Language Arts
42 Spectrum Test Prep Grade 8

42

Name ______________________ Date ______________

English Language Arts

Write an Informative Text

Writing

DIRECTIONS: Read the passage from a student's informative essay. Then, answer the questions that follow.

> One of the most fascinating figures on ancient artifacts is that of Kokopelli. Kokopelli is compelling, not only because he is cute and vibrant, but because he is everywhere. Several Native American tribes, including the Hopi, Zuni, Winnebago, and Anasazi, tell stories and depict images of the flute playing, hunch-backed little man. Each tribe's ideas about Kokopelli are a little different. Some say his back is humped because he is carrying a sack. In some versions, the sack is filled with trade goods like parrot feathers. In others, the sack holds rain clouds that water the crops. Whatever his origin, images of the little dude are now popular throughout the Southwestern United States. His image appears on t-shirts and in artworks, and he has even been turned into a doll. Kokopelli has replaced the howling coyote, the lizard, and the saguaro cactus as the main symbol of the Southwest.

Strategy Plan the structure of your informative writing before you begin to write. Common structures are main idea and details, cause and effect, and problem-solution.

1. What structure did the student use to organize this introductory paragraph?

Ⓐ compare-contrast
● main idea and details
Ⓒ space order
Ⓓ time order

2. The student summarizes two different explanations of why Kokopelli carries a sack. What idea is supported by these examples?

Possible Answer: the story of Kokopelli has many variants

3. The student describes several versions of the Kokopelli based on different tribes. Why is that important to include?

Ⓐ Including details that disagree is a feature of main idea and detail structure.
Ⓑ The details are not important to the main idea, but they are very interesting.
Ⓒ Each tribe has dramatically different descriptions and ideas of Kokopelli.
● Including all the tribes' descriptions gives a complete picture of Kokopelli.

4. Most of the language the student uses is formal. How would you rewrite this sentence to replace the informal expression with more formal language?

"Whatever his origin, images of the little dude are now popular throughout the Southwestern United States."

Possible Answer: Answers may suggest replacing "the little dude" with "Kokopelli" or "the figure."

5. Why is the last sentence important to the passage?

Possible Answer: It explains the significance and importance of Kokopelli as a symbol of the Southwest.

Spectrum Test Prep Grade 8 English Language Arts
43

43

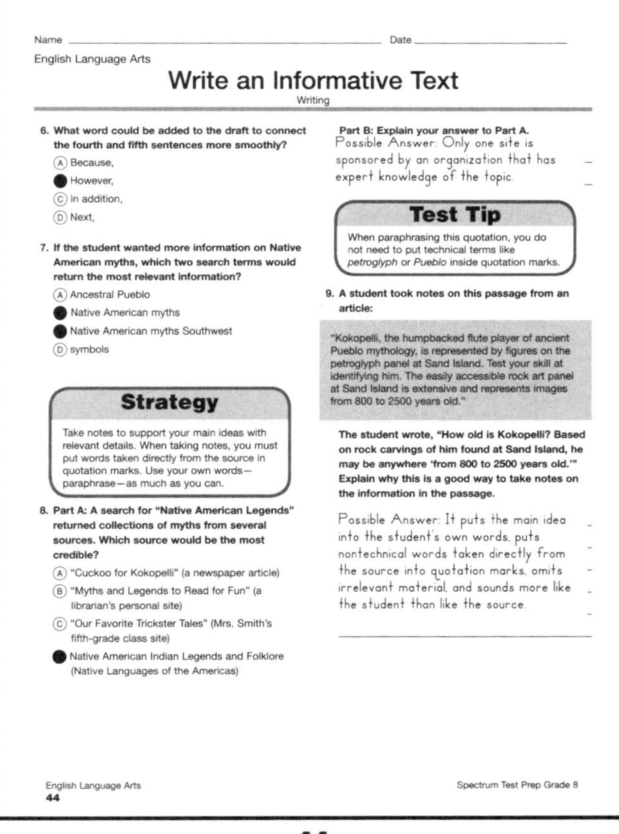

Name ______________________ Date ______________

English Language Arts

Write an Informative Text

Writing

6. What word could be added to the draft to connect the fourth and fifth sentences more smoothly?

Ⓐ Because,
● However,
Ⓒ In addition,
Ⓓ Next,

7. If the student wanted more information on Native American myths, which two search terms would return the most relevant information?

Ⓐ Ancestral Pueblo
● Native American myths
● Native American myths Southwest
Ⓓ symbols

Strategy Take notes to support your main ideas with relevant details. When taking notes, you must put words taken directly from the source in quotation marks. Use your own words—paraphrase—as much as you can.

8. Part A: A search for "Native American Legends" returned collections of myths from several sources. Which source would be the most credible?

Ⓐ "Cuckoo for Kokopelli" (a newspaper article)
Ⓑ "Myths and Legends to Read for Fun" (a librarian's personal site)
Ⓒ "Our Favorite Trickster Tales" (Mrs. Smith's fifth-grade class site)
● Native American Indian Legends and Folklore (Native Languages of the Americas)

Part B: Explain your answer to Part A.

Possible Answer: Only one site is sponsored by an organization that has expert knowledge of the topic.

Test Tip When paraphrasing this quotation, you do not need to put technical terms like *petroglyph* or *Pueblo* inside quotation marks.

9. A student took notes on this passage from an article:

> "Kokopelli, the humpbacked flute player of ancient Pueblo mythology, is represented by figures on the petroglyph panel at Sand Island. Test your skill at identifying him. The easily accessible rock art panel at Sand Island is extensive and represents images from 800 to 2500 years old."

The student wrote, "How old is Kokopelli? Based on rock carvings of him found at Sand Island, he may be anywhere 'from 800 to 2500 years old.'" Explain why this is a good way to take notes on the information in the passage.

Possible Answer: It puts the main idea into the student's own words, puts nontechnical words taken directly from the source into quotation marks, omits irrelevant material, and sounds more like the student than like the source.

English Language Arts
44 Spectrum Test Prep Grade 8

44

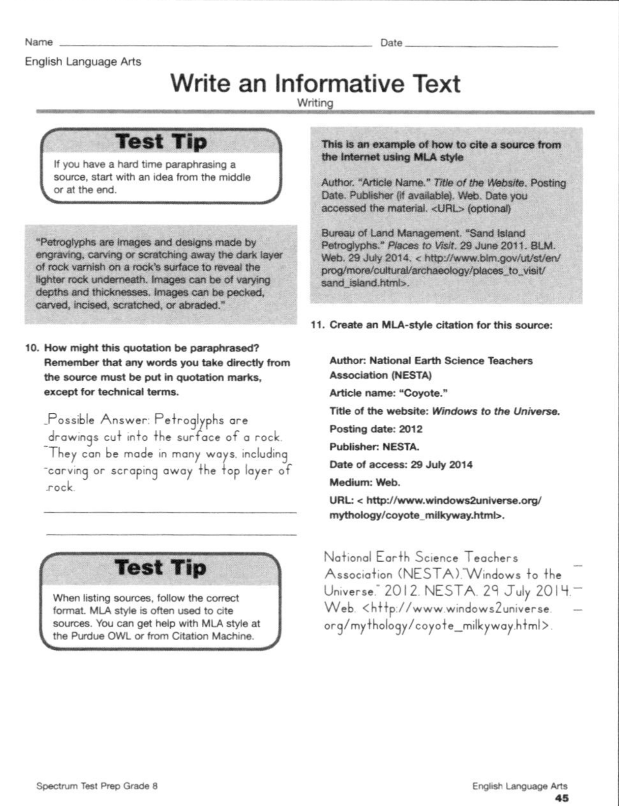

Name ______________________ Date ______________

English Language Arts

Write an Informative Text

Writing

Test Tip If you have a hard time paraphrasing a source, start with an idea from the middle or at the end.

> "Petroglyphs are images and designs made by engraving, carving or scratching away the dark layer of rock varnish on a rock's surface to reveal the lighter rock underneath. Images can be of varying depths and thicknesses. Images can be pecked, carved, incised, scratched, or abraded."

10. How might this quotation be paraphrased? Remember that any words you take directly from the source must be put in quotation marks, except for technical terms.

Possible Answer: Petroglyphs are drawings cut into the surface of a rock. They can be made in many ways, including carving or scraping away the top layer of rock.

Test Tip When listing sources, follow the correct format. MLA style is often used to cite sources. You can get help with MLA style at the Purdue OWL or from Citation Machine.

This is an example of how to cite a source from the Internet using MLA style

Author. "Article Name." *Title of the Website*. Posting Date. Publisher (if available). Web. Date you accessed the material. <URL> (optional)

Bureau of Land Management. "Sand Island Petroglyphs." *Places to Visit*. 29 June 2011. BLM. Web. 29 July 2014. < http://www.blm.gov/ut/st/en/prog/more/cultural/archaeology/places_to_visit/sand_island.html>.

11. Create an MLA-style citation for this source:

Author: National Earth Science Teachers Association (NESTA)
Article name: "Coyote."
Title of the website: *Windows to the Universe*.
Posting date: 2012
Publisher: NESTA.
Date of access: 29 July 2014
Medium: Web.
URL: < http://www.windows2universe.org/mythology/coyote_milkyway.html>.

National Earth Science Teachers Association (NESTA). "Windows to the Universe." 2012. NESTA. 29 July 2014. Web. <http://www.windows2universe.org/mythology/coyote_milkyway.html>.

Spectrum Test Prep Grade 8 English Language Arts
45

45

Name ______________________ Date ____________

English Language Arts

Write an Informative Text

Writing

DIRECTIONS: Write three paragraphs about a character in a Native American myth or another informational topic. Include the following:

- Information from at least two sources
- Facts about your topic
- Definitions and examples to help readers understand your topic
- A correctly formatted list of all the sources you used at the end

Plan your informative article by looking up at least two sources on your topic. Then, choose an organizational plan (cause-effect, compare-contrast, time order, etc.) Use your organizational plan to put your notes in order.

Answer: Paragraphs will vary.

English Language Arts 46 — Spectrum Test Prep Grade 8

46

Name ______________________ Date ____________

English Language Arts

Write a Narrative

Writing

DIRECTIONS: Read the fable and then, answer the questions.

> [1] A lion used to prowl about a field in which four oxen grazed. [2] Every time he tried to attack one, they turned their tails to one another. [3] Whichever way he approached, he was met by horns. [4] The oxen began quarrelling among themselves, and each went off in a huff to his own corner of the field. [5] The lion then attacked them one by one and soon made an end of all four.

Strategy Plan your narrative writing by deciding on characters, setting, and plot events. Who will be in your story, and what conflict will they face? How will they resolve the conflict?

Test Tip You can use narrative techniques such as dialogue and descriptive details to make stories more interesting.

1. What does the first sentence do?

- (A) describe the time and the place
- (B) establish a second-person point of view
- ● introduce the characters and the conflict
- (D) preview the order in which events happen

2. Which phrase could be added to sentence 4 to create a better connection with sentence 3?

- (A) Next,
- (B) Even if,
- (C) Instead,
- ● After a time,

3. Rewrite sentence 3 so that it includes descriptive details.

Whichever way he approached, he was met by their sharp, deadly horns.

4. Add one or more sentences before sentence 5 to show what the lion thinks to himself after the oxen stop working together.

Possible Answer: "Finally!" thought the lion. "My claws and fangs are no match for four oxen. But if the silly beasts think they are a match for me one on one, I can easily prove them wrong."

5. Fables usually end with a moral that states the lesson readers are intended to learn. Write a moral for this fable.

Possible Answer: United we stand, divided we fall.

Spectrum Test Prep Grade 8 — English Language Arts 47

47

Name ______________________ Date ____________

English Language Arts

Write a Narrative

Writing

DIRECTIONS: A narrative is a story that tells about real or imagined events. Write a narrative about a challenge you overcame. The challenge can be real or imagined. Write your paragraph on the lines. Your paragraph should have the following:

- A narrator and/or characters
- A natural sequence of events
- Dialogue
- Descriptions of actions, thoughts, and feelings
- Time words and phrases to show the order of events
- Concrete words and sensory details
- A sentence to end your paragraph

Strategy Plan a narrative by choosing people, places, and events that will be in the story. Use an outline to keep your ideas organized and to make sure you have details.

Test Tip Choosing the right words makes a narrative more interesting to read. Use exact words and phrases and figurative language.

Answer: Paragraphs will vary.

English Language Arts 48 — Spectrum Test Prep Grade 8

48

Name ______________________ Date ____________

English Language Arts

Understand Editing and Revising

Writing

1. Part A: Which sentence contains a gerund?

- (A) "When Yager was leaving Cheyenne, he was hoping to outrun an approaching thunderstorm."
- ● "Flying in the early days was difficult enough, but for Frank Yager and the other air mail pilots, flying at night would turn out to be a real adventure."
- (C) "The beacons were installed on towers built on 50-foot-long concrete arrows pointing the way to the next beacon."
- (D) "On a clear night, the beacons could be seen from 60 to 150 miles away, depending on their size and weather conditions."

Part B: Write a sentence that uses the word you identified in Part A as a gerund as a different part of speech.

Possible answer: He went flying through the air.

2. What punctuation mark should you use to show that words have been left out of a quotation?

- (A) colon
- (B) dash
- ● ellipses
- (D) hyphen

3. What verb form should be used in the first sentence of the second paragraph?

- ● left
- (B) had left
- (C) were leaving
- (D) would have been leaving

4. Part A: Suppose the third sentence in the second paragraph was rewritten to read "Chappell, Nebraska, was where he landed." How would the change from active to passive voice change the emphasis of the sentence?

Possible Answer: The emphasis is now on the place where he landed, not on Yager's decision to land.

PART B: Change this sentence from passive to active voice: "The airway was illuminated by lighted beacons and floodlights."

Possible Answer: Lighted beacons and floodlights illuminated the airway.

5. How would you correct the spelling error in the last sentence of the third paragraph?

Change *there* to *their*.

English Language Arts 50 — Spectrum Test Prep Grade 8

50

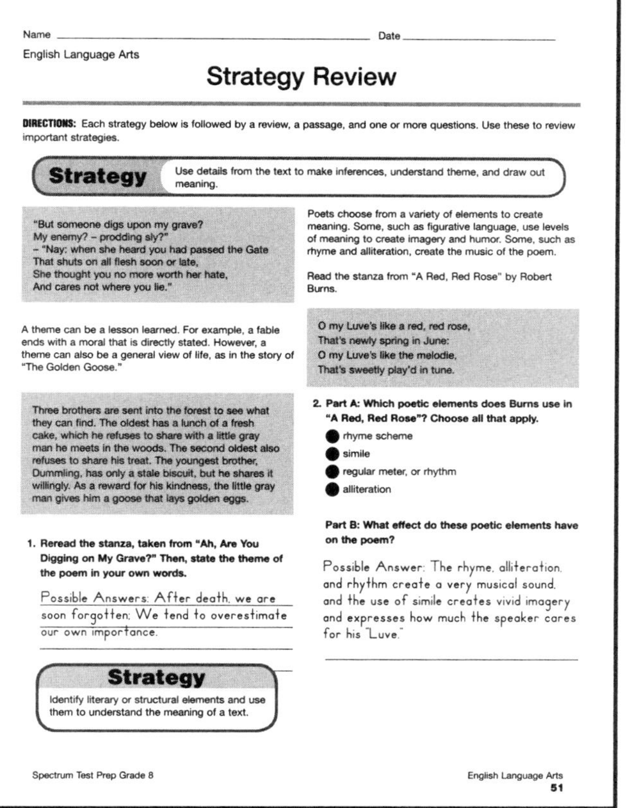

Name ______________________ Date ______________

English Language Arts

Strategy Review

DIRECTIONS: Each strategy below is followed by a review, a passage, and one or more questions. Use these to review important strategies.

Strategy Use details from the text to make inferences, understand theme, and draw out meaning.

"But someone digs upon my grave?
My enemy? – prodding sly?"
– "Nay: when she heard you had passed the Gate
That shuts on all flesh soon or late,
She thought you no more worth her hate,
And cares not where you lie."

A theme can be a lesson learned. For example, a fable ends with a moral that is directly stated. However, a theme can also be a general view of life, as in the story of "The Golden Goose."

Three brothers are sent into the forest to see what they can find. The oldest has a lunch of a fresh cake, which he refuses to share with a little gray man he meets in the woods. The second oldest also refuses to share his treat. The youngest brother, Dummling, has only a stale biscuit, but he shares it willingly. As a reward for his kindness, the little gray man gives him a goose that lays golden eggs.

1. **Reread the stanza, taken from "Ah, Are You Digging on My Grave?" Then, state the theme of the poem in your own words.**

Possible Answers: After death, we are soon forgotten; We tend to overestimate our own importance.

Strategy Identify literary or structural elements and use them to understand the meaning of a text.

Poets choose from a variety of elements to create meaning. Some, such as figurative language, use levels of meaning to create imagery and humor. Some, such as rhyme and alliteration, create the music of the poem.

Read the stanza from "A Red, Red Rose" by Robert Burns.

O my Luve's like a red, red rose,
That's newly spring in June:
O my Luve's like the melodie,
That's sweetly play'd in tune.

2. **Part A: Which poetic elements does Burns use in "A Red, Red Rose"? Choose all that apply.**
   - ● rhyme scheme
   - ● simile
   - ● regular meter, or rhythm
   - ● alliteration

Part B: What effect do these poetic elements have on the poem?

Possible Answer: The rhyme, alliteration, and rhythm create a very musical sound, and the use of simile creates vivid imagery and expresses how much the speaker cares for his "Luve."

Spectrum Test Prep Grade 8 — English Language Arts 51

51

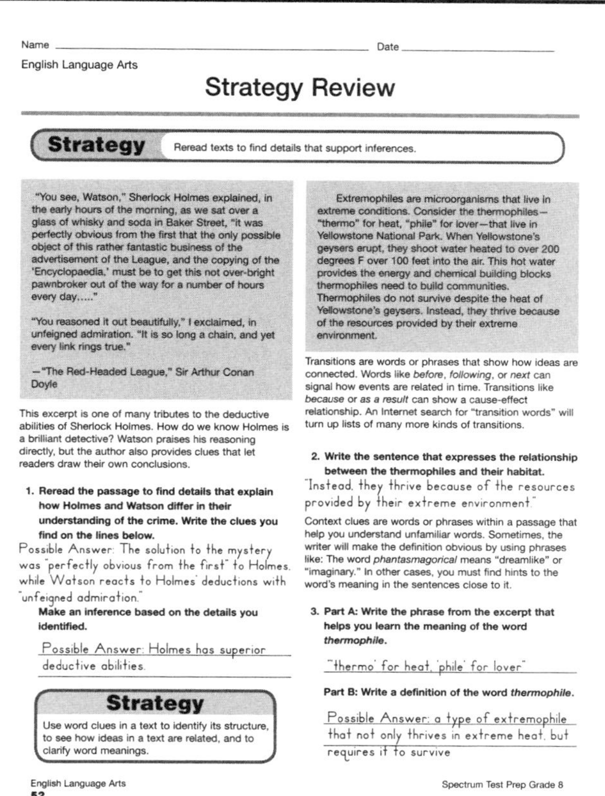

Name ______________________ Date ______________

English Language Arts

Strategy Review

Strategy Reread texts to find details that support inferences.

"You see, Watson," Sherlock Holmes explained, in the early hours of the morning, as we sat over a glass of whisky and soda in Baker Street, "it was perfectly obvious from the first that the only possible object of this rather fantastic business of the advertisement of the League, and the copying of the 'Encyclopaedia,' must be to get this not over-bright pawnbroker out of the way for a number of hours every day....."

"You reasoned it out beautifully," I exclaimed, in unfeigned admiration. "It is so long a chain, and yet every link rings true."

–"The Red-Headed League," Sir Arthur Conan Doyle

This excerpt is one of many tributes to the deductive abilities of Sherlock Holmes. How do we know Holmes is a brilliant detective? Watson praises his reasoning directly, but the author also provides clues that let readers draw their own conclusions.

1. **Reread the passage to find details that explain how Holmes and Watson differ in their understanding of the crime. Write the clues you find on the lines below.**

Possible Answer: The solution to the mystery was "perfectly obvious from the first" to Holmes, while Watson reacts to Holmes' deductions with "unfeigned admiration."

Make an inference based on the details you identified.

Possible Answer: Holmes has superior deductive abilities.

Strategy Use word clues in a text to identify its structure, to see how ideas in a text are related, and to clarify word meanings.

Extremophiles are microorganisms that live in extreme conditions. Consider the thermophiles—"thermo" for heat, "phile" for lover—that live in Yellowstone National Park. When Yellowstone's geysers erupt, they shoot water heated to over 200 degrees F over 100 feet into the air. This hot water provides the energy and chemical building blocks thermophiles need to build communities. Thermophiles do not survive despite the heat of Yellowstone's geysers. Instead, they thrive because of the resources provided by their extreme environment.

Transitions are words or phrases that show how ideas are connected. Words like *before*, *following*, or *next* can signal how events are related in time. Transitions like *because* or *as a result* can show a cause-effect relationship. An Internet search for "transition words" will turn up lists of many more kinds of transitions.

2. **Write the sentence that expresses the relationship between the thermophiles and their habitat.**

"Instead, they thrive because of the resources provided by their extreme environment."

Context clues are words or phrases within a passage that help you understand unfamiliar words. Sometimes, the writer will make the definition obvious by using phrases like: The word *phantasmagorical* means "dreamlike" or "imaginary." In other cases, you must find hints to the word's meaning in the sentences close to it.

3. **Part A: Write the phrase from the excerpt that helps you learn the meaning of the word *thermophile*.**

"thermo" for heat, "phile" for lover"

Part B: Write a definition of the word *thermophile*.

Possible Answer: a type of extremophile that not only thrives in extreme heat, but requires it to survive

English Language Arts 52 — Spectrum Test Prep Grade 8

52

Name ______________________ Date ______________

English Language Arts

Strategy Review

Strategy When writing, use details to support, explain, or clarify your main ideas.

Despite their name, jellyfish are not true fish. They are really zooplankton—simple animals that spend their lives floating in water. The hundreds of jellyfish species vary greatly in size. Some are about the size of a fingernail, while others are over 7 feet long. The blue whale, which is the largest mammal on earth, is over 110 feet long. Despite this variation in size, most jellyfish have a similar structure: transparent bodies shaped like a bell, with tentacles dangling below. Jellyfish are simple creatures, lacking bones, brains, blood, or hearts. They do have an elementary nervous system, or nerve net, that allows them to smell, detect light, and respond to other stimuli.

Details can be either helpful or distracting. If your readers have never seen a jellyfish, adding relevant details can help them understand these unusual creatures. However, adding details that don't relate to the main idea may confuse readers.

1. **Which in the list below would be least helpful to readers who want to know more about jellyfish?**
   - ● Jellyfish are about 95% water.
   - Ⓑ Like jelly shoes, jellyfish are sometimes called "jellies."
   - Ⓒ Jellyfish can sting, although their sting is not usually fatal to humans.
   - Ⓓ Jellyfish are members of the same animal kingdom as sea anemones and corals.

2. **Identify the irrelevant detail that could be left out of the paragraph.**

Answer: the size of the blue whale

Strategy Use an outline to plan your writing.

Scratch Outline for Argument

My claim: Solar energy is a green energy source that could reduce the need to use fossil fuels to produce electricity.

Evidence for my claim	**Evidence against my claim**
1. Solar power is a green energy source.	1. Solar power pollutes less than coal or natural gas, but making solar panels produces hazardous waste.
2. Homeowners who install solar panels can create their own free electricity	2.
3. Solar power is a renewable energy source.	3.

Conclusion: The U.S. government should promote efforts to increase the percentage of electricity generated by solar power.

While you can do a formal outline, complete with Roman numerals *I*, *II*, and *III*, often a scratch outline is enough. These outlines get their name from the way they're written—very quickly and informally. A quick look at Robbie's outline shows that his arguments are not balanced.

3. **Based on the outline, what does Robbie need to do before drafting his argument on wind energy?**

Possible Answer: Robbie only has one argument against his claim. He needs to do more research so that he is more familiar with arguments people might make against his position and is prepared to counter them.

Spectrum Test Prep Grade 8 — English Language Arts 53

53

Name ______________________ Date ______________

English Language Arts

Strategy Review

Strategy Use transitions to show how ideas are related in an argument.

People usually assume that cats purr because they're happy. In reality, the sound is far more complex. Cats purr when recovering from injury, and scientists suspect the sound helps strengthen their bones. Cats also purr when they want food. In fact, some have perfected a "manipulative meow," which embeds a sound like a baby's cry inside their normal low-frequency purr. They use the sound to influence humans to give them food.

When your assignment is to write an argument, you may be asked to include a *counterargument*. A counterargument is an argument against your position. One reason to include a counterargument is to give you a chance to show why the other side is wrong. To do this, you need to use transitions that signal disagreement. Transitions that show contrast include *but*, *on the other hand*, *actually*, or *the truth is....*

1. **Write the phrase from the passage above that is used to contrast the counterargument and what the author believes to be the truth.**

in reality

Strategy Revise to make sure your writing is clear and makes sense. Then, edit to fix errors.

In *Bird by Bird*, writer Anne Lamott describes how she begins writing. She advises, "Start by getting something—anything—down on paper." This first step is the "down draft": at this stage, you're just trying to capture your ideas, or get them down, in some format. The next draft is the "up draft." At this stage of the process, you go back and "fix up" your first draft to make it clear and complete once your ideas are clear, it's time for the "dental draft." In this draft, you check your writing for punctuation, spelling, and missing words as thoroughly as your dentist checks your teeth.

2. **Why does Lamott write more than one draft?**

Possible Answer: Each draft has a different purpose. The first is to capture ideas in a rough form, the second is to make the ideas in the rough draft clear and complete; the final is to polish and correct errors.

3. **Part A: Which sentence in the paragraph contains an error?**
   - Ⓐ "*In Bird by Bird*, writer Anne Lamott describes how she begins writing."
   - Ⓑ "She advises, 'Start by getting something—anything—down on paper.'"
   - ● "At this stage of the process, you go back and 'fix up' your first draft to make it clear and complete once your ideas are clear, it's time for the 'dental draft.'"
   - Ⓓ "In this draft, you check your writing for punctuation, spelling, and missing words as thoroughly as your dentist checks your teeth."

Part B: Rewrite the sentence to correct the error.

Possible Answer: At this stage of the process, you go back and "fix up" your first draft to make it clear and complete. Once your ideas are clear, it's time for the "dental draft."

English Language Arts 54 — Spectrum Test Prep Grade 8

54

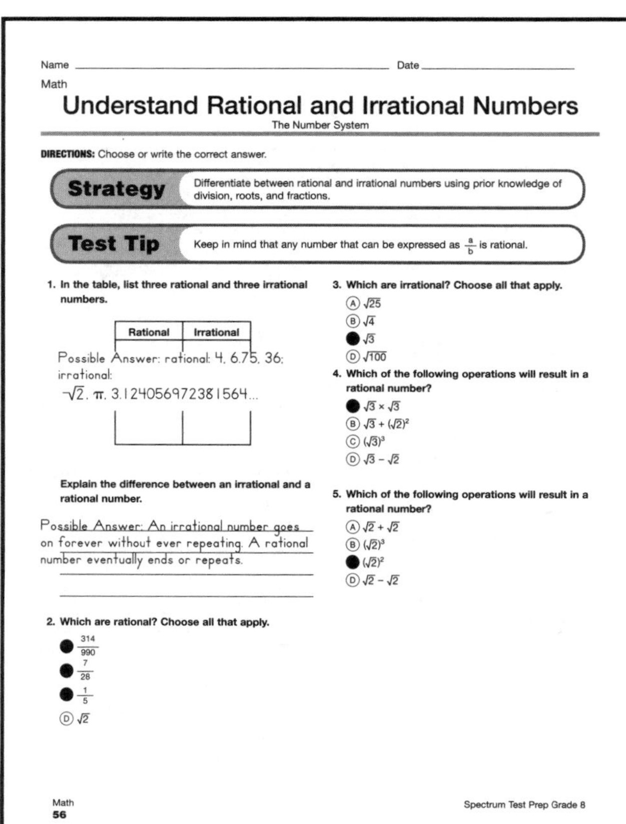

Name ______ Date ______

Math

Understand Rational and Irrational Numbers

The Number System

DIRECTIONS: Choose or write the correct answer.

Strategy Differentiate between rational and irrational numbers using prior knowledge of division, roots, and fractions.

Test Tip Keep in mind that any number that can be expressed as $\frac{a}{b}$ is rational.

1. In the table, list three rational and three irrational numbers.

Rational	Irrational

Possible Answer: rational: 4, 6.75, 36; irrational: $-\sqrt{2}$, π, 3.12405697238 1564...

Explain the difference between an irrational and a rational number.

Possible Answer: An irrational number goes on forever without ever repeating. A rational number eventually ends or repeats.

2. Which are rational? Choose all that apply.

● $\frac{314}{990}$

● $\frac{7}{28}$

● $\frac{1}{5}$

Ⓓ $\sqrt{2}$

3. Which are irrational? Choose all that apply.

Ⓐ $\sqrt{25}$

Ⓑ $\sqrt{4}$

● $\sqrt{3}$

Ⓓ $\sqrt{100}$

4. Which of the following operations will result in a rational number?

● $\sqrt{3} \times \sqrt{3}$

Ⓑ $\sqrt{3} + (\sqrt{2})^2$

Ⓒ $(\sqrt{3})^3$

Ⓓ $\sqrt{3} - \sqrt{2}$

5. Which of the following operations will result in a rational number?

Ⓐ $\sqrt{2} + \sqrt{2}$

Ⓑ $(\sqrt{2})^3$

● $(\sqrt{2})^2$

Ⓓ $\sqrt{2} - \sqrt{2}$

Math 56 Spectrum Test Prep Grade 8

56

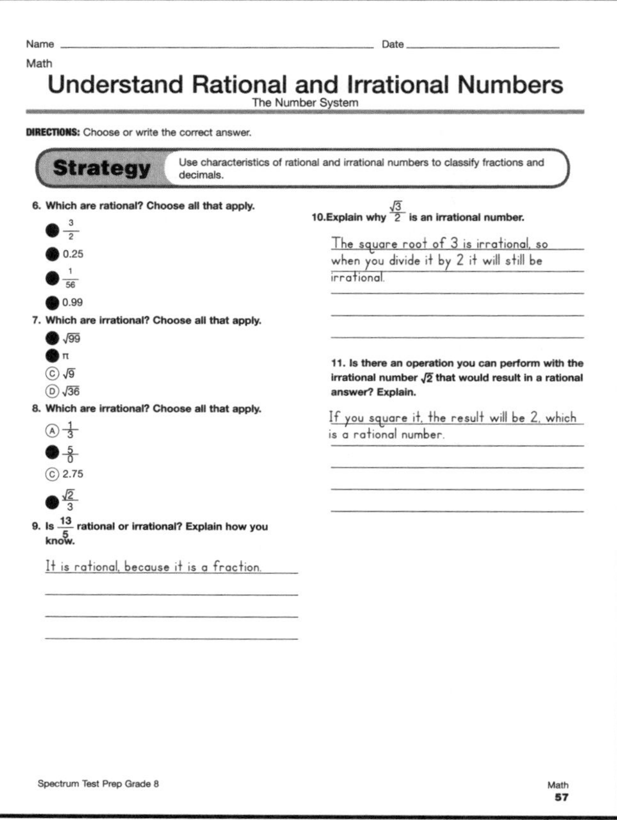

Name ______ Date ______

Math

Understand Rational and Irrational Numbers

The Number System

DIRECTIONS: Choose or write the correct answer.

Strategy Use characteristics of rational and irrational numbers to classify fractions and decimals.

6. Which are rational? Choose all that apply.

● $\frac{3}{2}$

● 0.25

● $\frac{1}{56}$

● 0.99

7. Which are irrational? Choose all that apply.

● $\sqrt{99}$

● π

Ⓒ $\sqrt{9}$

Ⓓ $\sqrt{36}$

8. Which are irrational? Choose all that apply.

Ⓐ $\frac{1}{3}$

● $\frac{5}{0}$

Ⓒ 2.75

● $\frac{\sqrt{2}}{3}$

9. Is $\frac{13}{5}$ rational or irrational? Explain how you know.

It is rational, because it is a fraction.

10. Explain why $\frac{\sqrt{3}}{2}$ is an irrational number.

The square root of 3 is irrational, so when you divide it by 2 it will still be irrational.

11. Is there an operation you can perform with the irrational number $\sqrt{2}$ that would result in a rational answer? Explain.

If you square it, the result will be 2, which is a rational number.

Spectrum Test Prep Grade 8 Math 57

57

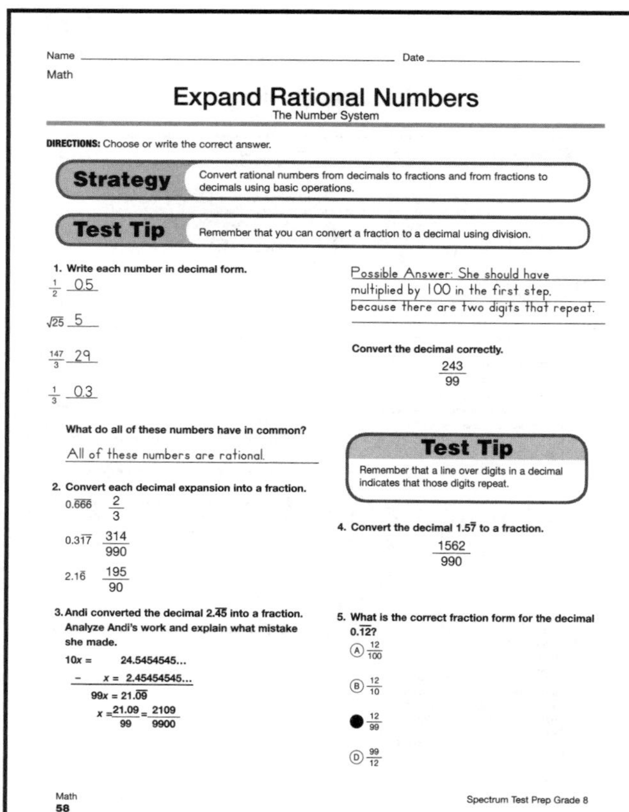

Name ______ Date ______

Math

Expand Rational Numbers

The Number System

DIRECTIONS: Choose or write the correct answer.

Strategy Convert rational numbers from decimals to fractions and from fractions to decimals using basic operations.

Test Tip Remember that you can convert a fraction to a decimal using division.

1. Write each number in decimal form.

$\frac{1}{2}$ 0.5

$\sqrt{25}$ 5

$\frac{147}{3}$ 29

$\frac{1}{3}$ 0.3

What do all of these numbers have in common?

All of these numbers are rational.

2. Convert each decimal expansion into a fraction.

$0.\overline{666}$ $\frac{2}{3}$

$0.3\overline{17}$ $\frac{314}{990}$

$2.1\overline{6}$ $\frac{195}{90}$

3. Andi converted the decimal $2.\overline{45}$ into a fraction. Analyze Andi's work and explain what mistake she made.

$10x = 24.5454545...$

$-\quad x = 2.45454545...$

$99x = 21.\overline{09}$

$x = \frac{21.09}{99} = \frac{2109}{9900}$

Possible Answer: She should have multiplied by 100 in the first step, because there are two digits that repeat.

Convert the decimal correctly.

$\frac{243}{99}$

Test Tip Remember that a line over digits in a decimal indicates that those digits repeat.

4. Convert the decimal $1.5\overline{7}$ to a fraction.

$\frac{1562}{990}$

5. What is the correct fraction form for the decimal $0.\overline{12}$?

Ⓐ $\frac{12}{100}$

Ⓑ $\frac{12}{10}$

● $\frac{12}{99}$

Ⓓ $\frac{99}{12}$

Math 58 Spectrum Test Prep Grade 8

58

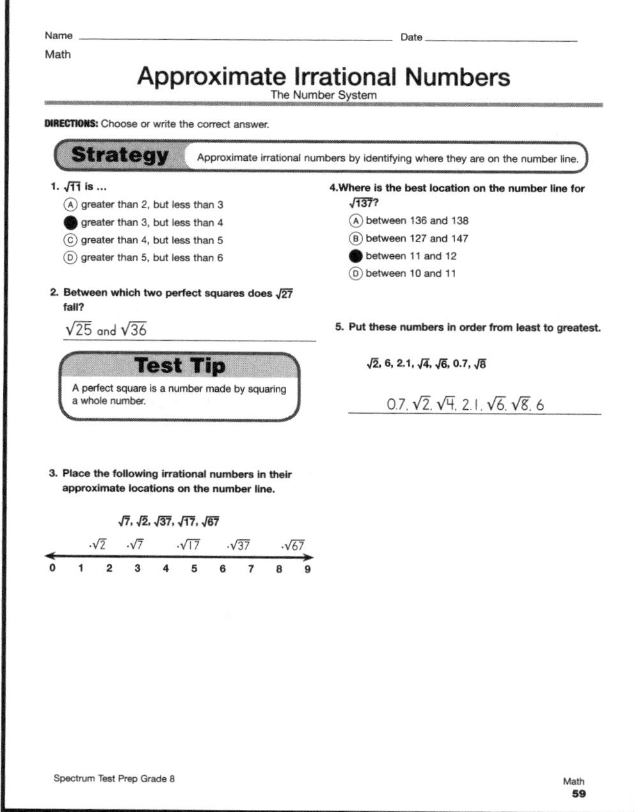

Name ______ Date ______

Math

Approximate Irrational Numbers

The Number System

DIRECTIONS: Choose or write the correct answer.

Strategy Approximate irrational numbers by identifying where they are on the number line.

1. $\sqrt{11}$ is ...

Ⓐ greater than 2, but less than 3

● greater than 3, but less than 4

Ⓒ greater than 4, but less than 5

Ⓓ greater than 5, but less than 6

2. Between which two perfect squares does $\sqrt{27}$ fall?

$\sqrt{25}$ and $\sqrt{36}$

Test Tip A perfect square is a number made by squaring a whole number.

3. Place the following irrational numbers in their approximate locations on the number line.

$\sqrt{7}$, $\sqrt{2}$, $\sqrt{37}$, $\sqrt{17}$, $\sqrt{67}$

4. Where is the best location on the number line for $\sqrt{137}$?

Ⓐ between 136 and 138

Ⓑ between 127 and 147

● between 11 and 12

Ⓓ between 10 and 11

5. Put these numbers in order from least to greatest.

$\sqrt{2}$, 6, 2.1, $\sqrt{4}$, $\sqrt{6}$, 0.7, $\sqrt{8}$

0.7, $\sqrt{2}$, $\sqrt{4}$, 2.1, $\sqrt{6}$, $\sqrt{8}$, 6

Spectrum Test Prep Grade 8 Math 59

59

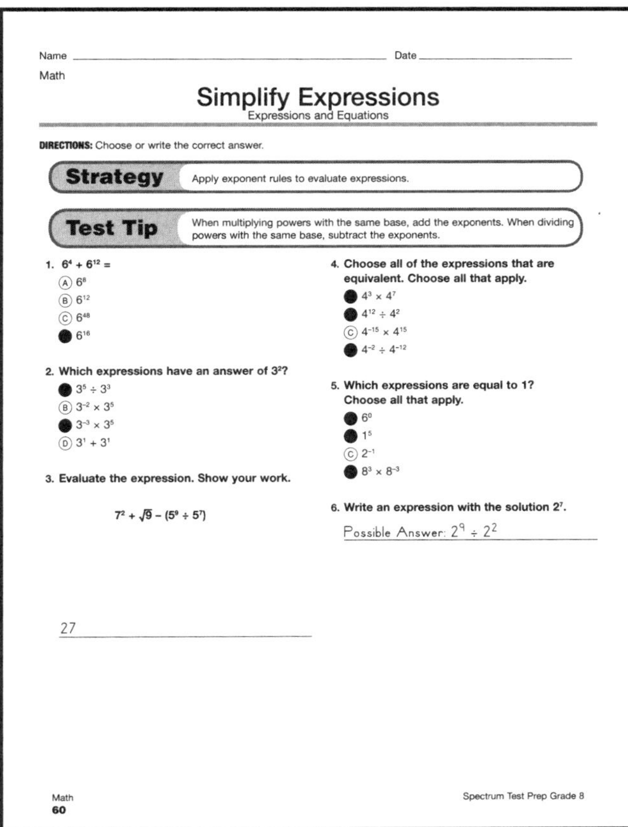

Name ______________________ Date ______________
Math

Simplify Expressions
Expressions and Equations

DIRECTIONS: Choose or write the correct answer.

Strategy Apply exponent rules to evaluate expressions.

Test Tip When multiplying powers with the same base, add the exponents. When dividing powers with the same base, subtract the exponents.

1. $6^4 + 6^{12}$ =
- (A) 6^8
- (B) 6^{12}
- (C) 6^{48}
- ● 6^{16}

2. Which expressions have an answer of 3^2?
- ● $3^5 \div 3^3$
- (B) $3^{-2} \times 3^5$
- ● $3^{-3} \times 3^5$
- (D) $3^1 + 3^1$

3. Evaluate the expression. Show your work.

$7^2 + \sqrt{9} - (5^9 \div 5^7)$

27

4. Choose all of the expressions that are equivalent. Choose all that apply.
- ● $4^3 \times 4^7$
- ● $4^{12} \div 4^2$
- (C) $4^{-15} \times 4^{15}$
- ● $4^{-2} \div 4^{-12}$

5. Which expressions are equal to 1? Choose all that apply.
- ● 6^0
- ● 1^5
- (C) 2^{-1}
- ● $8^3 \times 8^{-3}$

6. Write an expression with the solution 2^7.

Possible Answer: $2^9 \div 2^2$

Math 60 Spectrum Test Prep Grade 8

60

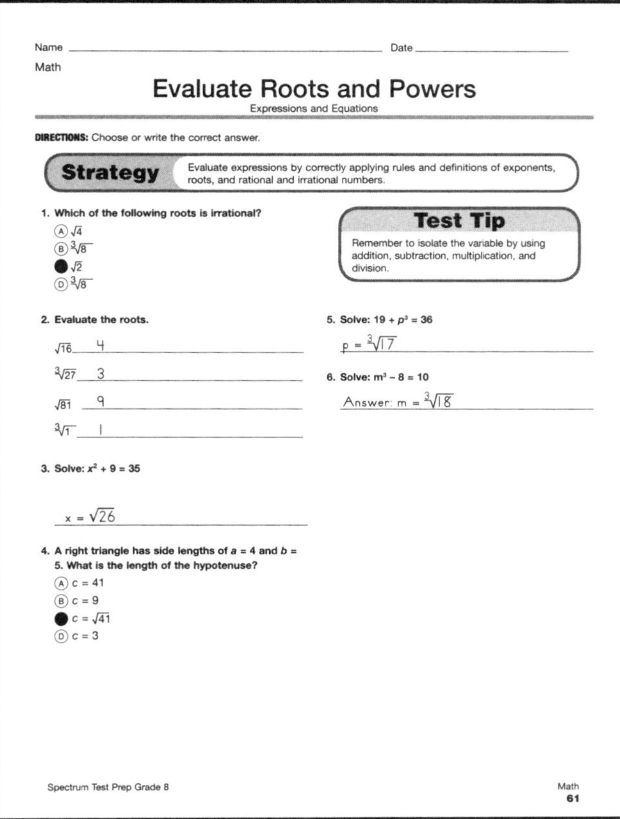

Name ______________________ Date ______________
Math

Evaluate Roots and Powers
Expressions and Equations

DIRECTIONS: Choose or write the correct answer.

Strategy Evaluate expressions by correctly applying rules and definitions of exponents, roots, and rational and irrational numbers.

Test Tip Remember to isolate the variable by using addition, subtraction, multiplication, and division.

1. Which of the following roots is irrational?
- (A) $\sqrt{4}$
- (B) $\sqrt[3]{8}$
- ● $\sqrt{2}$
- (D) $\sqrt[3]{8}$

2. Evaluate the roots.

$\sqrt{16}$ 4

$\sqrt[3]{27}$ 3

$\sqrt{81}$ 9

$\sqrt[3]{1}$ 1

3. Solve: $x^2 + 9 = 35$

$x = \sqrt{26}$

4. A right triangle has side lengths of $a = 4$ and $b = 5$. What is the length of the hypotenuse?
- (A) $c = 41$
- (B) $c = 9$
- ● $c = \sqrt{41}$
- (D) $c = 3$

5. Solve: $19 + p^3 = 36$

$p = \sqrt[3]{17}$

6. Solve: $m^3 - 8 = 10$

Answer: $m = \sqrt[3]{18}$

Spectrum Test Prep Grade 8 Math 61

61

Name ______________________ Date ______________
Math

Evaluate Roots and Powers
Expressions and Equations

DIRECTIONS: Choose or write the correct answer.

Strategy Combine knowledge of powers, roots, and rational and irrational numbers to evaluate and interpret expressions.

7. $\sqrt{81} - \sqrt{16}$ =
- (A) $\sqrt{65}$
- ● 5
- (C) $\sqrt{5}$
- (D) 2.5

Is the solution rational or irrational? Write how you know.

The solution is rational, because 5 is a rational number.

8. Which expression shows that $\sqrt[3]{64} = 4$?
- (A) $64 \div 3$
- (B) 4×3
- (C) $3 \times 3 \times 3 \times 3$
- ● $4 \times 4 \times 4$

9. Evaluate the expression. Show your work.

$\frac{x^3 + 8}{3} = 25$

$x = \sqrt[3]{67}$

How can you determine if the answer is rational or irrational?

Possible Answer: I can try different numbers for x and see if a rational number works in the equation.

10. List the first 5 perfect squares and perfect cubes in the table.

Perfect squares	Perfect cubes
1	1
4	8
9	27
16	64
25	125

Math 62 Spectrum Test Prep Grade 8

62

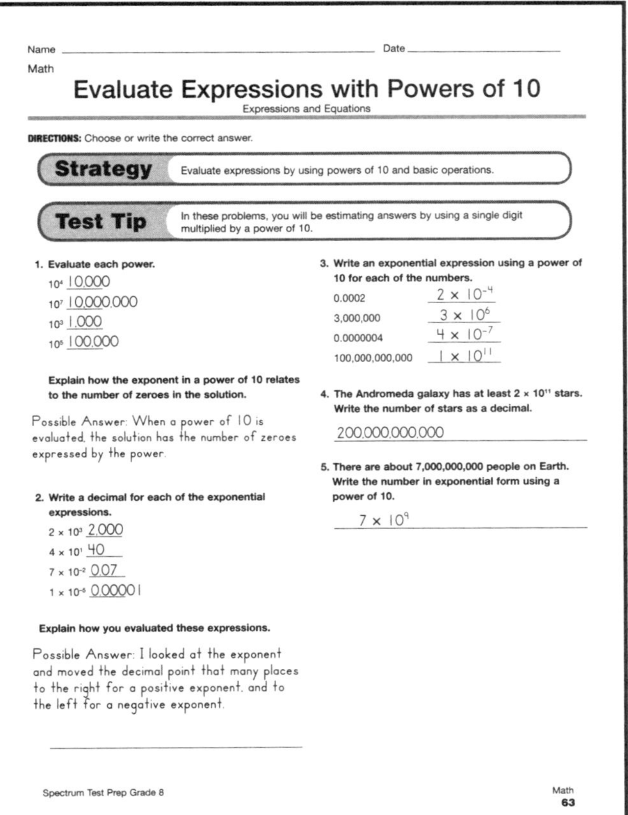

Name ______________________ Date ______________
Math

Evaluate Expressions with Powers of 10
Expressions and Equations

DIRECTIONS: Choose or write the correct answer.

Strategy Evaluate expressions by using powers of 10 and basic operations.

Test Tip In these problems, you will be estimating answers by using a single digit multiplied by a power of 10.

1. Evaluate each power.

10^4 10,000

10^7 10,000,000

10^3 1,000

10^5 100,000

Explain how the exponent in a power of 10 relates to the number of zeroes in the solution.

Possible Answer: When a power of 10 is evaluated, the solution has the number of zeroes expressed by the power.

2. Write a decimal for each of the exponential expressions.

2×10^3 2,000

4×10^1 40

7×10^{-2} 0.07

1×10^{-5} 0.00001

Explain how you evaluated these expressions.

Possible Answer: I looked at the exponent and moved the decimal point that many places to the right for a positive exponent, and to the left for a negative exponent.

3. Write an exponential expression using a power of 10 for each of the numbers.

0.0002 2×10^{-4}

3,000,000 3×10^6

0.0000004 4×10^{-7}

100,000,000,000 1×10^{11}

4. The Andromeda galaxy has at least 2×10^{11} stars. Write the number of stars as a decimal.

200,000,000,000

5. There are about 7,000,000,000 people on Earth. Write the number in exponential form using a power of 10.

7×10^9

Spectrum Test Prep Grade 8 Math 63

63

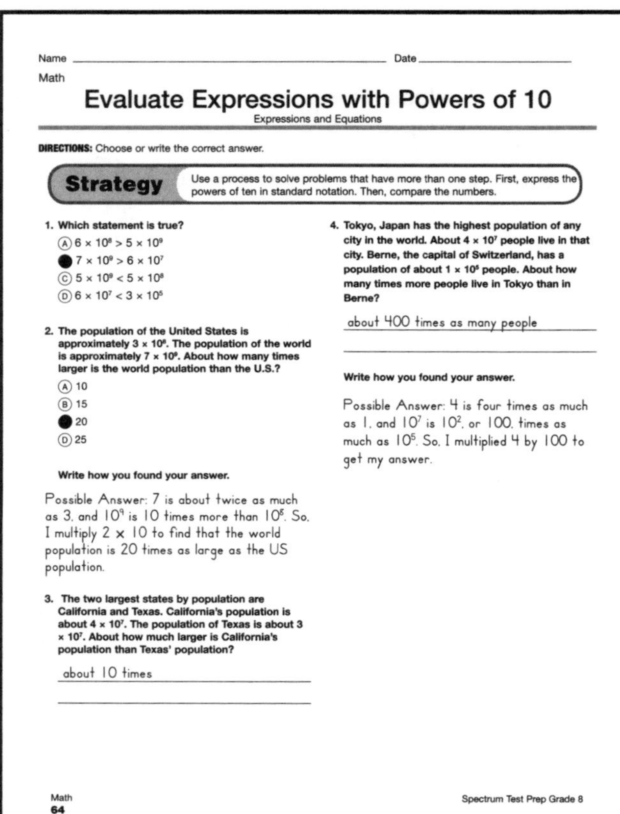

Name ______________________ Date ____________

Math

Evaluate Expressions with Powers of 10

Expressions and Equations

DIRECTIONS: Choose or write the correct answer.

Strategy Use a process to solve problems that have more than one step. First, express the powers of ten in standard notation. Then, compare the numbers.

1. Which statement is true?

Ⓐ $6 \times 10^8 > 5 \times 10^9$
● $7 \times 10^9 > 6 \times 10^7$
Ⓒ $5 \times 10^9 < 5 \times 10^8$
Ⓓ $6 \times 10^7 < 3 \times 10^5$

2. The population of the United States is approximately 3×10^8. The population of the world is approximately 7×10^9. About how many times larger is the world population than the U.S.?

Ⓐ 10
Ⓑ 15
● 20
Ⓓ 25

Write how you found your answer.

Possible Answer: 7 is about twice as much as 3, and 10^9 is 10 times more than 10^8. So, I multiply 2×10 to find that the world population is 20 times as large as the US population.

3. The two largest states by population are California and Texas. California's population is about 4×10^7. The population of Texas is about 3×10^7. About how much larger is California's population than Texas' population?

about 10 times

4. Tokyo, Japan has the highest population of any city in the world. About 4×10^7 people live in that city. Berne, the capital of Switzerland, has a population of about 1×10^5 people. About how many times more people live in Tokyo than in Berne?

about 400 times as many people

Write how you found your answer.

Possible Answer: 4 is four times as much as 1, and 10^7 is 10^2, or 100, times as much as 10^5. So, I multiplied 4 by 100 to get my answer.

Math 64 Spectrum Test Prep Grade 8

64

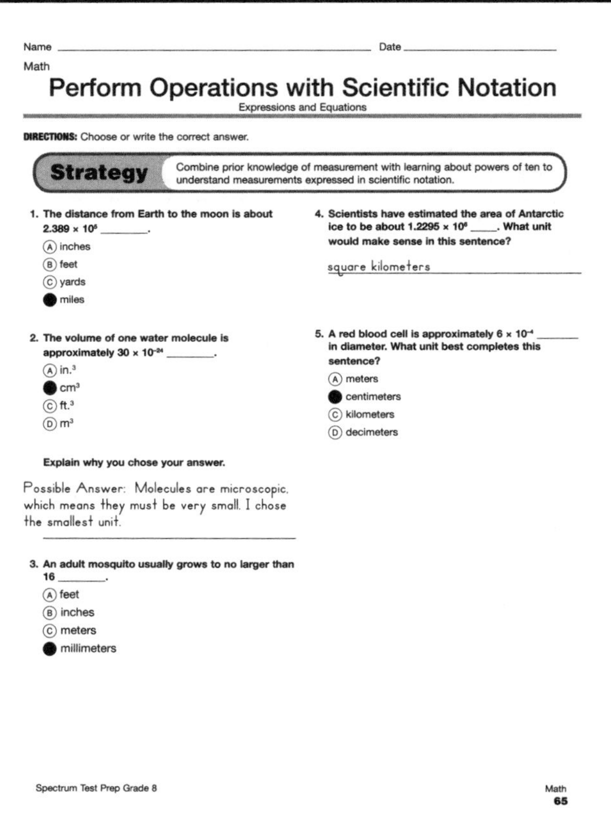

Name ______________________ Date ____________

Math

Perform Operations with Scientific Notation

Expressions and Equations

DIRECTIONS: Choose or write the correct answer.

Strategy Combine prior knowledge of measurement with learning about powers of ten to understand measurements expressed in scientific notation.

1. The distance from Earth to the moon is about 2.389×10^5 ________.

Ⓐ inches
Ⓑ feet
Ⓒ yards
● miles

2. The volume of one water molecule is approximately 30×10^{-24} ________.

Ⓐ $in.^3$
● cm^3
Ⓒ $ft.^3$
Ⓓ m^3

Explain why you chose your answer.

Possible Answer: Molecules are microscopic, which means they must be very small. I chose the smallest unit.

3. An adult mosquito usually grows to no larger than 16 ________.

Ⓐ feet
Ⓑ inches
Ⓒ meters
● millimeters

4. Scientists have estimated the area of Antarctic ice to be about 1.2295×10^6 ____. What unit would make sense in this sentence?

square kilometers

5. A red blood cell is approximately 6×10^{-4} ______ in diameter. What unit best completes this sentence?

Ⓐ meters
● centimeters
Ⓒ kilometers
Ⓓ decimeters

Spectrum Test Prep Grade 8 Math 65

65

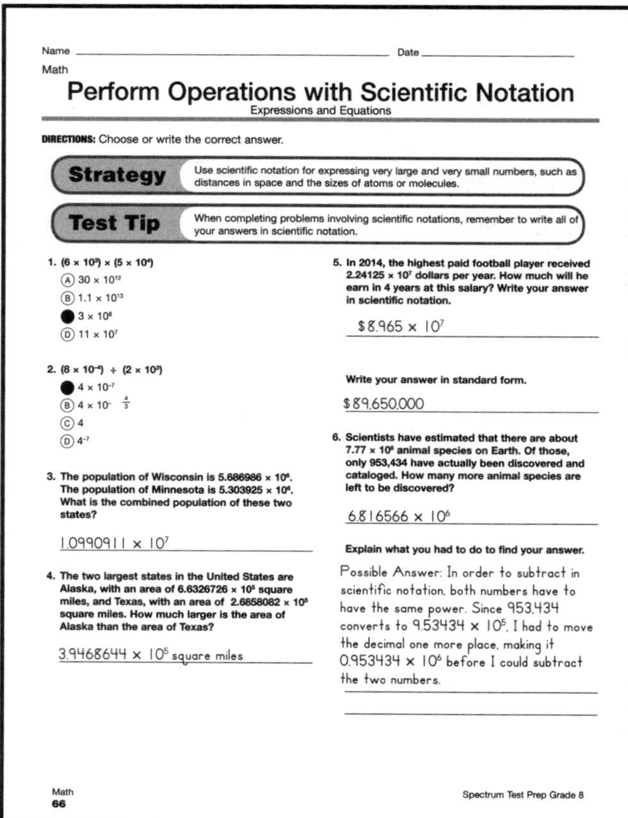

Name ______________________ Date ____________

Math

Perform Operations with Scientific Notation

Expressions and Equations

DIRECTIONS: Choose or write the correct answer.

Strategy Use scientific notation for expressing very large and very small numbers, such as distances in space and the sizes of atoms or molecules.

Test Tip When completing problems involving scientific notations, remember to write all of your answers in scientific notation.

1. $(6 \times 10^3) \times (5 \times 10^4)$

Ⓐ 30×10^{12}
Ⓑ 1.1×10^{13}
● 3×10^8
Ⓓ 11×10^7

2. $(8 \times 10^{-4}) \div (2 \times 10^3)$

● 4×10^{-7}
Ⓑ $4 \times 10^{-\frac{4}{3}}$
Ⓒ 4
Ⓓ 4^{-7}

3. The population of Wisconsin is 5.686986×10^6. The population of Minnesota is 5.303925×10^6. What is the combined population of these two states?

1.0990911×10^7

4. The two largest states in the United States are Alaska, with an area of 6.6326726×10^5 square miles, and Texas, with an area of 2.6858082×10^5 square miles. How much larger is the area of Alaska than the area of Texas?

3.9468644×10^5 square miles

5. In 2014, the highest paid football player received 2.24125×10^7 dollars per year. How much will he earn in 4 years at this salary? Write your answer in scientific notation.

$\$8.965 \times 10^7$

Write your answer in standard form.

$89,650,000

6. Scientists have estimated that there are about 7.77×10^6 animal species on Earth. Of those, only 953,434 have actually been discovered and cataloged. How many more animal species are left to be discovered?

6.816566×10^6

Explain what you had to do to find your answer.

Possible Answer: In order to subtract in scientific notation, both numbers have to have the same power. Since 953,434 converts to 9.53434×10^5, I had to move the decimal one more place, making it 0.953434×10^6 before I could subtract the two numbers.

Math 66 Spectrum Test Prep Grade 8

66

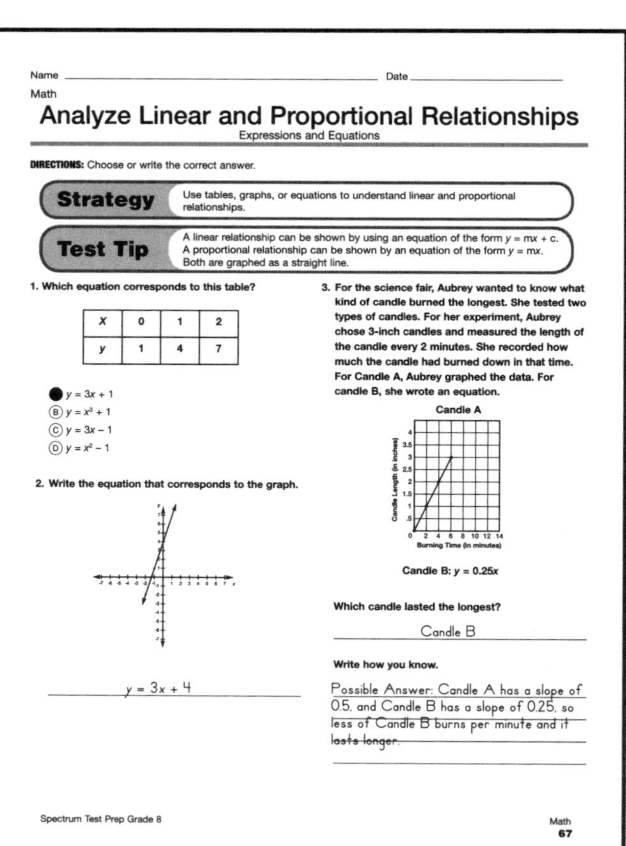

Name ______________________ Date ____________

Math

Analyze Linear and Proportional Relationships

Expressions and Equations

DIRECTIONS: Choose or write the correct answer.

Strategy Use tables, graphs, or equations to understand linear and proportional relationships.

Test Tip A linear relationship can be shown by using an equation of the form $y = mx + c$. A proportional relationship can be shown by an equation of the form $y = mx$. Both are graphed as a straight line.

1. Which equation corresponds to this table?

x	0	1	2
y	1	4	7

● $y = 3x + 1$
Ⓑ $y = x^3 + 1$
Ⓒ $y = 3x - 1$
Ⓓ $y = x^2 - 1$

2. Write the equation that corresponds to the graph.

$y = 3x + 4$

3. For the science fair, Aubrey wanted to know what kind of candle burned the longest. She tested two types of candles. For her experiment, Aubrey chose 3-inch candles and measured the length of the candle every 2 minutes. She recorded how much the candle had burned down in that time. For Candle A, Aubrey graphed the data. For candle B, she wrote an equation.

Candle B: $y = 0.25x$

Which candle lasted the longest?

Candle B

Write how you know.

Possible Answer: Candle A has a slope of 0.5, and Candle B has a slope of 0.25, so less of Candle B burns per minute and it lasts longer.

Spectrum Test Prep Grade 8 Math 67

67

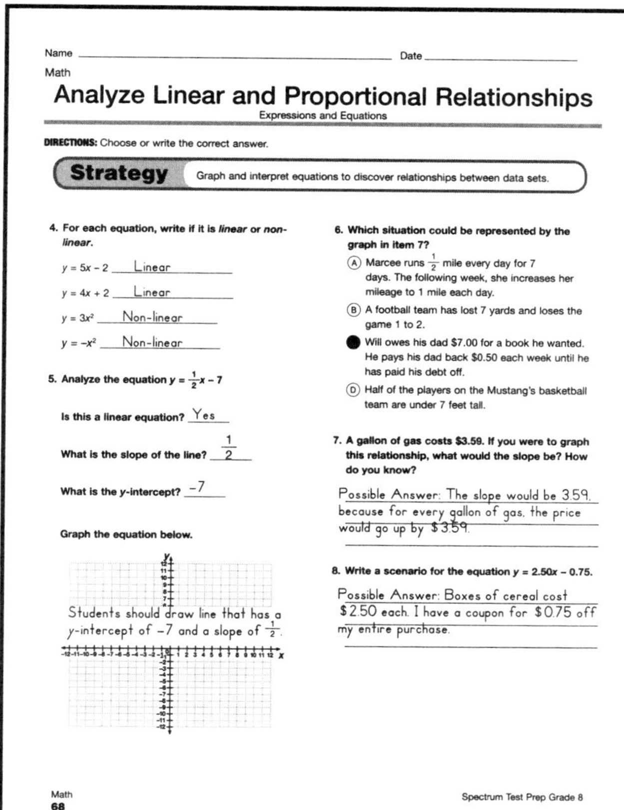

Name ______________________ Date ____________

Math

Analyze Linear and Proportional Relationships

Expressions and Equations

DIRECTIONS: Choose or write the correct answer.

Strategy Graph and interpret equations to discover relationships between data sets.

4. For each equation, write if it is *linear* or *non-linear*.

$y = 5x - 2$ Linear

$y = 4x + 2$ Linear

$y = 3x^2$ Non-linear

$y = -x^2$ Non-linear

5. Analyze the equation $y = \frac{1}{2}x - 7$

Is this a linear equation? Yes

What is the slope of the line? $\frac{1}{2}$

What is the *y*-intercept? -7

Graph the equation below.

Students should draw line that has a *y*-intercept of −7 and a slope of $\frac{1}{2}$.

6. Which situation could be represented by the graph in item 7?

- (A) Marcee runs $\frac{1}{2}$ mile every day for 7 days. The following week, she increases her mileage to 1 mile each day.
- (B) A football team has lost 7 yards and loses the game 1 to 2.
- ● Will owes his dad $7.00 for a book he wanted. He pays his dad back $0.50 each week until he has paid his debt off.
- (D) Half of the players on the Mustang's basketball team are under 7 feet tall.

7. A gallon of gas costs $3.59. If you were to graph this relationship, what would the slope be? How do you know?

Possible Answer: The slope would be 3.59, because for every gallon of gas, the price would go up by $3.59.

8. Write a scenario for the equation $y = 2.50x - 0.75$.

Possible Answer: Boxes of cereal cost $2.50 each. I have a coupon for $0.75 off my entire purchase.

Math 68 Spectrum Test Prep Grade 8

68

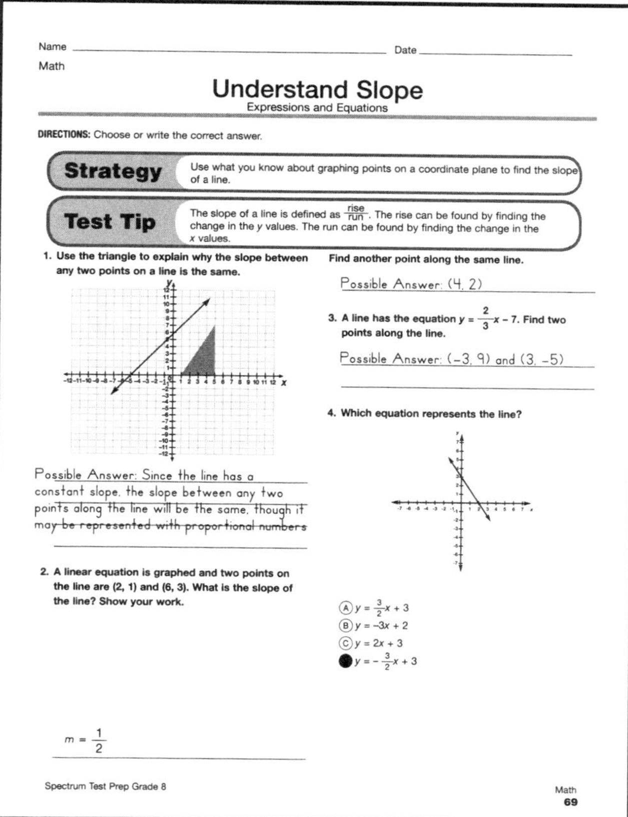

Name ______________________ Date ____________

Math

Understand Slope

Expressions and Equations

DIRECTIONS: Choose or write the correct answer.

Strategy Use what you know about graphing points on a coordinate plane to find the slope of a line.

Test Tip The slope of a line is defined as $\frac{rise}{run}$. The rise can be found by finding the change in the *y* values. The run can be found by finding the change in the *x* values.

1. Use the triangle to explain why the slope between any two points on a line is the same.

Possible Answer: Since the line has a constant slope, the slope between any two points along the line will be the same, though it may be represented with proportional numbers

2. A linear equation is graphed and two points on the line are (2, 1) and (6, 3). What is the slope of the line? Show your work.

$m = \frac{1}{2}$

Find another point along the same line.

Possible Answer: (4, 2)

3. A line has the equation $y = \frac{2}{3}x - 7$. Find two points along the line.

Possible Answer: (−3, 9) and (3, −5)

4. Which equation represents the line?

- (A) $y = \frac{3}{2}x + 3$
- (B) $y = -3x + 2$
- (C) $y = 2x + 3$
- ● $y = -\frac{3}{2}x + 3$

Spectrum Test Prep Grade 8 Math 69

69

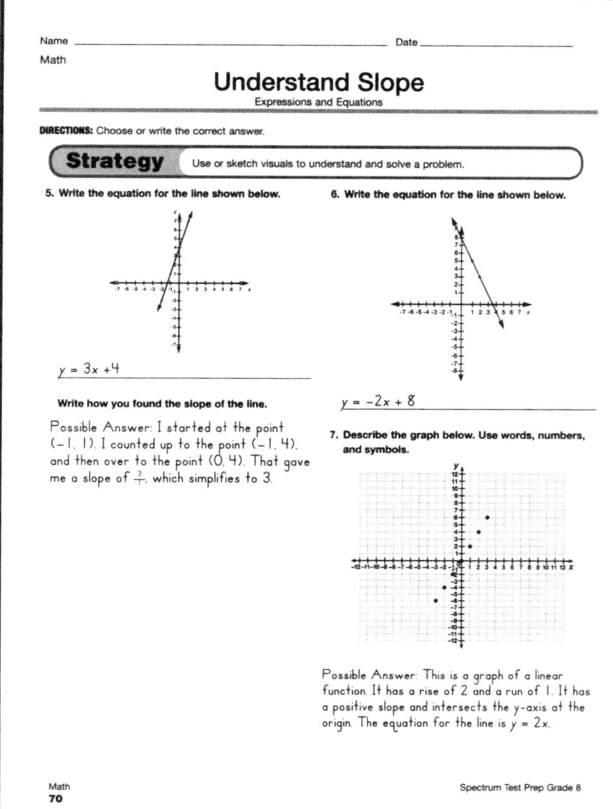

Name ______________________ Date ____________

Math

Understand Slope

Expressions and Equations

DIRECTIONS: Choose or write the correct answer.

Strategy Use or sketch visuals to understand and solve a problem.

5. Write the equation for the line shown below.

$y = 3x + 4$

Write how you found the slope of the line.

Possible Answer: I started at the point (−1, 1). I counted up to the point (−1, 4), and then over to the point (0, 4). That gave me a slope of $\frac{3}{1}$, which simplifies to 3.

6. Write the equation for the line shown below.

$y = -2x + 8$

7. Describe the graph below. Use words, numbers, and symbols.

Possible Answer: This is a graph of a linear function. It has a rise of 2 and a run of 1. It has a positive slope and intersects the *y*-axis at the origin. The equation for the line is $y = 2x$.

Math 70 Spectrum Test Prep Grade 8

70

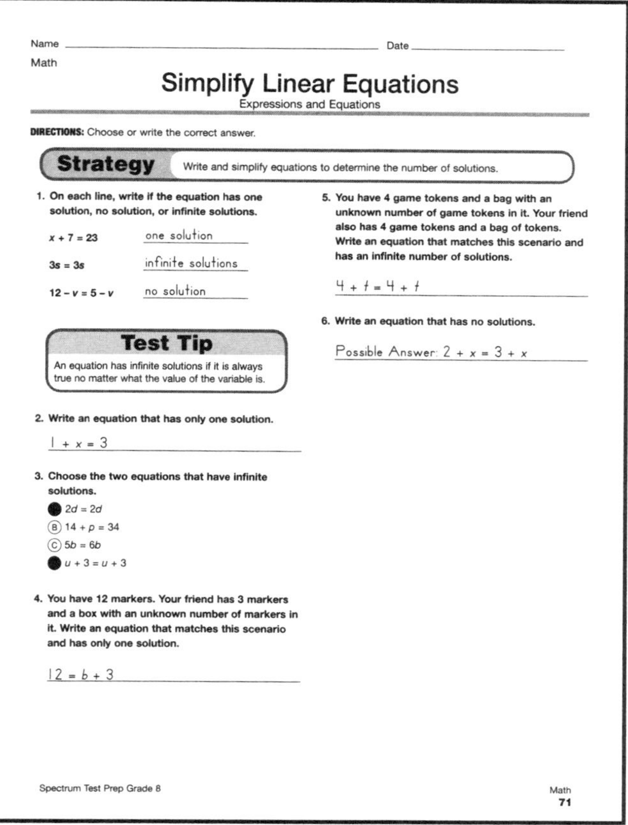

Name ______________________ Date ____________

Math

Simplify Linear Equations

Expressions and Equations

DIRECTIONS: Choose or write the correct answer.

Strategy Write and simplify equations to determine the number of solutions.

1. On each line, write if the equation has one solution, no solution, or infinite solutions.

$x + 7 = 23$ one solution

$3s = 3s$ infinite solutions

$12 - v = 5 - v$ no solution

Test Tip An equation has infinite solutions if it is always true no matter what the value of the variable is.

2. Write an equation that has only one solution.

$1 + x = 3$

3. Choose the two equations that have infinite solutions.

- ● $2d = 2d$
- (B) $14 + p = 34$
- (C) $5b = 6b$
- ● $u + 3 = u + 3$

4. You have 12 markers. Your friend has 3 markers and a box with an unknown number of markers in it. Write an equation that matches this scenario and has only one solution.

$12 = b + 3$

5. You have 4 game tokens and a bag with an unknown number of game tokens in it. Your friend also has 4 game tokens and a bag of tokens. Write an equation that matches this scenario and has an infinite number of solutions.

$4 + t = 4 + t$

6. Write an equation that has no solutions.

Possible Answer: $2 + x = 3 + x$

Spectrum Test Prep Grade 8 Math 71

71

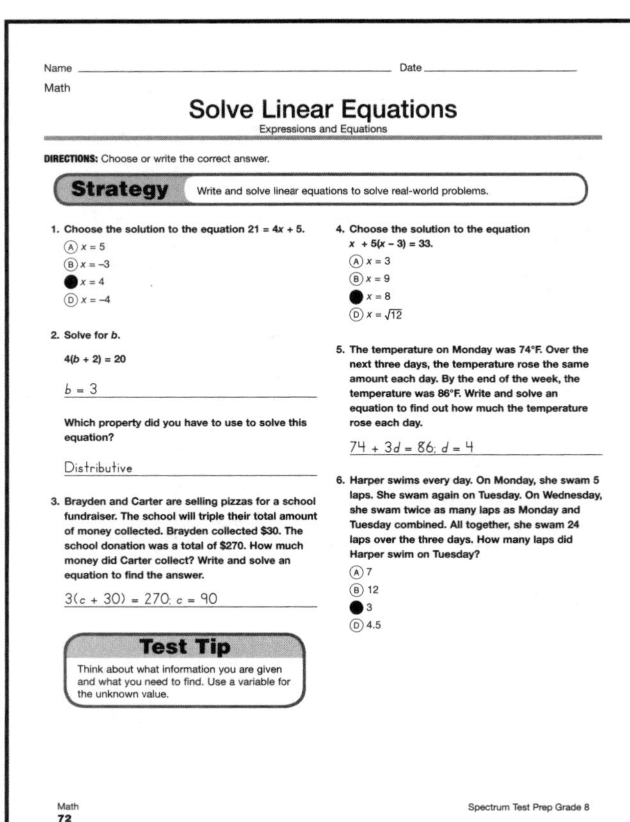
Name ______________________ Date __________

Math

Solve Linear Equations

Expressions and Equations

DIRECTIONS: Choose or write the correct answer.

Strategy Write and solve linear equations to solve real-world problems.

1. Choose the solution to the equation $21 = 4x + 5$.
   - Ⓐ $x = 5$
   - Ⓑ $x = -3$
   - ● $x = 4$
   - Ⓓ $x = -4$

2. Solve for *b*.

   $4(b + 2) = 20$

   $b = 3$

   Which property did you have to use to solve this equation?

   Distributive

3. Brayden and Carter are selling pizzas for a school fundraiser. The school will triple their total amount of money collected. Brayden collected $30. The school donation was a total of $270. How much money did Carter collect? Write and solve an equation to find the answer.

   $3(c + 30) = 270$; $c = 90$

Test Tip Think about what information you are given and what you need to find. Use a variable for the unknown value.

4. Choose the solution to the equation $x + 5(x - 3) = 33$.
   - Ⓐ $x = 3$
   - Ⓑ $x = 9$
   - ● $x = 8$
   - Ⓓ $x = \sqrt{12}$

5. The temperature on Monday was 74°F. Over the next three days, the temperature rose the same amount each day. By the end of the week, the temperature was 86°F. Write and solve an equation to find out how much the temperature rose each day.

   $74 + 3d = 86$; $d = 4$

6. Harper swims every day. On Monday, she swam 5 laps. She swam again on Tuesday. On Wednesday, she swam twice as many laps as Monday and Tuesday combined. All together, she swam 24 laps over the three days. How many laps did Harper swim on Tuesday?
   - Ⓐ 7
   - Ⓑ 12
   - ● 3
   - Ⓓ 4.5

Math 72 Spectrum Test Prep Grade 8

72

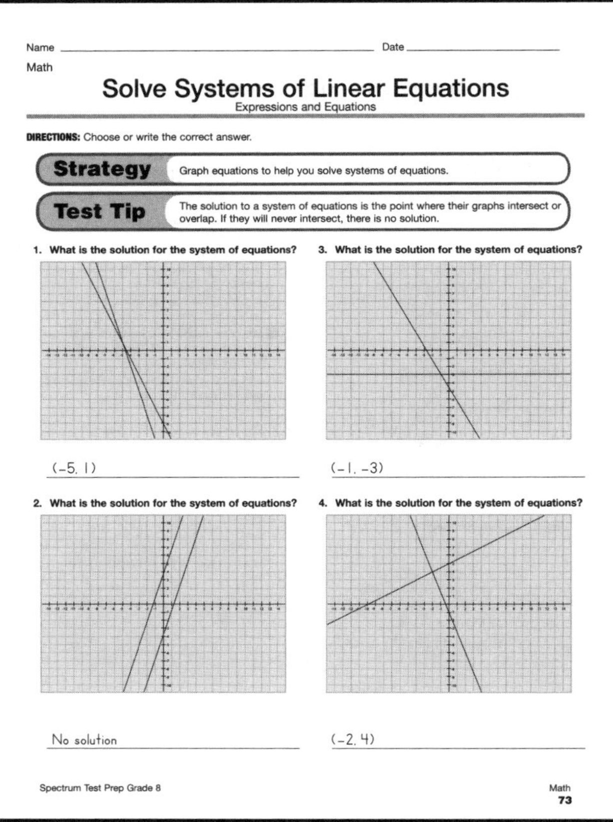
Name ______________________ Date __________

Math

Solve Systems of Linear Equations

Expressions and Equations

DIRECTIONS: Choose or write the correct answer.

Strategy Graph equations to help you solve systems of equations.

Test Tip The solution to a system of equations is the point where their graphs intersect or overlap. If they will never intersect, there is no solution.

1. What is the solution for the system of equations?

   (−5, 1)

2. What is the solution for the system of equations?

   No solution

3. What is the solution for the system of equations?

   (−1, −3)

4. What is the solution for the system of equations?

   (−2, 4)

Spectrum Test Prep Grade 8 Math 73

73

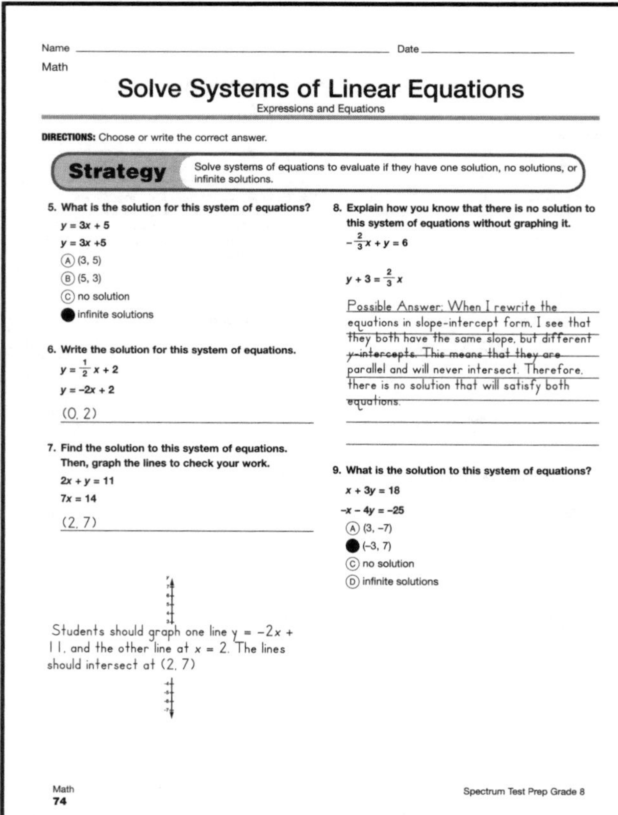
Name ______________________ Date __________

Math

Solve Systems of Linear Equations

Expressions and Equations

DIRECTIONS: Choose or write the correct answer.

Strategy Solve systems of equations to evaluate if they have one solution, no solutions, or infinite solutions.

5. What is the solution for this system of equations?

   $y = 3x + 5$

   $y = 3x + 5$
   - Ⓐ (3, 5)
   - Ⓑ (5, 3)
   - Ⓒ no solution
   - ● infinite solutions

6. Write the solution for this system of equations.

   $y = \frac{1}{2}x + 2$

   $y = -2x + 2$

   (0, 2)

7. Find the solution to this system of equations. Then, graph the lines to check your work.

   $2x + y = 11$

   $7x = 14$

   (2, 7)

   Students should graph one line $y = -2x + 11$, and the other line at $x = 2$. The lines should intersect at (2, 7)

8. Explain how you know that there is no solution to this system of equations without graphing it.

   $-\frac{2}{3}x + y = 6$

   $y + 3 = \frac{2}{3}x$

   Possible Answer: When I rewrite the equations in slope-intercept form, I see that they both have the same slope, but different y-intercepts. This means that they are parallel and will never intersect. Therefore, there is no solution that will satisfy both equations.

9. What is the solution to this system of equations?

   $x + 3y = 18$

   $-x - 4y = -25$
   - Ⓐ (3, −7)
   - ● (−3, 7)
   - Ⓒ no solution
   - Ⓓ infinite solutions

Math 74 Spectrum Test Prep Grade 8

74

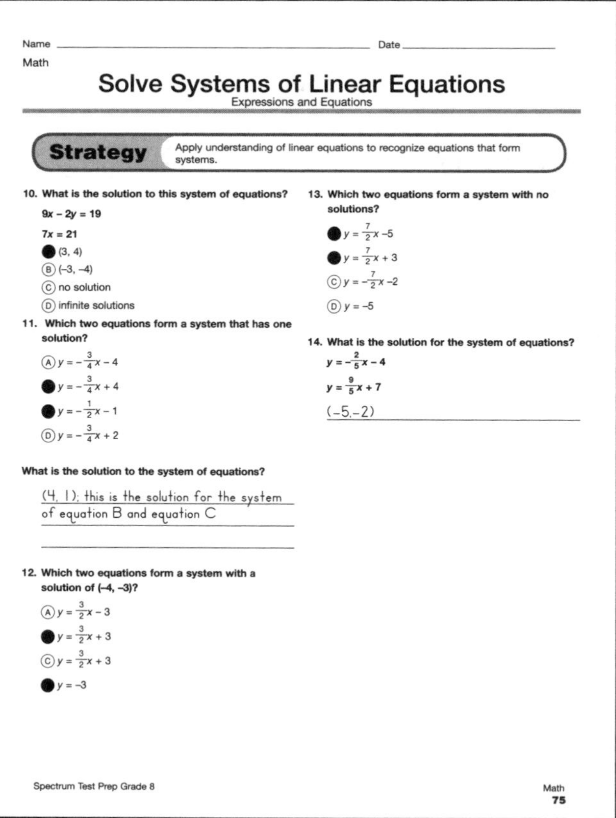
Name ______________________ Date __________

Math

Solve Systems of Linear Equations

Expressions and Equations

Strategy Apply understanding of linear equations to recognize equations that form systems.

10. What is the solution to this system of equations?

    $9x - 2y = 19$

    $7x = 21$
    - ● (3, 4)
    - Ⓑ (−3, −4)
    - Ⓒ no solution
    - Ⓓ infinite solutions

11. Which two equations form a system that has one solution?
    - Ⓐ $y = -\frac{3}{4}x - 4$
    - ● $y = -\frac{3}{4}x + 4$
    - ● $y = -\frac{1}{2}x - 1$
    - Ⓓ $y = -\frac{3}{4}x + 2$

    What is the solution to the system of equations?

    (4, 1); this is the solution for the system of equation B and equation C

12. Which two equations form a system with a solution of (−4, −3)?
    - Ⓐ $y = \frac{3}{2}x - 3$
    - ● $y = \frac{3}{2}x + 3$
    - Ⓒ $y = \frac{3}{2}x + 3$
    - ● $y = -3$

13. Which two equations form a system with no solutions?
    - ● $y = \frac{7}{2}x - 5$
    - ● $y = \frac{7}{2}x + 3$
    - Ⓒ $y = -\frac{7}{2}x - 2$
    - Ⓓ $y = -5$

14. What is the solution for the system of equations?

    $y = -\frac{2}{5}x - 4$

    $y = \frac{9}{5}x + 7$

    (−5, −2)

Spectrum Test Prep Grade 8 Math 75

75

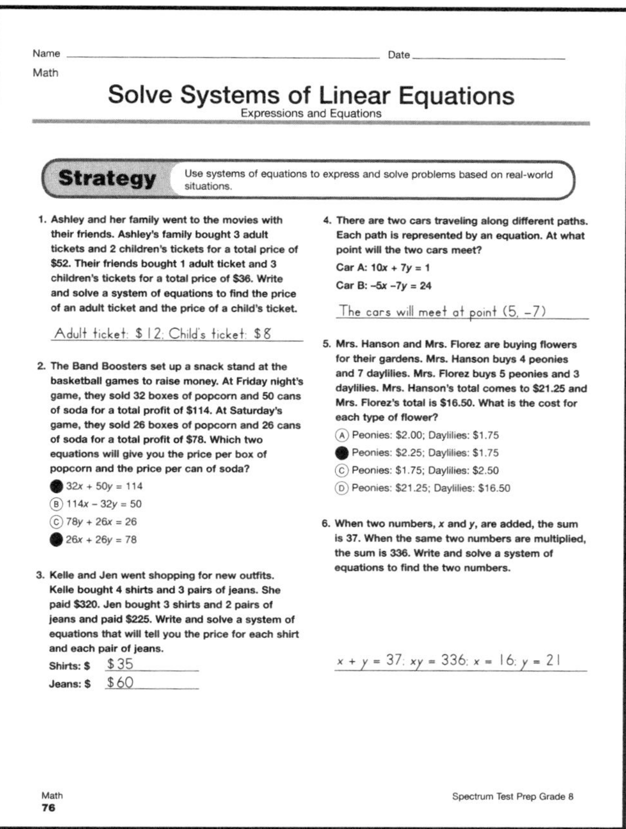

Name ______________________ Date ______________

Math

Solve Systems of Linear Equations

Expressions and Equations

Strategy Use systems of equations to express and solve problems based on real-world situations.

1. Ashley and her family went to the movies with their friends. Ashley's family bought 3 adult tickets and 2 children's tickets for a total price of \$52. Their friends bought 1 adult ticket and 3 children's tickets for a total price of \$36. Write and solve a system of equations to find the price of an adult ticket and the price of a child's ticket.

Adult ticket: \$12; Child's ticket: \$8

2. The Band Boosters set up a snack stand at the basketball games to raise money. At Friday night's game, they sold 32 boxes of popcorn and 50 cans of soda for a total profit of \$114. At Saturday's game, they sold 26 boxes of popcorn and 26 cans of soda for a total profit of \$78. Which two equations will give you the price per box of popcorn and the price per can of soda?

● $32x + 50y = 114$
Ⓑ $114x - 32y = 50$
Ⓒ $78y + 26x = 26$
● $26x + 26y = 78$

3. Kelle and Jen went shopping for new outfits. Kelle bought 4 shirts and 3 pairs of jeans. She paid \$320. Jen bought 3 shirts and 2 pairs of jeans and paid \$225. Write and solve a system of equations that will tell you the price for each shirt and each pair of jeans.

Shirts: \$ 35

Jeans: \$ 60

4. There are two cars traveling along different paths. Each path is represented by an equation. At what point will the two cars meet?

Car A: $10x + 7y = 1$

Car B: $-5x - 7y = 24$

The cars will meet at point (5, −7)

5. Mrs. Hanson and Mrs. Florez are buying flowers for their gardens. Mrs. Hanson buys 4 peonies and 7 daylilies. Mrs. Florez buys 5 peonies and 3 daylilies. Mrs. Hanson's total comes to \$21.25 and Mrs. Florez's total is \$16.50. What is the cost for each type of flower?

Ⓐ Peonies: \$2.00; Daylilies: \$1.75
● Peonies: \$2.25; Daylilies: \$1.75
Ⓒ Peonies: \$1.75; Daylilies: \$2.50
Ⓓ Peonies: \$21.25; Daylilies: \$16.50

6. When two numbers, x and y, are added, the sum is 37. When the same two numbers are multiplied, the sum is 336. Write and solve a system of equations to find the two numbers.

$x + y = 37$; $xy = 336$; $x = 16$; $y = 21$

Math 76 Spectrum Test Prep Grade 8

76

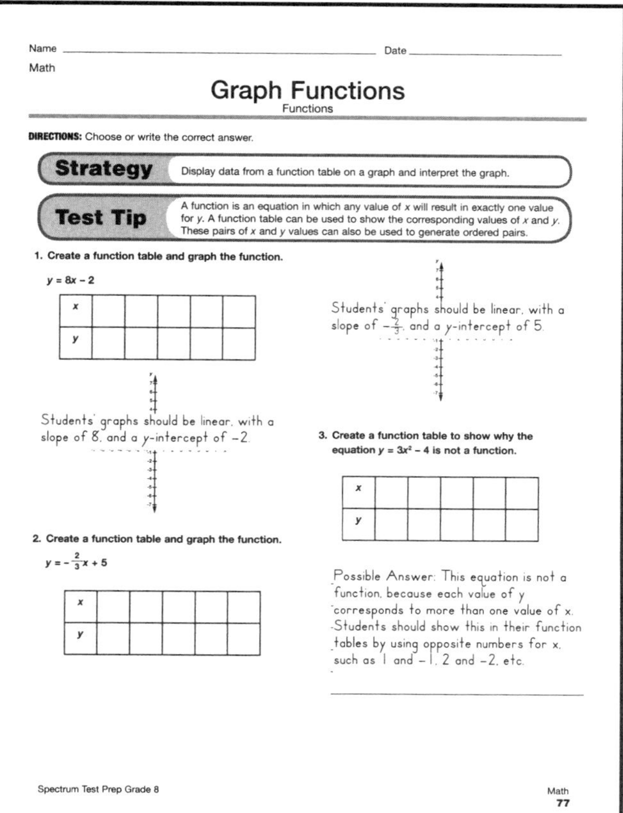

Name ______________________ Date ______________

Math

Graph Functions

Functions

DIRECTIONS: Choose or write the correct answer.

Strategy Display data from a function table on a graph and interpret the graph.

Test Tip A function is an equation in which any value of x will result in exactly one value for y. A function table can be used to show the corresponding values of x and y. These pairs of x and y values can also be used to generate ordered pairs.

1. Create a function table and graph the function.

$y = 8x - 2$

x						
y						

Students' graphs should be linear, with a slope of 8, and a y-intercept of −2.

2. Create a function table and graph the function.

$y = -\frac{2}{3}x + 5$

x						
y						

Students' graphs should be linear, with a slope of $-\frac{2}{3}$, and a y-intercept of 5.

3. Create a function table to show why the equation $y = 3x^2 - 4$ is not a function.

x					
y					

Possible Answer: This equation is not a function, because each value of y corresponds to more than one value of x. Students should show this in their function tables by using opposite numbers for x, such as 1 and −1, 2 and −2, etc.

Spectrum Test Prep Grade 8 Math 77

77

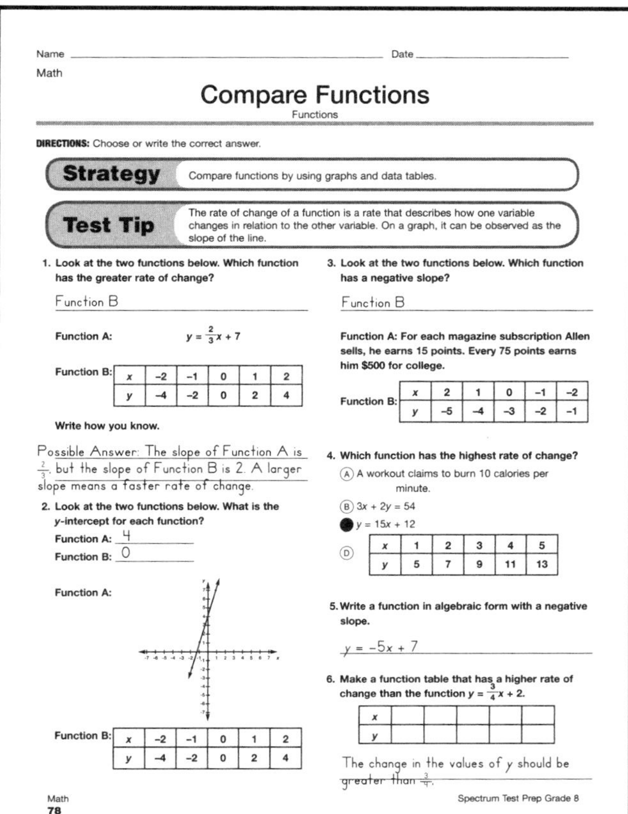

Name ______________________ Date ______________

Math

Compare Functions

Functions

DIRECTIONS: Choose or write the correct answer.

Strategy Compare functions by using graphs and data tables.

Test Tip The rate of change of a function is a rate that describes how one variable changes in relation to the other variable. On a graph, it can be observed as the slope of the line.

1. Look at the two functions below. Which function has the greater rate of change?

Function B

Function A: $y = \frac{2}{3}x + 7$

Function B:

x	−2	−1	0	1	2
y	−4	−2	0	2	4

Write how you know.

Possible Answer: The slope of Function A is $\frac{2}{3}$, but the slope of Function B is 2. A larger slope means a faster rate of change.

2. Look at the two functions below. What is the y-intercept for each function?

Function A: 4

Function B: 0

Function A: [graph]

Function B:

x	−2	−1	0	1	2
y	−4	−2	0	2	4

3. Look at the two functions below. Which function has a negative slope?

Function B

Function A: For each magazine subscription Allen sells, he earns 15 points. Every 75 points earns him \$500 for college.

Function B:

x	2	1	0	−1	−2
y	−5	−4	−3	−2	−1

4. Which function has the highest rate of change?

Ⓐ A workout claims to burn 10 calories per minute.
Ⓑ $3x + 2y = 54$
● $y = 15x + 12$
Ⓓ

x	1	2	3	4	5
y	5	7	9	11	13

5. Write a function in algebraic form with a negative slope.

$y = -5x + 7$

6. Make a function table that has a higher rate of change than the function $y = \frac{3}{4}x + 2$.

x						
y						

The change in the values of y should be greater than $\frac{3}{4}$.

Math 78 Spectrum Test Prep Grade 8

78

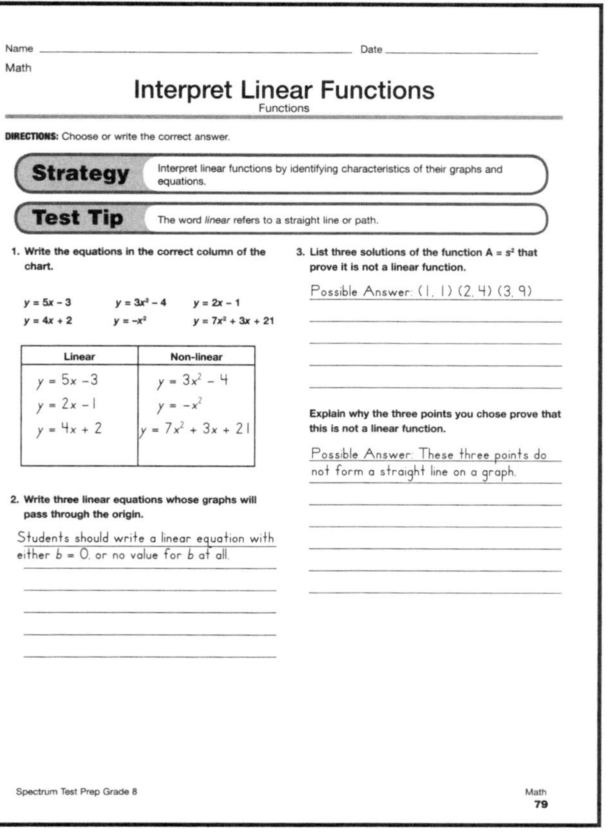

Name ______________________ Date ______________

Math

Interpret Linear Functions

Functions

DIRECTIONS: Choose or write the correct answer.

Strategy Interpret linear functions by identifying characteristics of their graphs and equations.

Test Tip The word *linear* refers to a straight line or path.

1. Write the equations in the correct column of the chart.

$y = 5x - 3$ $y = 3x^2 - 4$ $y = 2x - 1$

$y = 4x + 2$ $y = -x^2$ $y = 7x^2 + 3x + 21$

Linear	Non-linear
$y = 5x - 3$	$y = 3x^2 - 4$
$y = 2x - 1$	$y = -x^2$
$y = 4x + 2$	$y = 7x^2 + 3x + 21$

2. Write three linear equations whose graphs will pass through the origin.

Students should write a linear equation with either $b = 0$, or no value for b at all.

3. List three solutions of the function $A = s^2$ that prove it is not a linear function.

Possible Answer: (1, 1) (2, 4) (3, 9)

Explain why the three points you chose prove that this is not a linear function.

Possible Answer: These three points do not form a straight line on a graph.

Spectrum Test Prep Grade 8 Math 79

79

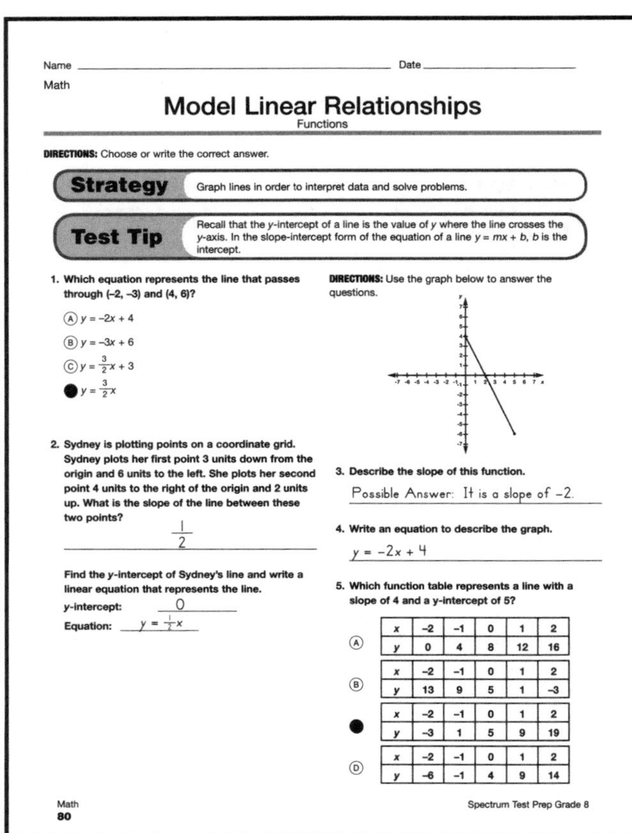

Name ______________________ Date ______________

Math

Model Linear Relationships

Functions

DIRECTIONS: Choose or write the correct answer.

Strategy Graph lines in order to interpret data and solve problems.

Test Tip Recall that the *y*-intercept of a line is the value of *y* where the line crosses the *y*-axis. In the slope-intercept form of the equation of a line $y = mx + b$, *b* is the intercept.

1. Which equation represents the line that passes through (–2, –3) and (4, 6)?

Ⓐ $y = -2x + 4$
Ⓑ $y = -3x + 6$
Ⓒ $y = \frac{3}{2}x + 3$
● $y = \frac{3}{2}x$

2. Sydney is plotting points on a coordinate grid. Sydney plots her first point 3 units down from the origin and 6 units to the left. She plots her second point 4 units to the right of the origin and 2 units up. What is the slope of the line between these two points?

$\frac{1}{2}$

Find the *y*-intercept of Sydney's line and write a linear equation that represents the line.

***y*-intercept:** 0

Equation: $y = \frac{1}{2}x$

DIRECTIONS: Use the graph below to answer the questions.

3. Describe the slope of this function.

Possible Answer: It is a slope of –2.

4. Write an equation to describe the graph.

$y = -2x + 4$

5. Which function table represents a line with a slope of 4 and a y-intercept of 5?

Ⓐ

x	–2	–1	0	1	2
y	0	4	8	12	16

Ⓑ

x	–2	–1	0	1	2
y	13	9	5	1	–3

●

x	–2	–1	0	1	2
y	–3	1	5	9	19

Ⓓ

x	–2	–1	0	1	2
y	–6	–1	4	9	14

Math 80 Spectrum Test Prep Grade 8

80

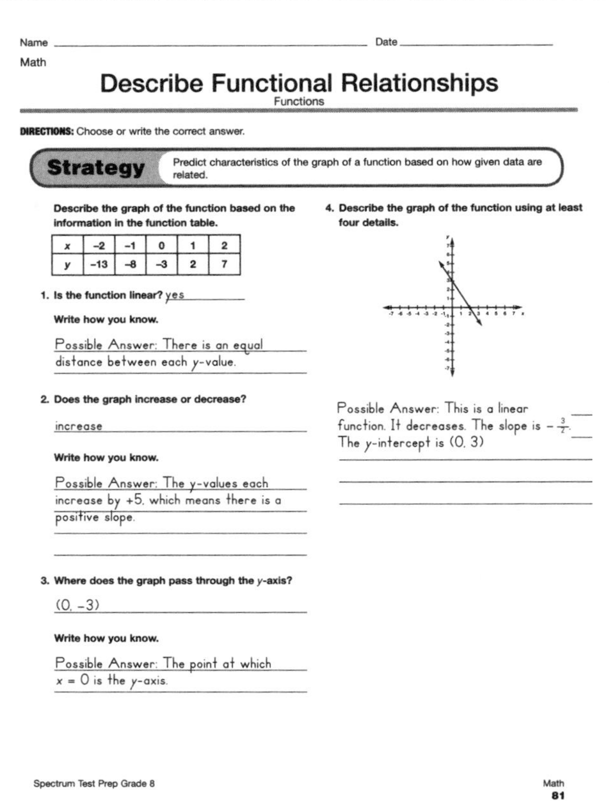

Name ______________________ Date ______________

Math

Describe Functional Relationships

Functions

DIRECTIONS: Choose or write the correct answer.

Strategy Predict characteristics of the graph of a function based on how given data are related.

Describe the graph of the function based on the information in the function table.

x	–2	–1	0	1	2
y	–13	–8	–3	2	7

1. Is the function linear? yes

Write how you know.

Possible Answer: There is an equal distance between each *y*-value.

2. Does the graph increase or decrease?

increase

Write how you know.

Possible Answer: The *y*-values each increase by +5, which means there is a positive slope.

3. Where does the graph pass through the *y*-axis?

(0, –3)

Write how you know.

Possible Answer: The point at which $x = 0$ is the *y*-axis.

4. Describe the graph of the function using at least four details.

Possible Answer: This is a linear function. It decreases. The slope is $-\frac{3}{2}$. The *y*-intercept is (0, 3)

Spectrum Test Prep Grade 8 Math 81

81

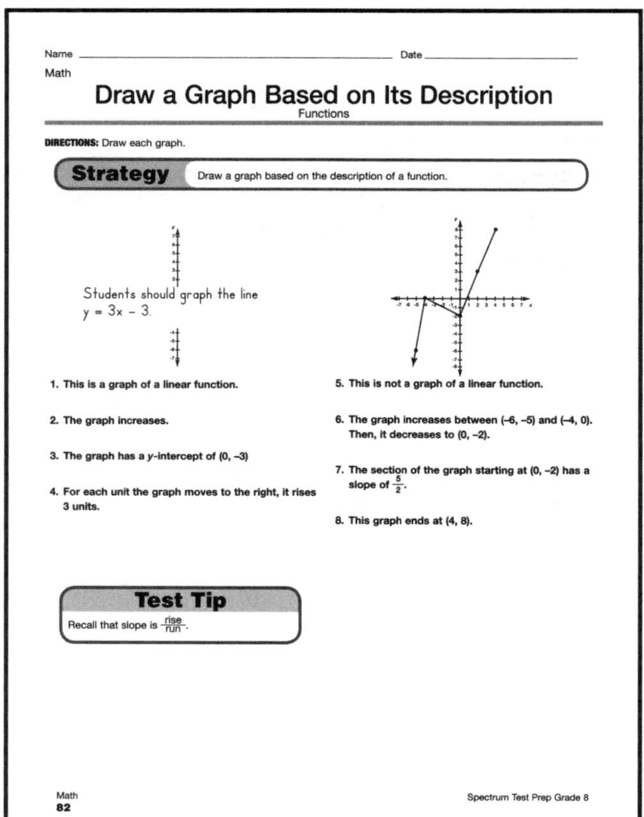

Name ______________________ Date ______________

Math

Draw a Graph Based on Its Description

Functions

DIRECTIONS: Draw each graph.

Strategy Draw a graph based on the description of a function.

Students should graph the line $y = 3x - 3$.

1. This is a graph of a linear function.
2. The graph increases.
3. The graph has a *y*-intercept of (0, –3)
4. For each unit the graph moves to the right, it rises 3 units.
5. This is not a graph of a linear function.
6. The graph increases between (–6, –5) and (–4, 0). Then, it decreases to (0, –2).
7. The section of the graph starting at (0, –2) has a slope of $\frac{5}{2}$.
8. This graph ends at (4, 8).

Test Tip Recall that slope is $\frac{\text{rise}}{\text{run}}$.

Math 82 Spectrum Test Prep Grade 8

82

Name ______________________ Date ______________

Math

Understand Rotations, Reflections, and Translations

Geometry

DIRECTIONS: Choose or write the correct answer.

Strategy Translate, rotate, and reflect figures on the coordinate plane.

Test Tip Rotations, reflections, and translations are all types of transformations that do not change the size of the figure.

1. Parallelogram QRST translated to a new position on the grid as shown. Which moves describe the translation?

● translated 1 right, 4 down
Ⓑ translated 1 right, 5 down
Ⓒ translated 2 right, 4 down
Ⓓ translated 1 right, 3 down

DIRECTIONS: Compare the following images to their transformation images. What type of transformation was performed? Be as specific as possible.

2. Possible Answer: translated 8 left, 2 down

3. Possible Answer: reflected across the *y*-axis

4. Possible Answer: reflected across the *x*-axis

Spectrum Test Prep Grade 8 Math 83

83

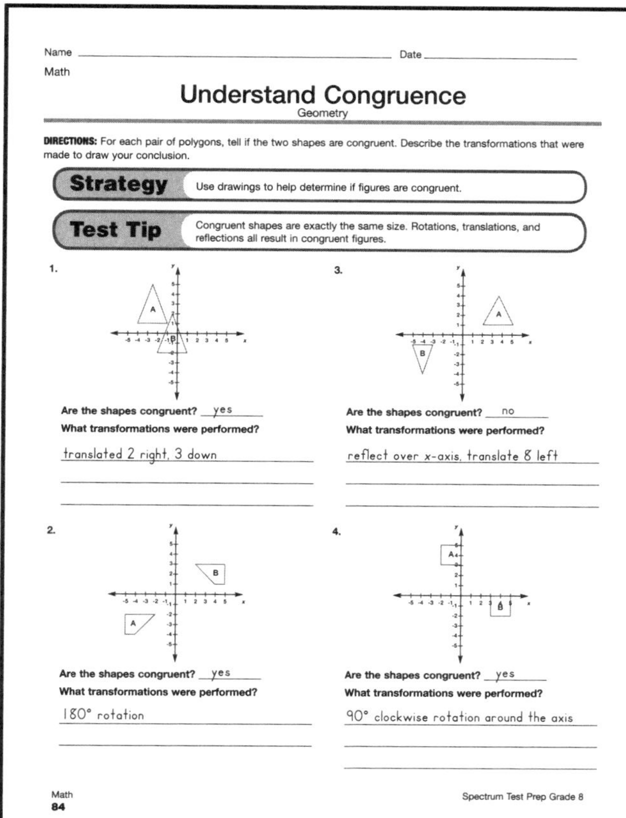

Name ______________________ Date ____________

Math

Understand Congruence

Geometry

DIRECTIONS: For each pair of polygons, tell if the two shapes are congruent. Describe the transformations that were made to draw your conclusion.

Strategy Use drawings to help determine if figures are congruent.

Test Tip Congruent shapes are exactly the same size. Rotations, translations, and reflections all result in congruent figures.

1\.

Are the shapes congruent? yes

What transformations were performed?

translated 2 right, 3 down

2\.

Are the shapes congruent? yes

What transformations were performed?

180° rotation

3\.

Are the shapes congruent? no

What transformations were performed?

reflect over x-axis, translate 8 left

4\.

Are the shapes congruent? yes

What transformations were performed?

90° clockwise rotation around the axis

Math 84 Spectrum Test Prep Grade 8

84

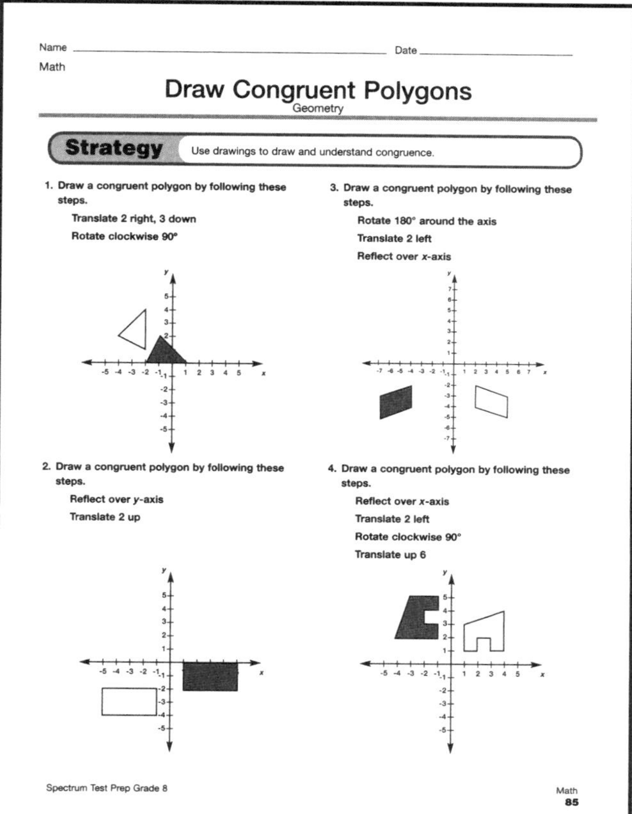

Name ______________________ Date ____________

Math

Draw Congruent Polygons

Geometry

Strategy Use drawings to draw and understand congruence.

1. Draw a congruent polygon by following these steps.

Translate 2 right, 3 down

Rotate clockwise 90°

2. Draw a congruent polygon by following these steps.

Reflect over *y*-axis

Translate 2 up

3. Draw a congruent polygon by following these steps.

Rotate 180° around the axis

Translate 2 left

Reflect over *x*-axis

4. Draw a congruent polygon by following these steps.

Reflect over *x*-axis

Translate 2 left

Rotate clockwise 90°

Translate up 6

Spectrum Test Prep Grade 8 Math 85

85

Name ______________________ Date ____________

Math

Use Coordinates to Describe Transformations

Geometry

DIRECTIONS: Choose or write the correct answer.

Strategy Transform figures by graphing the original figures and their transformations on a coordinate grid

Test Tip A dilation is a type of transformation that changes the size of the figure. A dilation can make a figure smaller or larger. If a figure is dilated, it is similar but no longer congruent to the original figure.

1\.

Write the coordinates for each point if the shape is reflected across the *x*-axis.

A' (−2, −4)

B' (−2, −2)

C' (3, −2)

D' (3, −4)

2\.

Write the coordinates for each point if the shape is dilated by a factor of 3.

A' (0, 12)

B' (0, 0)

C' (9, 0)

3. A triangle has the points A (−2, 1), B (2, 3), and C (4, 1). Write the coordinates for each point if the shape is dilated by a factor of $\frac{1}{2}$.

A' $-1, \frac{1}{2}$

B' $1, 1\frac{1}{2}$

C' $2, \frac{1}{2}$

Math 86 Spectrum Test Prep Grade 8

86

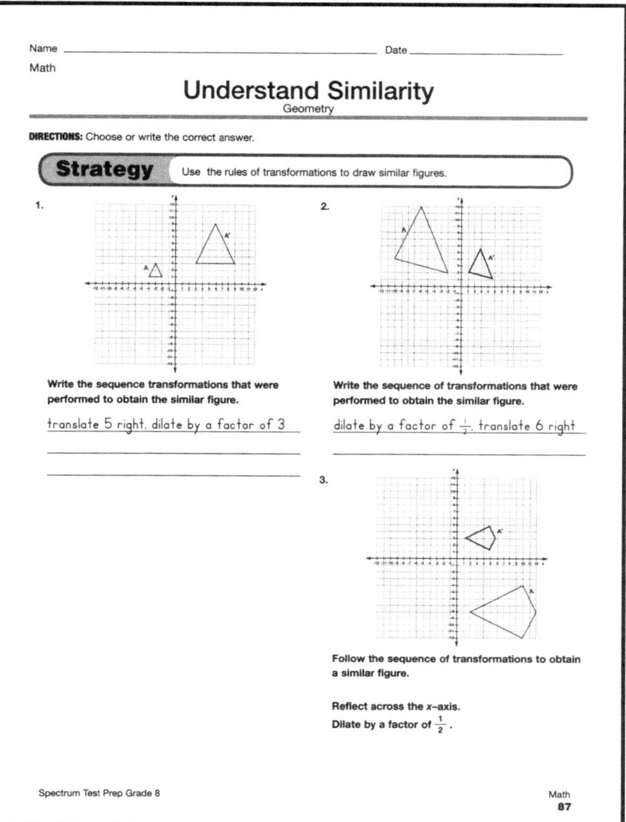

Name ______________________ Date ____________

Math

Understand Similarity

Geometry

DIRECTIONS: Choose or write the correct answer.

Strategy Use the rules of transformations to draw similar figures.

1\.

Write the sequence transformations that were performed to obtain the similar figure.

translate 5 right, dilate by a factor of 3

2\.

Write the sequence of transformations that were performed to obtain the similar figure.

dilate by a factor of $\frac{1}{2}$, translate 6 right

3\.

Follow the sequence of transformations to obtain a similar figure.

Reflect across the *x*-axis.

Dilate by a factor of $\frac{1}{2}$.

Spectrum Test Prep Grade 8 Math 87

87

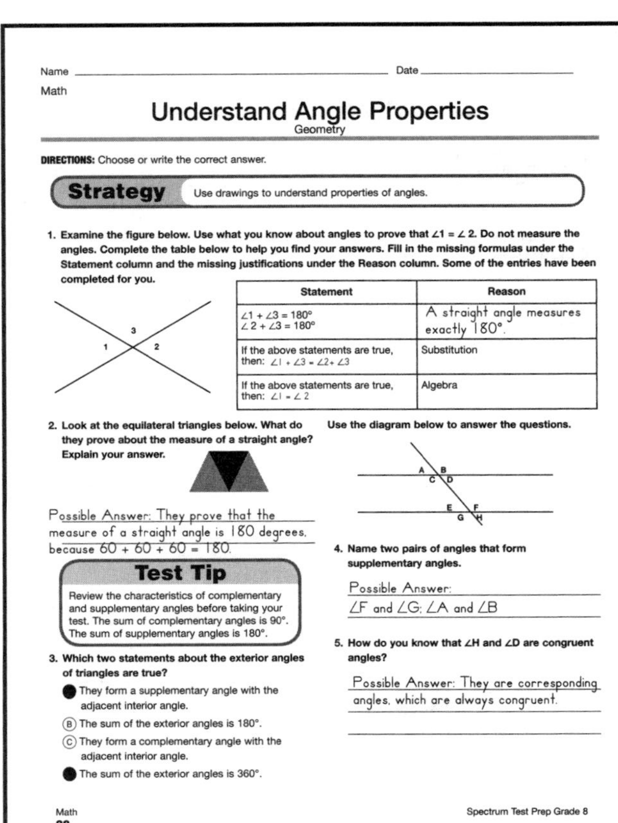

Name ______________________ Date ____________

Math

Understand Angle Properties

Geometry

DIRECTIONS: Choose or write the correct answer.

Strategy Use drawings to understand properties of angles.

1. Examine the figure below. Use what you know about angles to prove that ∠1 = ∠ 2. Do not measure the angles. Complete the table below to help you find your answers. Fill in the missing formulas under the Statement column and the missing justifications under the Reason column. Some of the entries have been completed for you.

Statement	Reason
∠1 + ∠3 = 180° ∠2 + ∠3 = 180°	A straight angle measures exactly 180°.
If the above statements are true, then: ∠1 + ∠3 = ∠2 + ∠3	Substitution
If the above statements are true, then: ∠1 = ∠2	Algebra

2. Look at the equilateral triangles below. What do they prove about the measure of a straight angle? Explain your answer.

Possible Answer: They prove that the measure of a straight angle is 180 degrees, because 60 + 60 + 60 = 180.

Test Tip

Review the characteristics of complementary and supplementary angles before taking your test. The sum of complementary angles is 90°. The sum of supplementary angles is 180°.

3. Which two statements about the exterior angles of triangles are true?

● They form a supplementary angle with the adjacent interior angle.

Ⓑ The sum of the exterior angles is 180°.

Ⓒ They form a complementary angle with the adjacent interior angle.

● The sum of the exterior angles is 360°.

Use the diagram below to answer the questions.

4. Name two pairs of angles that form supplementary angles.

Possible Answer: ∠F and ∠G; ∠A and ∠B

5. How do you know that ∠H and ∠D are congruent angles?

Possible Answer: They are corresponding angles, which are always congruent.

Math 88 Spectrum Test Prep Grade 8

88

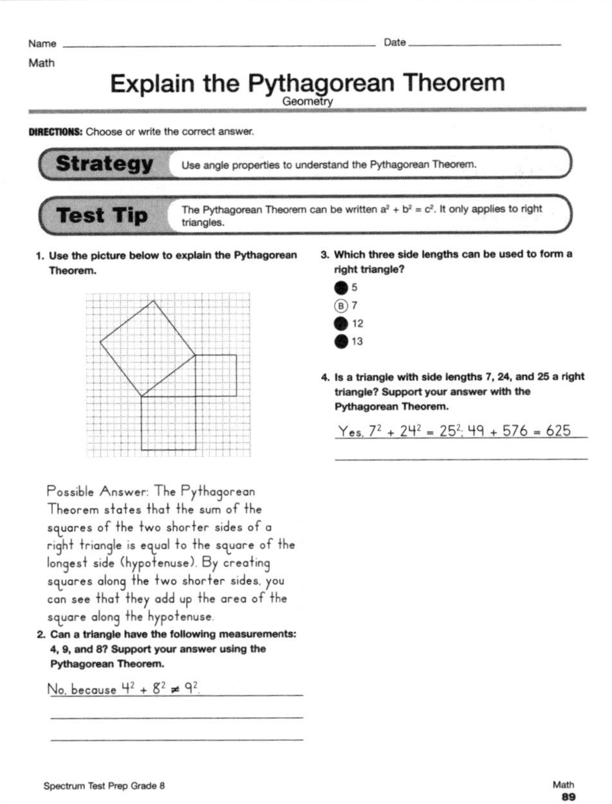

Name ______________________ Date ____________

Math

Explain the Pythagorean Theorem

Geometry

DIRECTIONS: Choose or write the correct answer.

Strategy Use angle properties to understand the Pythagorean Theorem.

Test Tip The Pythagorean Theorem can be written $a^2 + b^2 = c^2$. It only applies to right triangles.

1. Use the picture below to explain the Pythagorean Theorem.

Possible Answer: The Pythagorean Theorem states that the sum of the squares of the two shorter sides of a right triangle is equal to the square of the longest side (hypotenuse). By creating squares along the two shorter sides, you can see that they add up the area of the square along the hypotenuse.

2. Can a triangle have the following measurements: 4, 9, and 8? Support your answer using the Pythagorean Theorem.

No, because $4^2 + 8^2 \neq 9^2$.

3. Which three side lengths can be used to form a right triangle?

● 5

Ⓑ 7

● 12

● 13

4. Is a triangle with side lengths 7, 24, and 25 a right triangle? Support your answer with the Pythagorean Theorem.

Yes, $7^2 + 24^2 = 25^2$; $49 + 576 = 625$

Spectrum Test Prep Grade 8 Math 89

89

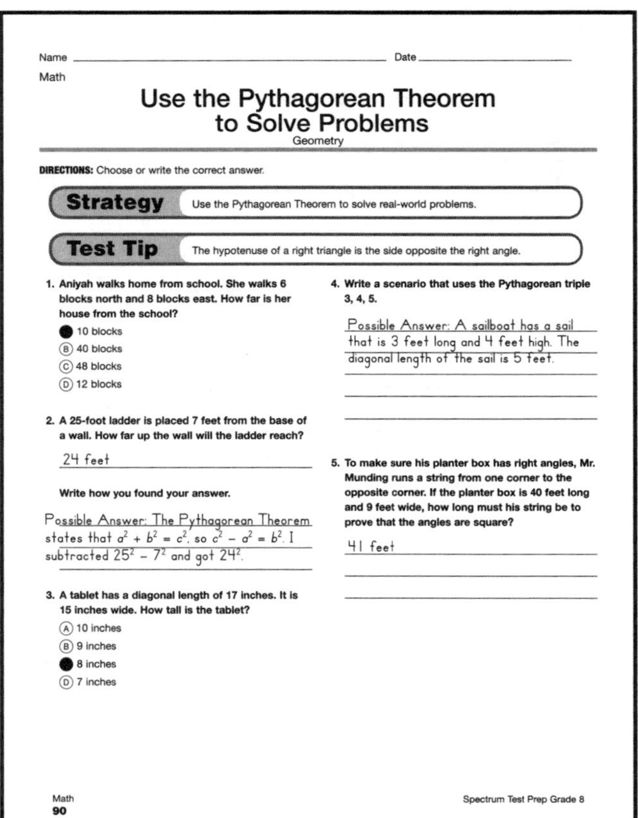

Name ______________________ Date ____________

Math

Use the Pythagorean Theorem to Solve Problems

Geometry

DIRECTIONS: Choose or write the correct answer.

Strategy Use the Pythagorean Theorem to solve real-world problems.

Test Tip The hypotenuse of a right triangle is the side opposite the right angle.

1. Aniyah walks home from school. She walks 6 blocks north and 8 blocks east. How far is her house from the school?

● 10 blocks

Ⓑ 40 blocks

Ⓒ 48 blocks

Ⓓ 12 blocks

2. A 25-foot ladder is placed 7 feet from the base of a wall. How far up the wall will the ladder reach?

24 feet

Write how you found your answer.

Possible Answer: The Pythagorean Theorem states that $a^2 + b^2 = c^2$, so $c^2 - a^2 = b^2$. I subtracted $25^2 - 7^2$ and got 24^2.

3. A tablet has a diagonal length of 17 inches. It is 15 inches wide. How tall is the tablet?

Ⓐ 10 inches

Ⓑ 9 inches

● 8 inches

Ⓓ 7 inches

4. Write a scenario that uses the Pythagorean triple 3, 4, 5.

Possible Answer: A sailboat has a sail that is 3 feet long and 4 feet high. The diagonal length of the sail is 5 feet.

5. To make sure his planter box has right angles, Mr. Munding runs a string from one corner to the opposite corner. If the planter box is 40 feet long and 9 feet wide, how long must his string be to prove that the angles are square?

41 feet

Math 90 Spectrum Test Prep Grade 8

90

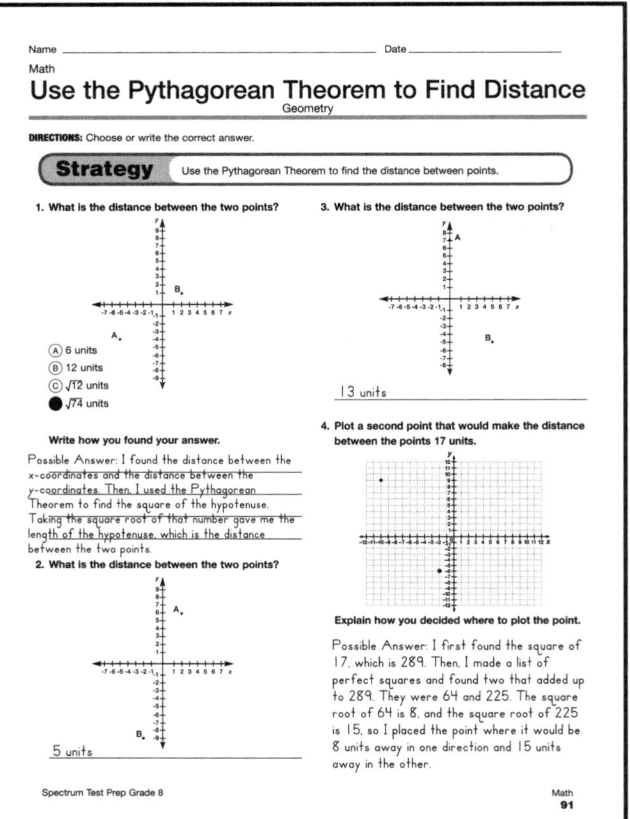

Name ______________________ Date ____________

Math

Use the Pythagorean Theorem to Find Distance

Geometry

DIRECTIONS: Choose or write the correct answer.

Strategy Use the Pythagorean Theorem to find the distance between points.

1. What is the distance between the two points?

Ⓐ 6 units

Ⓑ 12 units

Ⓒ $\sqrt{12}$ units

● $\sqrt{74}$ units

Write how you found your answer.

Possible Answer: I found the distance between the x-coordinates and the distance between the y-coordinates. Then, I used the Pythagorean Theorem to find the square of the hypotenuse. Taking the square root of that number gave me the length of the hypotenuse, which is the distance between the two points.

2. What is the distance between the two points?

5 units

3. What is the distance between the two points?

13 units

4. Plot a second point that would make the distance between the points 17 units.

Explain how you decided where to plot the point.

Possible Answer: I first found the square of 17, which is 289. Then, I made a list of perfect squares and found two that added up to 289. They were 64 and 225. The square root of 64 is 8, and the square root of 225 is 15, so I placed the point where it would be 8 units away in one direction and 15 units away in the other.

Spectrum Test Prep Grade 8 Math 91

91

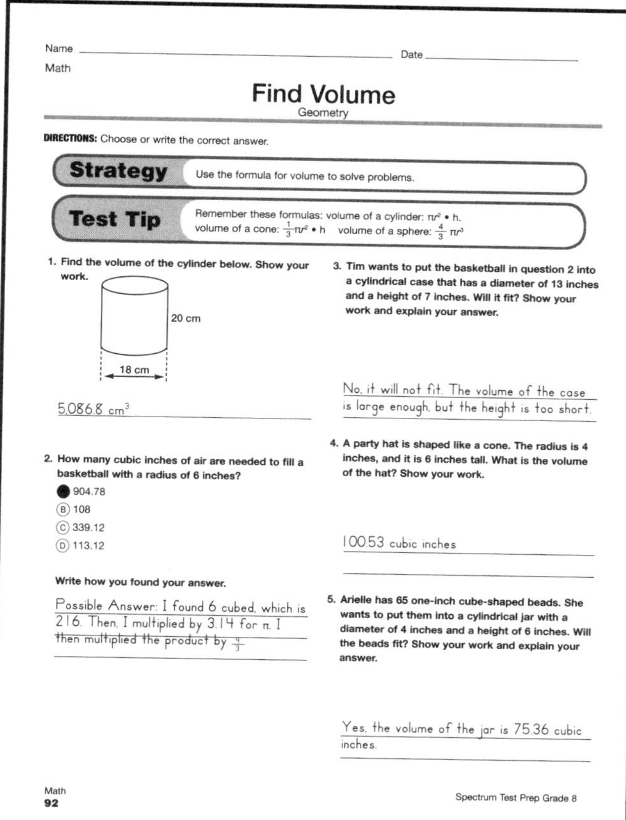

Name ______________________ Date __________

Math

Find Volume

Geometry

DIRECTIONS: Choose or write the correct answer.

Strategy Use the formula for volume to solve problems.

Test Tip Remember these formulas: volume of a cylinder: $\pi r^2 \bullet h$. volume of a cone: $\frac{1}{3}\pi r^2 \bullet h$ volume of a sphere: $\frac{4}{3}\pi r^3$

1. Find the volume of the cylinder below. Show your work.

20 cm
18 cm

$5{,}086.8$ cm³

2. How many cubic inches of air are needed to fill a basketball with a radius of 6 inches?

● 904.78
Ⓑ 108
Ⓒ 339.12
Ⓓ 113.12

Write how you found your answer.

Possible Answer: I found 6 cubed, which is 216. Then, I multiplied by 3.14 for π. I then multiplied the product by $\frac{4}{3}$.

3. Tim wants to put the basketball in question 2 into a cylindrical case that has a diameter of 13 inches and a height of 7 inches. Will it fit? Show your work and explain your answer.

No, it will not fit. The volume of the case is large enough, but the height is too short.

4. A party hat is shaped like a cone. The radius is 4 inches, and it is 6 inches tall. What is the volume of the hat? Show your work.

100.53 cubic inches

5. Arielle has 65 one-inch cube-shaped beads. She wants to put them into a cylindrical jar with a diameter of 4 inches and a height of 6 inches. Will the beads fit? Show your work and explain your answer.

Yes, the volume of the jar is 75.36 cubic inches.

Math 92 — Spectrum Test Prep Grade 8

92

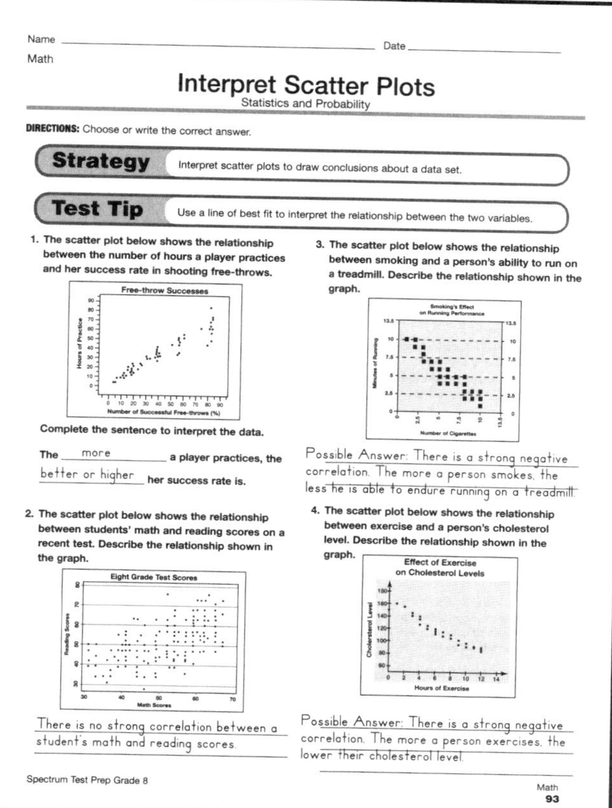

Name ______________________ Date __________

Math

Interpret Scatter Plots

Statistics and Probability

DIRECTIONS: Choose or write the correct answer.

Strategy Interpret scatter plots to draw conclusions about a data set.

Test Tip Use a line of best fit to interpret the relationship between the two variables.

1. The scatter plot below shows the relationship between the number of hours a player practices and her success rate in shooting free-throws.

Complete the sentence to interpret the data.

The __more__ a player practices, the __better or higher__ her success rate is.

2. The scatter plot below shows the relationship between students' math and reading scores on a recent test. Describe the relationship shown in the graph.

There is no strong correlation between a student's math and reading scores.

3. The scatter plot below shows the relationship between smoking and a person's ability to run on a treadmill. Describe the relationship shown in the graph.

Possible Answer: There is a strong negative correlation. The more a person smokes, the less he is able to endure running on a treadmill.

4. The scatter plot below shows the relationship between exercise and a person's cholesterol level. Describe the relationship shown in the graph.

Possible Answer: There is a strong negative correlation. The more a person exercises, the lower their cholesterol level.

Spectrum Test Prep Grade 8 — Math 93

93

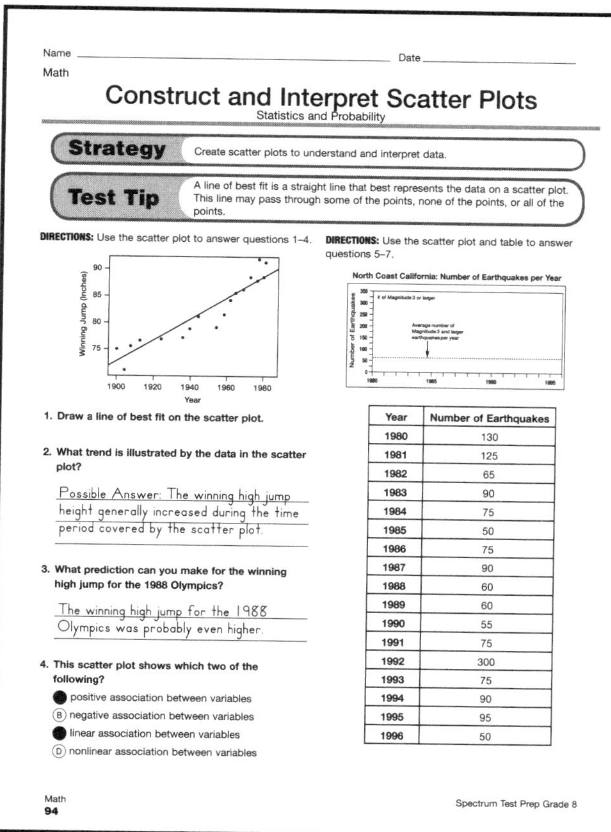

Name ______________________ Date __________

Math

Construct and Interpret Scatter Plots

Statistics and Probability

Strategy Create scatter plots to understand and interpret data.

Test Tip A line of best fit is a straight line that best represents the data on a scatter plot. This line may pass through some of the points, none of the points, or all of the points.

DIRECTIONS: Use the scatter plot to answer questions 1–4.

1. Draw a line of best fit on the scatter plot.

2. What trend is illustrated by the data in the scatter plot?

Possible Answer: The winning high jump height generally increased during the time period covered by the scatter plot.

3. What prediction can you make for the winning high jump for the 1988 Olympics?

The winning high jump for the 1988 Olympics was probably even higher.

4. This scatter plot shows which two of the following?

● positive association between variables
Ⓑ negative association between variables
● linear association between variables
Ⓓ nonlinear association between variables

DIRECTIONS: Use the scatter plot and table to answer questions 5–7.

North Coast California: Number of Earthquakes per Year

Year	Number of Earthquakes
1980	130
1981	125
1982	65
1983	90
1984	75
1985	50
1986	75
1987	90
1988	60
1989	60
1990	55
1991	75
1992	300
1993	75
1994	90
1995	95
1996	50

Math 94 — Spectrum Test Prep Grade 8

94

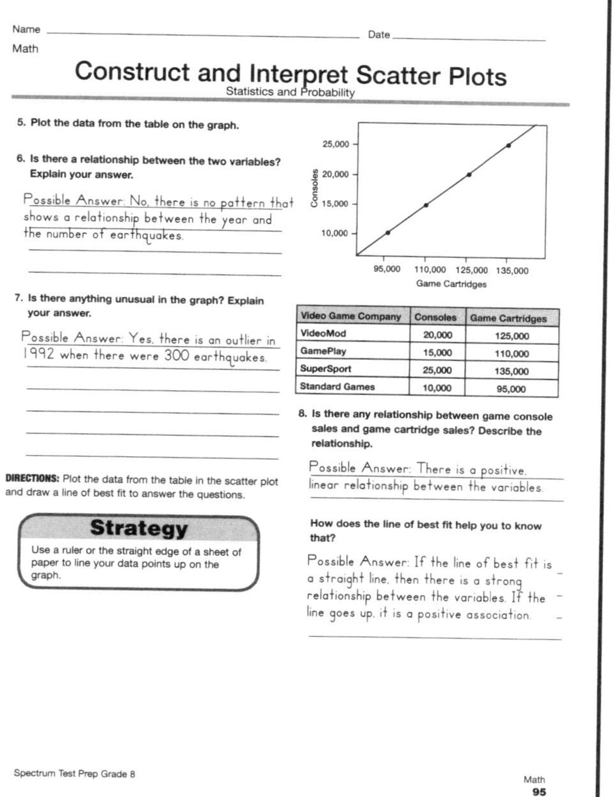

Name ______________________ Date __________

Math

Construct and Interpret Scatter Plots

Statistics and Probability

5. Plot the data from the table on the graph.

6. Is there a relationship between the two variables? Explain your answer.

Possible Answer: No, there is no pattern that shows a relationship between the year and the number of earthquakes.

7. Is there anything unusual in the graph? Explain your answer.

Possible Answer: Yes, there is an outlier in 1992 when there were 300 earthquakes.

DIRECTIONS: Plot the data from the table in the scatter plot and draw a line of best fit to answer the questions.

Strategy Use a ruler or the straight edge of a sheet of paper to line your data points up on the graph.

Video Game Company	Consoles	Game Cartridges
VideoMod	20,000	125,000
GamePlay	15,000	110,000
SuperSport	25,000	135,000
Standard Games	10,000	95,000

8. Is there any relationship between game console sales and game cartridge sales? Describe the relationship.

Possible Answer: There is a positive, linear relationship between the variables.

How does the line of best fit help you to know that?

Possible Answer: If the line of best fit is a straight line, then there is a strong relationship between the variables. If the line goes up, it is a positive association.

Spectrum Test Prep Grade 8 — Math 95

95

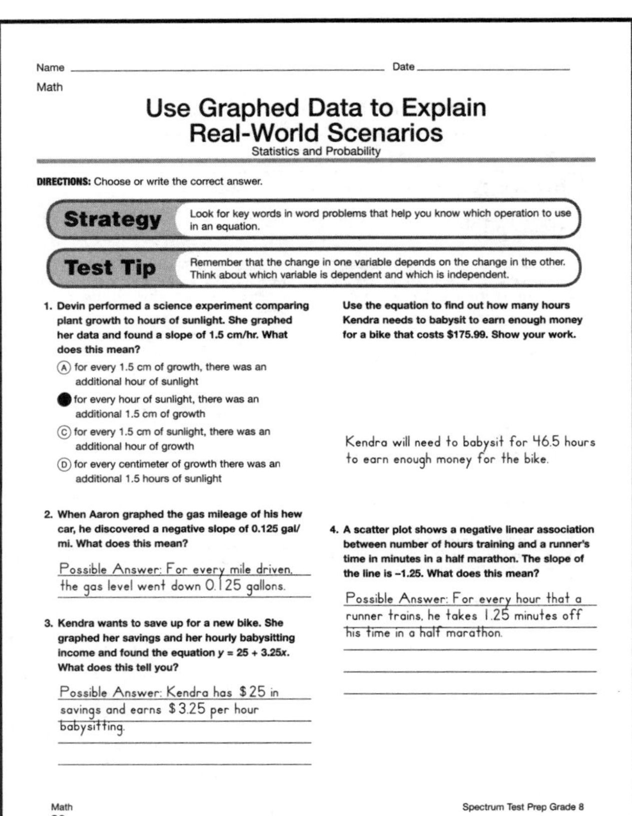

Name ______________________ Date __________

Math

Use Graphed Data to Explain Real-World Scenarios

Statistics and Probability

DIRECTIONS: Choose or write the correct answer.

Strategy Look for key words in word problems that help you know which operation to use in an equation.

Test Tip Remember that the change in one variable depends on the change in the other. Think about which variable is dependent and which is independent.

1. Devin performed a science experiment comparing plant growth to hours of sunlight. She graphed her data and found a slope of 1.5 cm/hr. What does this mean?

Ⓐ for every 1.5 cm of growth, there was an additional hour of sunlight

● for every hour of sunlight, there was an additional 1.5 cm of growth

Ⓒ for every 1.5 cm of growth, there was an additional hour of growth

Ⓓ for every centimeter of growth there was an additional 1.5 hours of sunlight

2. When Aaron graphed the gas mileage of his new car, he discovered a negative slope of 0.125 gal/mi. What does this mean?

Possible Answer: For every mile driven, the gas level went down 0.125 gallons.

3. Kendra wants to save up for a new bike. She graphed her savings and her hourly babysitting income and found the equation $y = 25 + 3.25x$. What does this tell you?

Possible Answer: Kendra has $25 in savings and earns $3.25 per hour babysitting.

Use the equation to find out how many hours Kendra needs to babysit to earn enough money for a bike that costs $175.99. Show your work.

Kendra will need to babysit for 46.5 hours to earn enough money for the bike.

4. A scatter plot shows a negative linear association between number of hours training and a runner's time in minutes in a half marathon. The slope of the line is –1.25. What does this mean?

Possible Answer: For every hour that a runner trains, he takes 1.25 minutes off his time in a half marathon.

Math 96 Spectrum Test Prep Grade 8

96

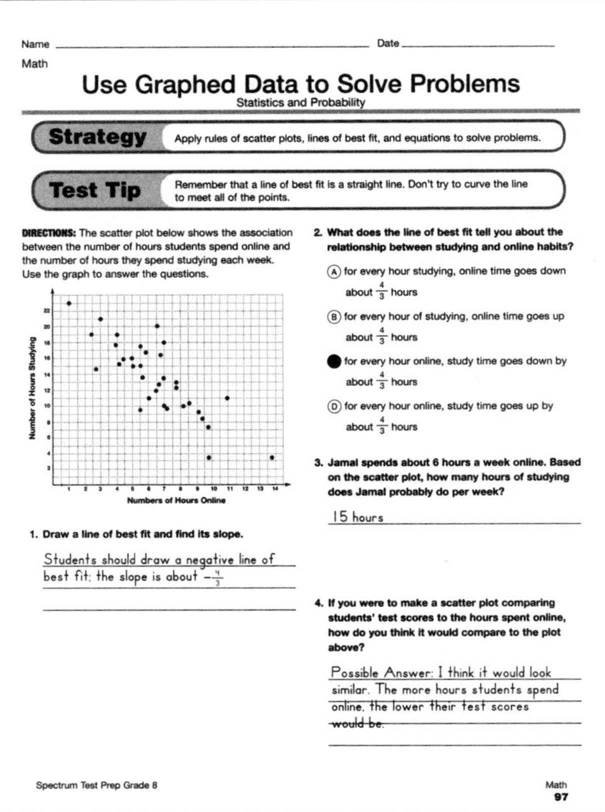

Name ______________________ Date __________

Math

Use Graphed Data to Solve Problems

Statistics and Probability

Strategy Apply rules of scatter plots, lines of best fit, and equations to solve problems.

Test Tip Remember that a line of best fit is a straight line. Don't try to curve the line to meet all of the points.

DIRECTIONS: The scatter plot below shows the association between the number of hours students spend online and the number of hours they spend studying each week. Use the graph to answer the questions.

1. Draw a line of best fit and find its slope.

Students should draw a negative line of best fit; the slope is about $-\frac{4}{3}$

2. What does the line of best fit tell you about the relationship between studying and online habits?

Ⓐ for every hour studying, online time goes down about $\frac{4}{3}$ hours

Ⓑ for every hour of studying, online time goes up about $\frac{4}{3}$ hours

● for every hour online, study time goes down by about $\frac{4}{3}$ hours

Ⓓ for every hour online, study time goes up by about $\frac{4}{3}$ hours

3. Jamal spends about 6 hours a week online. Based on the scatter plot, how many hours of studying does Jamal probably do per week?

15 hours

4. If you were to make a scatter plot comparing students' test scores to the hours spent online, how do you think it would compare to the plot above?

Possible Answer: I think it would look similar. The more hours students spend online, the lower their test scores ~~would be.~~

Spectrum Test Prep Grade 8 Math 97

97

Name ______________________ Date __________

Math

Interpret Bivariate Frequency Tables

Statistics and Probability

Strategy Organize and display data in frequency tables in order to interpret it.

Test Tip When answering the questions, decide whether the tally chart or the frequency table is going to give you the best information.

DIRECTIONS: Mrs. Weinstein asked her students if they play a sport or a musical instrument. She collected the data below. Use the data to answer the questions.

Student	1	2	3	4	5	6	7	8	9	10	11	12	13	14	15	16	17	18	19	20	21	22	23	24	25
Sport	X				X				X		X		X		X	X	X			X		X			X
Instrument	X	X			X		X		X		X		X		X		X	X		X		X		X	

1. Use the data to create a frequency table.

Students' tables should have a title such as "Students Extra-Curricular Activities"; they should be labeled with Sports and Musical Instrument. They should have 11 sports and 13 instruments.

2. Of the students who play a sport, what ratio also plays a musical instrument?

Possible Answer: $\frac{9}{11}$

3. Of the students who do not play a sport, what ratio also plays a musical instrument?

$\frac{4}{14}$

4. Based on this data, what correlation do you see between playing a sport and playing a musical instrument?

Possible Answer: Students who play a sport or a musical instrument often do the other as well. Students who do not ~~participate in either sports or music usually do not participate in the other~~ either.

Math 98 Spectrum Test Prep Grade 8

98

Name ______________________ Date __________

Math

Interpret Bivariate Frequency Tables

Statistics and Probability

Strategy Double check to make sure the numbers in your frequency table match the number of tallies in the tally chart.

DIRECTIONS: Eighth graders in one class were asked if they had chores or a curfew. Use the data to answer the questions.

Student	1	2	3	4	5	6	7	8	9	10	11	12	13	14	15	16	17	18	19	20	21	22	23	24	25
Curfew	X			X	X			X	X		X		X		X	X	X		X	X	X	X		X	X
Chores	X	X		X	X		X		X		X	X	X		X		X	X	X	X	X	X		X	

5. Use the data to create a frequency table.

Students' tables should have a title such as "Students With Curfews and Chores"; they should be labeled with Curfew and Chores. They should have 16 curfews and 17 chores.

6. Of students who have curfews, what ratio also has chores?

Ⓐ $\frac{16}{25}$

Ⓑ $\frac{16}{17}$

● $\frac{13}{16}$

Ⓓ $\frac{13}{17}$

7. Of students who do not have curfews, what ratio has chores?

$\frac{4}{9}$

8. What correlation can you make between having a curfew and having chores?

Possible Answer: Most students $\frac{13}{17}$ who have a curfew also have chores.

Spectrum Test Prep Grade 8 Math 99

99

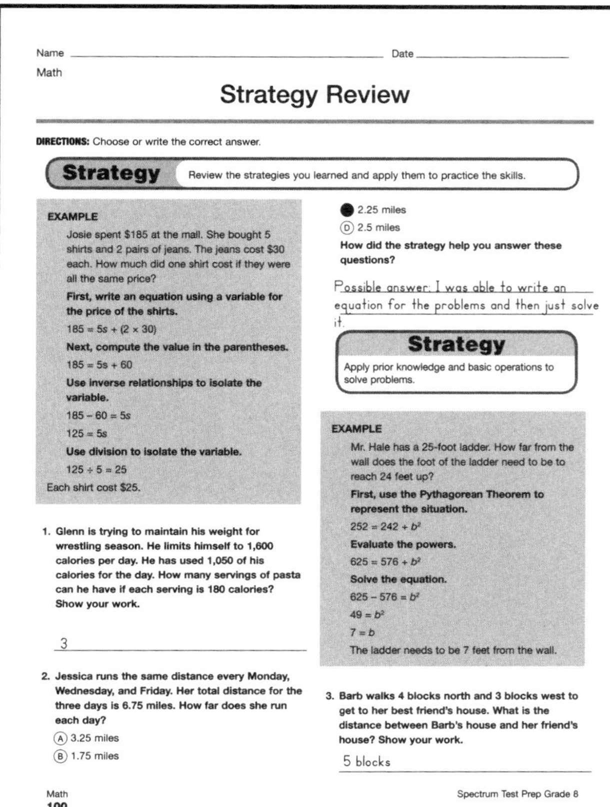

Name ______________________ Date ______________

Math

Strategy Review

DIRECTIONS: Choose or write the correct answer.

Strategy Review the strategies you learned and apply them to practice the skills.

EXAMPLE

Josie spent $185 at the mall. She bought 5 shirts and 2 pairs of jeans. The jeans cost $30 each. How much did one shirt cost if they were all the same price?

First, write an equation using a variable for the price of the shirts.

$185 = 5s + (2 \times 30)$

Next, compute the value in the parentheses.

$185 = 5s + 60$

Use inverse relationships to isolate the variable.

$185 - 60 = 5s$

$125 = 5s$

Use division to isolate the variable.

$125 \div 5 = 25$

Each shirt cost $25.

1. **Glenn is trying to maintain his weight for wrestling season. He limits himself to 1,600 calories per day. He has used 1,050 of his calories for the day. How many servings of pasta can he have if each serving is 180 calories? Show your work.**

   3

2. **Jessica runs the same distance every Monday, Wednesday, and Friday. Her total distance for the three days is 6.75 miles. How far does she run each day?**
   - Ⓐ 3.25 miles
   - Ⓑ 1.75 miles
   - ● 2.25 miles
   - Ⓓ 2.5 miles

How did the strategy help you answer these questions?

Possible answer: I was able to write an equation for the problems and then just solve it.

Strategy

Apply prior knowledge and basic operations to solve problems.

EXAMPLE

Mr. Hale has a 25-foot ladder. How far from the wall does the foot of the ladder need to be to reach 24 feet up?

First, use the Pythagorean Theorem to represent the situation.

$25^2 = 24^2 + b^2$

Evaluate the powers.

$625 = 576 + b^2$

Solve the equation.

$625 - 576 = b^2$

$49 = b^2$

$7 = b$

The ladder needs to be 7 feet from the wall.

3. **Barb walks 4 blocks north and 3 blocks west to get to her best friend's house. What is the distance between Barb's house and her friend's house? Show your work.**

   5 blocks

Math
100 — Spectrum Test Prep Grade 8

100

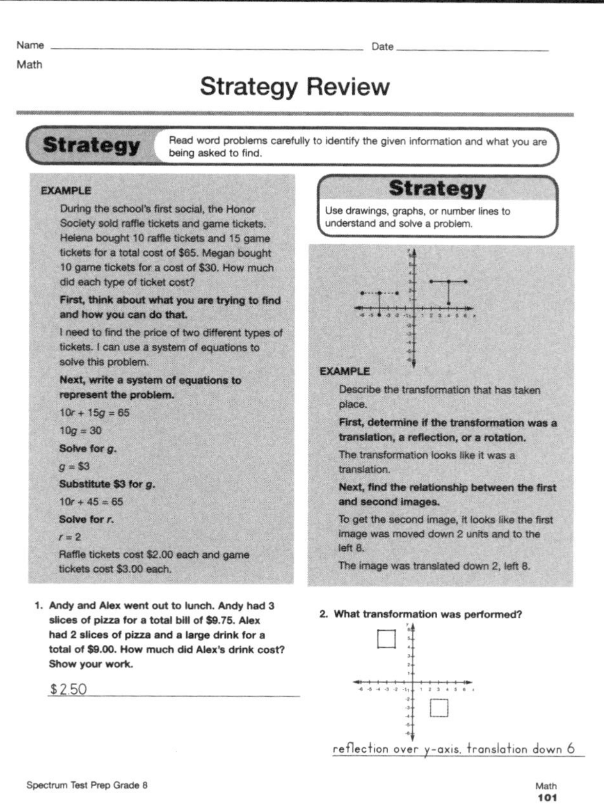

Name ______________________ Date ______________

Math

Strategy Review

Strategy Read word problems carefully to identify the given information and what you are being asked to find.

EXAMPLE

During the school's first social, the Honor Society sold raffle tickets and game tickets. Helena bought 10 raffle tickets and 15 game tickets for a total cost of $65. Megan bought 10 game tickets for a cost of $30. How much did each type of ticket cost?

First, think about what you are trying to find and how you can do that.

I need to find the price of two different types of tickets. I can use a system of equations to solve this problem.

Next, write a system of equations to represent the problem.

$10r + 15g = 65$

$10g = 30$

Solve for g.

$g = \$3$

Substitute $3 for g.

$10r + 45 = 65$

Solve for r.

$r = 2$

Raffle tickets cost $2.00 each and game tickets cost $3.00 each.

1. **Andy and Alex went out to lunch. Andy had 3 slices of pizza for a total bill of $9.75. Alex had 2 slices of pizza and a large drink for a total of $9.00. How much did Alex's drink cost? Show your work.**

   $2.50

Strategy

Use drawings, graphs, or number lines to understand and solve a problem.

EXAMPLE

Describe the transformation that has taken place.

First, determine if the transformation was a translation, a reflection, or a rotation.

The transformation looks like it was a translation.

Next, find the relationship between the first and second images.

To get the second image, it looks like the first image was moved down 2 units and to the left 8.

The image was translated down 2, left 8.

2. **What transformation was performed?**

   reflection over y-axis, translation down 6

Spectrum Test Prep Grade 8 — Math
101

101

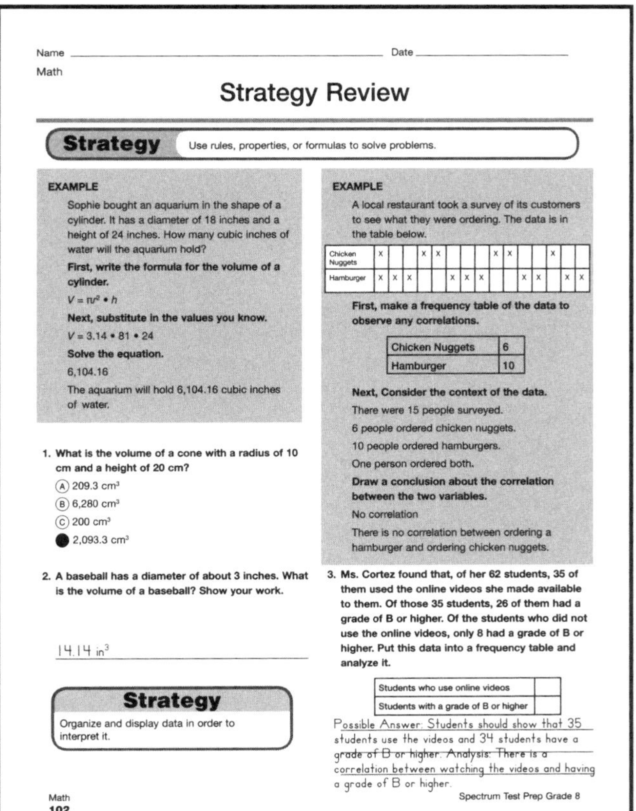

Name ______________________ Date ______________

Math

Strategy Review

Strategy Use rules, properties, or formulas to solve problems.

EXAMPLE

Sophie bought an aquarium in the shape of a cylinder. It has a diameter of 18 inches and a height of 24 inches. How many cubic inches of water will the aquarium hold?

First, write the formula for the volume of a cylinder.

$V = \pi r^2 \cdot h$

Next, substitute in the values you know.

$V = 3.14 \cdot 81 \cdot 24$

Solve the equation.

6,104.16

The aquarium will hold 6,104.16 cubic inches of water.

1. **What is the volume of a cone with a radius of 10 cm and a height of 20 cm?**
   - Ⓐ 209.3 cm^3
   - Ⓑ 6,280 cm^3
   - Ⓒ 200 cm^3
   - ● 2,093.3 cm^3

2. **A baseball has a diameter of about 3 inches. What is the volume of a baseball? Show your work.**

   14.14 in^3

Strategy

Organize and display data in order to interpret it.

EXAMPLE

A local restaurant took a survey of its customers to see what they were ordering. The data is in the table below.

Chicken Nuggets	X			X	X				X	X			X		
Hamburger	X	X	X			X	X	X			X	X		X	X

First, make a frequency table of the data to observe any correlations.

Chicken Nuggets	6
Hamburger	10

Next, Consider the context of the data.

There were 15 people surveyed.

6 people ordered chicken nuggets.

10 people ordered hamburgers.

One person ordered both.

Draw a conclusion about the correlation between the two variables.

No correlation

There is no correlation between ordering a hamburger and ordering chicken nuggets.

3. **Ms. Cortez found that, of her 62 students, 35 of them used the online videos she made available to them. Of those 35 students, 26 of them had a grade of B or higher. Of the students who did not use the online videos, only 8 had a grade of B or higher. Put this data into a frequency table and analyze it.**

Students who use online videos	
Students with a grade of B or higher	

Possible Answer: Students should show that 35 students use the videos and 34 students have a grade of B or higher. Analysis: There is a correlation between watching the videos and having a grade of B or higher.

Math
102 — Spectrum Test Prep Grade 8

102

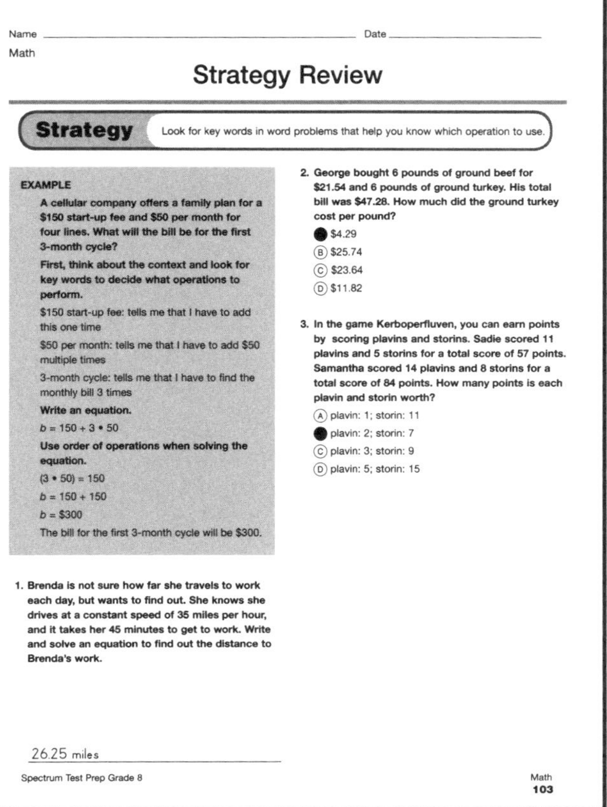

Name ______________________ Date ______________

Math

Strategy Review

Strategy Look for key words in word problems that help you know which operation to use.

EXAMPLE

A cellular company offers a family plan for a $150 start-up fee and $50 per month for four lines. What will the bill be for the first 3-month cycle?

First, think about the context and look for key words to decide what operations to perform.

$150 start-up fee: tells me that I have to add this one time

$50 per month: tells me that I have to add $50 multiple times

3-month cycle: tells me that I have to find the monthly bill 3 times

Write an equation.

$b = 150 + 3 \cdot 50$

Use order of operations when solving the equation.

$(3 \cdot 50) = 150$

$b = 150 + 150$

$b = \$300$

The bill for the first 3-month cycle will be $300.

1. **Brenda is not sure how far she travels to work each day, but wants to find out. She knows she drives at a constant speed of 35 miles per hour, and it takes her 45 minutes to get to work. Write and solve an equation to find out the distance to Brenda's work.**

   26.25 miles

2. **George bought 6 pounds of ground beef for $21.54 and 6 pounds of ground turkey. His total bill was $47.28. How much did the ground turkey cost per pound?**
   - ● $4.29
   - Ⓑ $25.74
   - Ⓒ $23.64
   - Ⓓ $11.82

3. **In the game Kerboperfluven, you can earn points by scoring plavins and storins. Sadie scored 11 plavins and 5 storins for a total score of 57 points. Samantha scored 14 plavins and 8 storins for a total score of 84 points. How many points is each plavin and storin worth?**
   - Ⓐ plavin: 1; storin: 11
   - ● plavin: 2; storin: 7
   - Ⓒ plavin: 3; storin: 9
   - Ⓓ plavin: 5; storin: 15

Spectrum Test Prep Grade 8 — Math
103

103